MY F
J O U R N Eʏ I N F I L M
from H O L L Y W O O D
to H I R O S H I M A

CHOOSING
LIFE

LESLIE A. SUSSAN

Print ISBN: 978-1-09831-453-8

eBook ISBN: 978-1-09831-454-5

Summer grasses:

All that remains of great soldiers'

Imperial dreams.

— Basho, translated by Sam Hamill,
from *The Little Book of Haiku* (B&N, 1995)

* * *

In truth, there is only one war. It is the struggle between the power of good and the power of evil in one's own heart and soul. All other wars spring from that source and, in the end, can only be resolved in that place.

— Michael Bonesteel, American Visionary Art Museum
http://www.avam.org/exhibitions/warandpeace.html (retrieved May 8, 2008)

DEDICATIONS

MY FATHER WISHED TO DEDICATE HIS story to his son, my brother, Paul Brinseley Sussan. He wrote that Paul "convinced me that young people want to see and know the truth about all this, written with the fervent hope that your children and mine — and all the generations to come — will never have to endure the horror and reality of nuclear attack . . . that man may eventually gain the knowledge and wisdom to save himself from total destruction."

I dedicate my part in this story to my daughter, Kendra Sheridan Parham, who has joined me through this long journey. My heartfelt prayer is that her children and their children may know a world filled with peace and love. *Gambatte, kudasai*!

This book as a whole is dedicated to all *hibakusha*, those who died quickly and those who survived to bear witness and seek peace.

TABLE OF CONTENTS

LIST OF PHOTOGRAPHS AND RECORDS

FOREWORD BY GREG MITCHELL

WHEN I MET HERB SUSSAN IN THE AUTUMN OF 1982, AND soon published the first article about him and his amazing atomic saga, the anti-nuclear movement in America (and around the world) was at its peak. Grassroots fervor for a "freeze" on building or deploying nuclear weapons, and then reducing their number, had inspired protest marches attracting record crowds. Long-established organizations such as SANE and Women's Strike for Peace were re-energized as thousands of local groups affiliated with numerous national networks popped up all over the country. Lobbying offices were established near Capitol Hill to press for arms control legislation making its way through Congress.

In this atmosphere, the profile of Herb in my magazine, *Nuclear Times*, spread like wildfire, and he was invited to tell it in person as well. Finally, the color footage he helped shoot and manage in Hiroshima and Nagasaki was drawing wide attention after decades of suppression. So many news outlets and documentary filmmakers were inquiring about the dozens of reels of footage at the National Archives (then in Washington, D.C.) that an archivist there told me they were now referring to them as "the *Nuclear Times* tapes." By then I had also tracked down the overall director of the atomic film project, Lt. Daniel A. McGovern, who confirmed details about the shooting and cover-up.

Herb soon realized his dream of returning to Hiroshima and sent me postcards of the Peace Park and A-Bomb Dome, expressing the profound nature of his experience there. Sadly, his health quickly worsened, and he passed away. The anti-nuclear movement also went into decline, although some of its checks on the arms race did reach fruition, and were then aided by the collapse of the Soviet

Union. Over the next three decades the number of nuclear warheads in the world declined but many remained on hair-trigger alert.

Through this, one thing remained constant — the steady use by news producers and filmmakers of that disturbing footage created by Herb and others in the two atomic cities. As the only color footage shot in Hiroshima and Nagasaki in the aftermath of the bombings it is always easy to identify it whenever it appears. Truly this was Herb's gift — in bringing it to public attention —and his legacy.

Official suppression of such images extended to black and white newsreel footage shot by a Japanese newsreel team, as well as to Hollywood studios (which I explore in my latest book, *The Beginning or the End*). Unfortunately, what happened in Hiroshima and Nagasaki is all the more relevant today, as the United States, in the Trump era, returns to a policy of planning new and more dangerous, as they are more "useable," nuclear weapons.

This has been accompanied by growing threats to use them. Indeed, the U.S. today maintains its "first-use" policy (initiated in 1945) which calls for meeting an enemy's "conventional" attack with a nuclear first strike on our part, if we wish. A new nuclear actor, North Korea, has emerged on the world stage, as the U.S. once again tries to bully Iran into refraining from exploring its own options. The danger of some sort of nuclear attack by terrorists grows every year. All of this led the *Bulletin of the Atomic Scientists* to move forward the hands of its famous "Doomsday Clock" to two minutes to midnight in 2019 — and a year later to just 100 seconds to midnight, the closest ever.

Surely, if Herb was still with us, this would make him angry, but on the other hand, his greatest fear — that nuclear weapons would be used again over large cities — has not come to pass. Surely, the wide, if belated, dissemination of his footage, among the most important images ever captured by anyone, has had at least some influence in helping to prevent a modern nuclear holocaust.

Greg Mitchell, author of "Atomic Cover-up," "The Beginning or the End," and co-author (with Robert Jay Lifton) of "Hiroshima in America."

INTRODUCTION

THE ATOM BOMBS THAT DROPPED ON HIROSHIMA AND Nagasaki in August 1945 form the center of this story. Everyone has seen the aerial photographs of the mushroom cloud, but few have heard the voices of those who saw it from below and survived in the ruins afterward. One person who listened to those voices first-hand was my father, Herbert Sussan. His assignment was to make the only color film record of the effectiveness of the atomic bombs, but he found a mission instead to record the human suffering they caused. It changed him.

More than forty years later, I retraced his journey and listened to the survivors reflect on how the bomb, and the filming, changed their lives. It changed me. One change both of us experienced, and that the survivors too reported, was a compelling need to tell the story in an effort to call the world to unite against ever using nuclear weapons again.

The use of the atomic bombs in the final days of World War II resulted from many political, military, and perhaps psychological factors, all of which have been explored by many authors. In this book, I focus instead on the ramifications of their use at a human scale. The questions I try to explore are about the effects on individuals and on families and how those effects ripple outward across generations and around the world. To understand this, I follow threads tying multiple generations of my own family to Hiroshima's people and their experience of the atom bomb.

When I was a teenager, my father seemed to me a depressed hypocrite in a business suit. He had been a pioneer in early television, producing award-winning shows, but he had a secret frustration eating away at him that had turned him bitter. The government had classified all of the atom bomb footage, and my father could never get access or make the film he thought would convince the world to give up nuclear weapons. I had no understanding of this undercurrent in his life.

As I grew older, my understanding of my father got more complicated. He had a cancer he attributed to his time in the atom-bombed cities, and he began to talk about his experiences. But it was only after my father died that I really got to know him. It was only then that I heard his full story and followed his footsteps. I met survivors of the bombing whom he had filmed. I heard the stories that changed him. And on that journey, I felt I met my real father for the first time.

The stories of those who were looking at the mushroom cloud from below have seldom been heard and even less often heeded. Their voices are dying out with the passing years, but the urgency of their call for peace is even more compelling for today's world. I am grateful to those who entrusted their stories to me forty years after having encountered my father and his film crew. I have tried to be faithful to that trust in sharing them here.

Figure 1: Map of Japan. (Illustration by Pavalena/shutterstock.com) (Note: Okinawa, and the tiny island of Ie Shima on which my father saw the end of the war, would be located well below and to the left of this map. Okinawa is just over 530 miles south of Kyushu. Nagasaki is on the west coast of Kyushu island.)

CHAPTER ONE:

Peace Park

HIROSHIMA, JAPAN (1987) — IT IS ANOTHER HOT AUGUST morning in Hiroshima. The ground at Peace Park is hard and dusty where I stand between the rivers in a spot where my father once stood. Nearby a twisted parasol tree gives little shade.

A tiny but sturdy Japanese woman in a pleated skirt, her graying hair in a bun, navigates rapidly on crutches and her one remaining leg to her special place beside the tree. She roosts neatly on a small folding chair with her good leg tucked neatly under it. A group of teenagers settles around her. In their school uniforms, the young boys resemble straight-backed soldiers and the young women seem like doe-eyed sailor girls. Even sitting, they tower over the drab little woman, but they all lean forward to hear her. Despite their youth and good health, her energy and presence dwarf them. Her gentle smile and mischievous eyes belie the many sorrows of her seventy-plus years.

Suzuko Numata has been coming here almost daily for a decade. She is doing *kataribe*, meaning bearing witness to what happened here by sharing her story of the atomic bombing. I am in Hiroshima for the first time and have come with a volunteer interpreter to hear her *kataribe*.

She begins with the story of her marriage preparations. Two families had been scurrying to arrange a wedding on short notice under the worst of circumstances. Food, money, supplies, everything was scarce in Hiroshima after so many years of war. Nevertheless, the young soldier's letter promising a brief visit on August 8 drove them to pull together to enable him to marry his fiancée during his furlough. Numata-sensei then lived with her parents, two brothers, and a younger sister. She had seen her young man only twice before he went to war. Still, at twenty-one, she yearned for his return and dreamed of becoming a married lady.

At this point in her story, Numata-sensei holds up a fading photo once intended as an engagement present for her fiancé. He shipped out to China before she could give it to him. Her younger self gazes out of the photo unsmiling in a formal pose. Her hair is arranged in a traditional coif, and she wears a beautiful kimono meant for her wedding.

I was not expecting a love story. When I was invited to hear *kataribe*, I expected more of a lecture on the evils of those who drop nuclear weapons. I expected to squirm, knowing that only one country had ever used such weapons: mine.

Numata-sensei explains that she worked alongside her father and sister at the Hiroshima Telecommunications Bureau, a modern four-story concrete construction. She always felt especially secure working in such a strong steel-framed building. The night of August 5, she slept poorly, thinking of a new employee she had met that day. He had wangled a transfer away from Tokyo and fled instantly to his new post, desperate to get his pregnant wife and three children away from the constant fire-bombings. He arrived that morning without even ration tickets for his family. He offered her some of his little remaining money to find something for his children to eat, not an easy task in the strictly rationed city. Moved by pity, Numata-sensei ran home as fast as she could and scoured the family kitchen. Finding a shriveled old potato and a little rice, she wrapped them in a cloth and dashed back across the three bridges to her workplace.

The grateful father wept and prayed a blessing on her for feeding his little ones that day. Numata-sensei would always remember this as the last time in her life that she ran on two good legs.

Her sleep was troubled not only by that memory and the anticipation of the coming wedding but also by repeated air raid alarms. Each of them turned out to signal only reconnaissance planes, though, and the morning dawned particularly beautiful, without a cloud in sight. Numata-sensei set out for work carrying her air raid hood and small first-aid kit, as she always did. She heard her best friend, Noriko-chan, calling to her. Usually, they loved to chat together about their upcoming marriages, but today Numata-sensei was in too much of a rush to stop and gossip, so she just waved. Later she would reflect on how casually their last chance to talk together was lost.

She was in the hall about to fill her bucket from the sink before cleaning the offices, when a beautiful light spread before her eyes. The flash was brilliant, with shades of orange, yellow, and red predominating, mixed with all the colors of the rainbow. Like the magnesium explosion of an old-fashioned camera flashbulb, the large, round ball of light came directly into her eyes. The next instant, the whole world went black.

When she reaches this part of her story, Numata-sensei closes her eyes and then suddenly opens them wide, throws her hands out, and blows out a big burst of air. The students lean back as if they feel a tiny blast pushing them.

I stand on the outside of the circle dipping my head to hear the translation. The miniature shock wave hits me too. I am big, blue-eyed, and clumsy. For a moment, it seems the circle has turned its back against my intrusion.

After pausing, Numata-sensei returns to her story. Her focus drifts to how she came to awareness in a dark room — not the hallway in which she had been standing before. The crushing weight of something heavy collapsed upon her. The sounds of calls and cries echoed from far off. She suddenly thought to scream for help. A man found her and dragged her out of the wreckage, hoisting her onto his back. She felt nothing; yet, her left ankle was severed through the bone and her foot dangled from mere shreds of skin. Blood poured down her rescuer's back. They struggled through the doorway into the corridor. Strange-smelling smoke enveloped them as they staggered down four floors to emerge into the yard. Behind her, she saw large flames flickering out of all the windows like red curtains. All around was burning bright red, even the surrounding trees and the neighboring hospital. Had her rescuer come even a few seconds later, she tells us, she "would not have survived, but would instead have perished there in anguish and tears of hate."

Her father had managed to rescue her sister and now ran amid the panicking crowd, half-crazed with fear, looking for Numata-sensei. "Where is my daughter? I can't find my daughter!" he shouted over and over.

The heat in the yard soared as fires raged on all sides. The wounded stampeded in every direction looking for escape. When Numata-sensei's father found her and pulled her onto a *tatami* mat, he was shocked by the sight of her barely attached foot. Ignoring the injuries of the others around him, he appealed for aid until someone helped him carry the mat with her limp body away from the flames to the spot where her sister waited. Glass shards stuck out from every side of her sister's upper body. Her flesh looked black from the blood drying around the glass. Nevertheless, she bent over Numata-sensei's legs crying, "Sister! Sister!"

Numata-sensei tilts her head and peers around the circle of young faces. She squeezes her eyes shut and begins reciting in a strange chant what she observed around her as she floated in and out of consciousness lying on the tatami mat:

> What I saw there was truly a picture of Hell. People burned so that they no longer looked human. Man and woman could not be distinguished among the sufferers. They screamed in anguish, calling for water, for help, for their mothers…and dying, one after another. I have no words to describe that horrible scene, like something from another world . . . All of a sudden, the sky turned black and it began to rain. We had no place to hide, and lay as we were, letting the rain fall as it would. I remember the rain falling on the stump of my leg and the fact that, strangely enough, it did not hurt at all.

The eerie black rain that fell that day haunted every account I was to hear from survivors in Hiroshima. Nature itself seemed to run backwards as the sky became dark at midday. The rain made the world dirtier, not cleaner. It rode the westerly breeze, spreading radioactive ashes over a wide area. Rain fell on the wounded and the whole, the injured and their rescuers, but washed no one clean that day. I heard about it for the first time that day listening to Numata-sensei.

The mass of suffering people in the yard included doctors and nurses who fled the destruction of the adjoining hospital. They were in no condition to do much in the way of medical relief. Nevertheless, later in the evening, one doctor responded to Numata-sensei's father's pleas to help with her ankle. Without any drugs or medicine, he determined he could only amputate the remaining connections and wrap the stump in gauze to stop the bleeding. Only then did Numata-sensei understand that she had lost her left foot forever.

That night, rumors spread that another air attack was coming. Those who could still move jammed themselves into the entrance of the shell of the Telecommunications Bureau building, as if that might protect them. This time the expected attack never came.

People lived or died unattended. Wounds festered and filled with maggots. One day, Numata-sensei saw a pregnant woman holding hands with a man. Both were burned over their whole bodies, their faces grotesque and swollen. Suddenly, they both fell over. The woman gave birth to a baby born covered with purple spots. The baby soon died, and the mother followed him. The man died a day later. Only after he was dead did Numata-sensei realize that he was the father to whom she had given food. All three other children had already died.

Hearing this, I feel cheated, as if I had cheered for these particular children to be fed only to have them snatched away from me. I am not sure I have a right to be eavesdropping on these agonies. I am not sure I can do anything else after this but listen to them over and over.

As she lay in the hospital, Numata-sensei learned that even at the time she first read the letter from her fiancé with excitement and joy, he had already died in battle in China. With that, she lost all desire to live. She spent her days staring blankly at the walls, disassociated from everyone and everything, unable even to think. In the fall, a typhoon passed through Hiroshima, piling misery on misery for the survivors. Her mother urged her on, saying, "You can still do anything with your two good hands." Numata-sensei lay unmoved and unmoving.

In March 1946, the nurses told her, with no explanation, that she was to go to the roof to be photographed. Her mother made them wait until she could dress Numata-sensei in her one intact kimono, the one intended for her wedding. It was faded and stained by dirt and water, but Numata-sensei's mother carefully washed and dried it so that it could be worn.

Numata-sensei had not tried to stand or walk since her injury. Now, she struggled for the first time to use crutches. When she reached the roof, she saw at last with her own eyes the ruins of atom-bombed Hiroshima. She cried, "Everything's gone! Nothing matters now!" Then she noticed an American man standing near an enormous camera.

"This is the man I saw," Numata-sensei says to the youngsters. She holds up an 8 by 10 photograph, a black and white close-up of a man's face. It is a picture of my father.

Numata-sensei does not look at me. She does not know yet who I am. My cheeks flush. I have changed in that instant from spectator to participant. And I do not know my part.

Numata-sensei was small and slight even then, she tells us. When she saw the tall American soldier for the first time, she was petrified.

> He was such a big man, with such big round eyes. He was the first American I had seen since the war ended. He said, "I'm sorry, it must be very painful, but we want to film you. So please take the bandage off."

> I did. When he saw the stump of my leg, he said, "It must really hurt very much."

So, I felt that he was kind at heart.

Numata-sensei was mortified to be seen in that condition and hated to be filmed. Even so, she says she is now grateful that this record exists. In fact, she says, this bit of film changed her life completely.

She never married or had children, and she lived her life with her sister and their darling cats. She became a math teacher and loved her work and her students. (The title of -*sensei* generally refers to a teacher or respected master in a field.) Her injuries were not as obviously bomb-related as those of burn victims with their raised keloid scars. Many people were afraid of *hibakusha*, the Japanese word for those affected by the atomic bomb. Afraid to hire people who might become sick. Afraid to marry people who might have bloodlines "tainted" from the radiation. Even afraid that the sicknesses or just the bad luck might be contagious. So Numata-sensei did not tell anyone that she was *hibakusha*.

Forty years later, a call came. A group from Tokyo managed to obtain the footage taken on that hospital rooftop and was trying to contact all the patients who were filmed. They wanted her to be filmed again, to speak about what had happened to her. She was old now, she thought, she was retired, and she was not going to marry. So, she decided to do it.

When the documentary appeared, she heard from many of her old students. "We were so close," they said, "but you did not tell us the most important thing about you." She felt their reproaches were justified. How could she have failed to tell them what war meant and how important peace was? So she dedicated the rest of her life to performing *kataribe* for students, tourists, any visitors to Peace Park.

Figure 2: Author meeting with Numata-sensei who is showing the photograph of Herbert Sussan that she uses in her kataribe. (Photo provided by The Chugoku Shimbum and used by permission).

I met Numata-sensei that first time not far from where my father first met her more than forty years before. I had come to Japan tracing my father's footsteps. He and I came down different paths to arrive at the same place. We were such different people, and the times in which each of us came of age were so different. We fought so much. We hardly talked after I left home, and I never followed his lead in anything. Yet here I was where he had been.

Encountering him like this in Peace Park convinced me that I was on the right path, following his ghost even if I did not know where it was heading. His own path to Hiroshima, though, began on a train heading west from New York City.

CHAPTER TWO:

Hurray for Hollywood

NEW YORK CITY (1939) — DESPITE THE EVENING HOUR, Grand Central Station felt hot and sticky. Vents to the street could barely move the air, much less counteract the heat pouring from the bodies of commuters and travelers pushing past. Tall but overweight, my father, Herb, dripped sweat, but he was too excited to care about the suffocating crowds. His red hair drooped, darkened by perspiration until it looked less out of place with the big Jewish nose that always embarrassed him. It did not bother him now. He was eighteen, and his real life had begun at last.

Clutching the ticket in one hand and his father's old suitcase in the other, he pushed forward to the gate. He would have to sit up for more than three days because his mother could not afford a sleeping berth for him. He did not want to sleep through any of it anyway.

This train trip to California was his first true adventure, nothing like riding the Manhattan subways or heading out to Coney Island or Jones Beach for the day. Even vacations in upstate New York or weekend outings to Cape May could not compare to watching the wide country pass by outside the rattling windows like a show staged especially for him. And California was the place where his Hollywood visions would take flesh, and live and breathe.

His dream caught him young. Saturday mornings at Radio City Music Hall, he slid down in his seat, the lights went dark and the screen lit up. The audience quieted down around him. Movie stars came to life, newly presented in full color and living sound. Busby

Berkeley musicals in which girls in flashy bathing suits and white caps formed stars and circles with their limbs pale against the blue pools or showgirls in glitter and feathers made dizzying kaleidoscopes. Double features and cartoons all for the price of a single admission. Screwball comedies or huge-cast epic stories, Charlie Chaplin miming or the Marx Brothers madcaps, Mae West flirting or W.C. Fields growling . . . anything on the flickering screen hypnotized him. The only thing he ever wanted to do in life was make movies.

His mother gave him quarters to see new movies. He knew she thought him safe at the theater, away from the street with the rough boys. The rest of the time she kept him indoors practicing piano or studying his schoolwork while other kids freely played stickball in the city streets. He was her only child. With her husband dead, the boy had to become the man of the family, so she told him over and over. He was all she had left.

* * *

I LEARNED ABOUT MY FATHER'S EARLY DAYS MOSTLY from scribbled notes I found after his death, after I had nagged him to write down the story of his filming Hiroshima and how the films were suppressed. He rarely talked to me about his youth, or about Hiroshima, when I was growing up. When I pressed him later in life to make a record of what happened to the film, he would say that the only way for him to tell the story was to edit the footage into movies to reach the American public. But he was never able to get access to the film he had helped shoot. It turned out, though, that he did hire a student to help him and tried to make the record I asked for, but all I found were scraps of typing and cryptic notecards.

Only fifteen years after he died did I discover that the student had also made audio recordings of her interviews with him. He never told me they existed. The student submitted them to the Columbia Oral History Archives, but my father never signed the release to make them publicly available. So, they sat untouched from 1985 until 2007. Reading a newsletter, *The Biographer's Craft*, I found a link to a database of oral histories and, on impulse, put in my father's name. I was stunned to find a hit, but details were only available by subscription. Librarians are my heroes – a crossbreed of bloodhounds and bulldogs once given a problem to solve. Luckily, I was then taking a graduate school program at University of Maryland. A persistent librarian there found an institutional subscription and discovered that the oral history was housed at Columbia. As my father's executor, I was able to obtain a transcript and hear my father's voice finally telling not just the bare facts of his upbringing and his experiences in Japan, but what those events meant to him. All the stories he never told me.

Listening to the recordings, I try to imagine my grandfather, Paul (for whom my brother is named). I never knew him except as a photo on my grandmother's wall. I remember my grandmother, Nanny, talking about him while she fixed stuffing for her piroshky or stirred borscht on her stove – not the cold beet kind, but the hot Ukrainian style, redolent of cabbage and onions. Her braided hair, wound into a bun, still showed more brown than grey when I was a child visiting her. Her voice softened and her eyes focused far off whenever she talked about him, so different from her usual practical intensity. The young woman in love peeked through her eyes. She swore that everyone said he looked like Tsar Nicholas. I found it hard to see the resemblance in the framed photo, but she admired his aristocratic mien.

Nanny described him as thin, a nervous intellectual with a bad stomach. He suffered from a "weak metabolism" because his stepmother never fed him enough. His own father was a Jewish tailor in Latvia who already had a large family when his first wife died in childbirth. He could never make enough money to feed all the children well, and his new wife favored her own babies. Grandfather Paul's mind, Nanny told me, was brilliant and his heart kind, but his health was never strong.

Figure 3: Herbert Sussan's parents: Paul Sussan and Clara Goldreyer, circa 1920.

My grandmother seemed driven to make up for Paul's ancient hunger by feeding and caring for everyone in sight. I remember her carrying soup down the hall to the "old lady" who turned out to be more than a decade younger than Nanny herself. Nanny explained that the neighbor *was* old because she did not go out at all and paid attention only to her own troubles. By that standard, Nanny never got old. When she was 93 and lay dying in the hospital, she worried about the "poor man" in the next bed suffering so much from an ulcer and missing time from work he needed to take care of his family. She called my father on the night before she died to apologize that she was not strong enough to help him anymore.

When I was girl visiting her co-op apartment on the West Side overlooking the Hudson River, she would make my favorite food

– salmon steaks in a jellied sauce with carrots and raisins – which I have never eaten anywhere else. She would buy sweet red peppers from the sidewalk grocers for me to eat like apples with red juice dripping down my chin. When I was at college, she would send me care packages: coffee cans lined with wax paper and full of home-made crescent-shaped poppy seed cookies. I never asked what she sent my father at college, but I cannot believe she would have failed to supply him with food made by her own hands.

Grandfather Paul was a genius, as Nanny told it, a civil engineer and inventor of an eye exercise system. He helped design a Consolidated Edison power station in lower Manhattan that my father used to point out to me regularly. Nanny was head nurse in a maternity center when she met Paul. My father told me that Nanny gave orders to her maternity staff about how to handle the birth even as she was in labor and never stopped giving instructions to everyone after that. But when it came to her husband, she never argued with him. Whatever he did was right. On the evenings and weekends, he saw patients for eye treatment with Nanny as his nurse; my father said that they had a "waiting room" instead of a "living room." When I was a girl, Nanny still had the machines he created set up in one room and continued to see loyal patients.

*   *   *

WHEN HERB WAS A YOUNG BOY, HIS FAMILY MOVED TO Brooklyn, relieved to leave behind the noisy tenements of the Lower East Side, crowded with new immigrants fresh from Eastern Europe. Their new neighborhood was a jigsaw of concrete plots with taller apartment buildings separated by wider avenues. From his bedroom window, Herb could see lighted rectangles in the apartment buildings and brownstone houses all around him. Other people with other lives appeared and vanished from view as he watched. Far off, a fairyland of glittering lights spread across New York. Every light had a story behind it. The people living in those apartments and houses, passing the open windows or hidden behind Venetian blinds, might be loving or weeping, giddy or somber, kind or cruel, rich or poor. He would fall asleep imagining all the stories to be told about other people's lives.

Herb proudly came to the Torah when he turned 13. The ceremony conferred on him the stature and responsibilities of a man in the Jewish community. Shortly after, his father took sick and lay in bed for three weeks. It was the first time Herb had known his papa to lie down in the daytime.

At two in the morning, a scream pierced his dreams, coming from his parents' room. Shivering with chill dread, he stumbled down the hallway, half asleep. He hesitated a moment at the strangeness of opening their door at night. He found his father looking content and asleep with his mother's body thrown full length across him. She wailed, "Get a doctor! *Do* something!"

Herb realized then that his father was not asleep. In robe and slippers, he ran out into the broad street and blinked. Not a soul was in sight. What was he to do? Something, but what? The apartment buildings in both directions formed a giant tunnel through which not a single car moved. Each building housed doctors' offices on the ground level, but no lights appeared in their windows at this hour. No one responded to shouts or knocks. If the family had a telephone at that point, no one thought to use it, and it could not have made a difference.

[My father never said what made him realize it was too late anyway. The knowledge must have slowly crept up his spine that his father was already dead. His papa would never take him on the trip he had always promised they would take together someday. From the day of his father's funeral, my father never set foot in a synagogue again. Decades later, when I wanted to join a synagogue, he railed against it. I did not know what God had done to him so I did not understand why he could not forgive God.]

* * *

HERB HAD LONG AGO MADE UP HIS MIND ABOUT HIS life, and now he was eager to get started on his plans. He wanted to go to the University of Southern California. USC offered the only degree in cinematography then available. Only there could a kid go to college to make movies. USC was near Hollywood and drew on all the best talent from the Academy of Motion Pictures. It was everything wonderful that Herb could imagine, and it actually existed.

Figure 4: Herbert Sussan, high school graduation picture. (Photo from collection of author's grandmother, photographer unknown)

Nanny felt it was fine for a boy to go to the shows and get dreamy about *Hooray for Hollywood*. But such things had nothing to do with the serious business of life as a man. She had not struggled to send Herb to Stuyvesant High School, among the best academic schools in the city, for him to devote his life to making foolish films. The son of an engineer and nurse should obviously be a doctor and contribute to the world. Night after night, they quarreled.

Furthermore, she could not face letting her precious child go off to the other end of the country when he graduated from high school, and him not yet seventeen at that. Nor could she understand why he would want to run after such crazy ideas. They both talked like New Yorkers, fast, loud, and with hands waving to emphasize their points — even more so when they got worked up.

"So, what kind of a school is this USC, which I never heard of this USC? There aren't enough good colleges in New York that you have to run across the whole country for a nothing school?" I can hear Nanny's voice echo in my head today, with its Yiddish rhythm and its Russian accent.

True enough, USC in those days was hardly an academic powerhouse, known mostly for its football team and its country club campus, hosting the lower-achieving scions of wealthy California families.

Knowing her, the next tack would have been, "It isn't enough what I have done for you that you want to leave me here all alone, a widow? Would Papa have approved of you running off this way?"

"I am not running off. I am going to school to do what I was born to do. USC is the only college that teaches what I want to learn. Besides, this is New York, not Russia; nobody is going to bother you. Your work is here; your friends are here. You will be fine here. I promise I will always take care of you. All the time with the worry!"

"How do you think you will take care of me, much less some-day a wife and children, on such fairy tale stuff as movies? You need to get an education for a real job; you're a man now, *nu*?" [Even when I knew her as my Nanny, she never ended a sentence with a period if a question mark could do.]

"You don't understand. I *know* I can do this. Making movies is the only thing I want to do."

Finally, they reached an agreement. Herb would enter the pre-med program at New York University the following fall after turning seventeen. He could not defy what his mother wanted so badly. She agreed that, if he were still as adamant after one year at NYU, she would allow him to attend USC. It was not the end of the arguments. Once she had him at NYU, she was sure she could persuade him to see the sense of her perspective before the year was out. But Herb was equally persistent, and finally she let him go.

That year, Herb had at least one reason to be glad he was still in New York: The World's Fair. Nanny no doubt held tightly to his hand as they took the five-cent subway ride to Flushing Meadow to see the wonders. The future was going to be amazing. RCA displayed the invention of visible radio transmission: the earliest televisions with images reflected from a mirror in the lid. Herb surely saw his tomor-row in those images. The Trylon and Perisphere structure (a huge globe connected by a moving sidewalk to a tall spire with the world's longest escalator) served as the talisman of the fair. Soon, its metal would be melted down for the war effort, but the bright excitement of progress could still push those shadows aside in 1939. And by the end of the year, he was free to go in search of bright tomorrows.

* * *

HERB WAS NOT THINKING ABOUT WAR AS HE BOARDED his train to dreamland and found his seat.

The tall buildings of Manhattan disappeared into the background. His breath fogged the window as he leaned forward to peer at the changing landscape. Pennsylvania farmlands ripening with miles of fall crops, interrupted only by silos and barns. Forests and towns across the Midwest. Straw-colored prairies with huge starry skies at night. Horizons that seemed unimaginably distant to someone used to the vertical lines of tall buildings. The train cut across snow-topped Western mountains and slid through deserts with air so pristine that a tree in the distance was indistinguishable from a bush in the foreground, before it finally rumbled into the Los Angeles train station.

At every stop along the route, Herb eagerly climbed down to the platform. He was less interested in buying food or stretching his legs than in exploring the amazing diversity of people. Folks chatting with their twangs or flat vowels, wearing their Amish bonnets or cowboy hats. They all looked, acted, and spoke differently than New Yorkers. Yet they were all Americans too. He would never forget how big the country was and how wide the world after this astonishing discovery merged in his heart with the pure joy of being young.

*   *   *

AS I READ THROUGH MY FATHER'S NOTES ABOUT THAT trip, I tried to picture him so young, so curious, so joyful. I remembered him as distant, disappointed, and often angry. He feared that my studying Russian and Chinese would made us targets of government agents; he found my pacifism foolish; he disapproved of me marrying a Black man. He seemed to mistrust everyone for little reason I could see. His mantra was "coulda, shoulda, woulda," a refrain of frustration and a lament for all that remained undone. I loved him and wanted him to be proud of me, but I did not seem to ever fit his image for his daughter. I was not sure whether he was angrier at me or at himself sometimes, but I never thought of joy when I thought of him.

It is true he was always New Yorker to the core despite years of living in Los Angeles. He never had a driver's license. Broadway and Wall Street were real places, not symbols or metaphors, to him. That part of him remained consistent with the young man leaving Grand Central Station. But what happened to that enthusiastic embrace of the rest of the world?

When I went to Hiroshima after he died, I had many reasons, including carrying out his wishes and hoping to preserve a story of humanity in the face of the horrors of nuclear war. But I also went to try to find some remnant of this other father that I had never met in life.

CHAPTER THREE:

Losing the man I never knew

NEW YORK CITY (1985) — FOR ME, THE JOURNEY TO Numata-sensei's *kataribe* began with my father's death. When he first got sick, no one knew what was wrong with him. First, the doctors suspected heart trouble, then pancreatitis, then cancer of some kind, but which? He worsened, and, after many days in the hospital, he was often delirious and at last plainly dying. Doctors struggled to decide what to do as one test after another came back without clear answers, leaving us in a twilight limbo between a straightforward negative and a devastating positive. My mother begged them to do something, anything. The same painful loop repeated:

"We think that the most likely diagnosis is non-Hodgkin's lymphoma, but the bone marrow test is also non-diagnostic." "What the hell does 'non-diagnostic' mean?" "It means that the results are not negative, so we can't rule out the diagnosis. But we can't definitely confirm it either."

At last, on a Thursday evening, five of us crowded into a small conference room – my mother, my brother, me, and the main doctor on my father's case, accompanied by another of the uncountable doctors that drifted through — interns, residents, consultants, and specialists. Tension and fear pinged off the walls and ricocheted among us. Even the doctors seemed irritable, as if annoyed that my father's sickness was stubbornly not giving up its secrets to their skill.

"Well, what else could he have?" My mother sounded shrill.

"There are a few other possibilities that we've been testing for. Most of them have already been ruled out. The most likely one is still the non-Hodgkins." "Well, then why aren't you treating him for it?" I asked. "He is just getting worse and worse and all you do is one awful test after another!"

They explained that they could not treat him for something that they were not sure he had when the treatments themselves were toxic. The doctor leaned forward.

"If we gave him chemotherapy and he got sicker from it, and then it turned out he hadn't had lymphoma, well, that could be a problem." Problem? I wondered who would have the problem.

"And what happens if you don't treat him?"

The room was an island of distress somehow isolated in the sea of suppressed panic flowing throughout the ICU. Through the open door drifted the Sputnik beeps of monitors, the race-walk bustle of rubber-soled nurses, and the muffled rings of phones and buzzes of alarms and call buttons. A faint aroma of disinfectant in the over-conditioned air bleached out the fruity, sweaty smells of organic life. People murmured in clusters outside open glass compartments, each containing some loved one in the center of a web of tubes and wires.

"He is weakening fast," the doctors told us. "We believe something has to be done this weekend at the latest or he may not be able to withstand either the illness or the treatment."

"You are telling us that you can't treat him without a definite diagnosis because you might get in trouble for that, but that if you don't treat him soon, he will die from the illness anyhow?" I started asking this as a question, but by the end my voice rose to a protest. "Well, we are hoping that we will be able to get a clear diagnostic result from one of the tests scheduled over the next day or two. That will clarify the situation and let us move forward." "But," I pointed out, "it is already Thursday."

The doctor turned to me slowly. We gazed at each other. His eyes were narrowed and wary. I realized then that my mother must have told him that I was a lawyer. A chill ran through me. It was my fault that the doctors were paralyzed by their own fear of litigation. Suddenly, I was angry. I never saw myself as *that* kind of lawyer — the hired-gun kind bent on extracting money. My lifework was using the tools of the law to serve those pushed to the edges of society — abused children, vulnerable old people, migrant farmworkers. Still, I could not let their defensive medicine make my profession the reason my father died.

I decided it was time to channel the tougher type of lawyer to help my father in his fight for his life. "Okay, I will make this easy. You are right. If you treat him and it turns out you treated him for the wrong thing, we might sue for malpractice. But I guarantee you, that if you don't start providing him with some treatment *now*, I *will* sue for neglect and malpractice and anything else I can think of. Since you face legal trouble either way, do what is best for him medically and do it now."

*　*　*

THEY BEGAN CHEMOTHERAPY THAT DAY BASED ON THE non-Hodgkin's lymphoma theory. Maybe they would have anyway. Almost immediately, my father started to respond. His response finally confirmed the diagnosis. His cancer was in his spleen, his lymph glands, and his brain. When he became a little stronger, they began to blast his head with radiation to fight the cancer cells in his brain and spinal fluid. A shunt was inserted surgically to medicate the brain case directly, since drugs do not cross the blood-brain barrier efficiently.

The successive "insults to the brain" (as the doctors referred to the cancer, the radiation, the implantation of a shunt, and several bouts of infection that followed) caused a frightening range of psychological effects. He was terrified of Martians who spoke to him through the small television that could be pulled over his bed on a metal arm. He believed the nurses were trying to kill him. He was furious with my mother for putting him in prison. Most of all, he screamed that radiation was poisoning him and fought every time he was taken for radiation therapy. He hovered between lucidity and delusion, between recovery and relapse.

My mother believed in macro-vitamins and alternative therapy. My father remembered how Japanese people would drink green tea to protect themselves from radiation sickness. His doctors were not keen on having their hard-won successes attributed to snake oil, but they finally agreed to allow my mother to bring in juices, teas, and supplements so long as we ensured that he also complied with medical treatments.

My mother consulted Dr. William Hitzig who supported the laughter-and-vitamin-C treatment Norman Cousins described in his book *Anatomy of an Illness*. Cousins had been a central figure in the story of the *Genbaku Otome* or Hiroshima Maidens. After the war ended, a Japanese Christian minister, Reverend Kiyoshi Tanimoto, grew concerned about the plight of schoolgirls with terrible burns from the atomic bombing. Many had been hidden away by their parents and rejected by employers because of their unsightly injuries. Worse, marriage was impossible because of the widespread belief that they could only give birth to genetic monstrosities. Rev. Tanimoto sought to publicize their situation and raise money for treatment.

Cousins visited Japan with his wife, and Reverend Tanimoto introduced them to the young women. Cousins launched a project to bring them to the United States for surgery. Dr. Hitzig, who had been Cousins' personal physician, recruited other surgeons in New York to help. In 1955, a contingent of twenty-five Maidens arrived in the United States. The Maidens were welcomed into various Quaker homes to stay while they underwent treatment. The results of their many operations varied, but the bridges built between Americans and these courageous girls were often enduring.

Knowing that Dr. Hitzig played a role in the Hiroshima Maidens project, my parents told him about my father's experiences in Japan at the end of World War II. They explained that he had been stationed on an island off the coast of Okinawa. He was sent to Tokyo and tapped for a special assignment for the Strategic Bombing Survey. His crew traveled by train beginning in December of 1945 to film the results of bombing on Japan cities. They spent months in the atom-bombed cities. Talking to Dr. Hitzig, my father became convinced that his cancer was the late-life effect of his exposure to residual radiation in Nagasaki and Hiroshima.

* * *

CONTROVERSY STILL EXISTS OVER WHAT LEVEL OF RADI-ation remained in the atom-bombed cities by then and whether such exposure could cause malignancy decades later. My point in sharing this part of his story, though, is not to prove that my father was right in believing that he was, in the end, a victim of the bomb himself. My point is that this belief resurrected the memories that haunted him all his life. They became a burning presence in his final years.

As far as I could ascertain from the oncologists treating my father, they viewed the premise as neither impossible nor provable.

From my perspective, the significance of my father's belief was that he identified even more with the bomb survivors because he felt himself damaged by the atom bomb, now physically as well as psychologically.

My father began speaking publicly about his memories of filming the aftermath of the atomic bombings only after he got sick. In 1983, journalist Greg Mitchell wrote an article about him in *Nuclear Times* magazine and later included a chapter about his experiences in the book, *Hiroshima in America*, he co-authored with Robert Jay Lifton. My father explained to Greg that, for thirty years, he had been told repeatedly that the films were classified, secret, unavailable. After his illness, my father told Greg, he had connected with a Japanese group that fought to get the footage released.

My father traveled to Japan in 1983 and met again the survivors he had filmed. He found travel exhausting, as his own health remained fragile and he was mourning the death of my mother earlier that year. I was not able to go with him because I had a new baby at home. During that visit, he came to identify as a *hibakusha* himself – yet another person deeply affected by the atomic bomb.

Although he went public at that point, he still never talked directly to his family about what he saw and how it affected him. I pressed him to write down his memories while he was able. I thought, there should be at least some record of what happened and of what became of the only color film of the aftermath. This idea did not seem to interest him. He kept saying that film was his language, not words. He was depressed about his life, questioning the point of anything he had accomplished. He had never made the documentary to end nuclear weapons he imagined when he took the footage. Instead, he left the military frustrated when he was told the film he shot was now classified above his level to even view it. Now, it was too late. He said he was collecting material with the student he hired to help, but I heard little more about this project that that. And then he had to be hospitalized again. This time he did not regain enough strength to go home. The doctors proudly said the autopsy showed he died cancer-free, as if that validated their work. Maybe so, but he was dead.

I was not with him when he died in September of 1985. My younger brother, Paul, was. After the funeral, we went to our father's apartment. Although he had died in the hospital, the air seemed flat and musty, as if a whiff of death had reached here. We opened file cabinets and rifled through desk drawers. I glanced sideways at my brother, wondering if he too felt like an intruder. These spaces felt private, but, after all, you do not need privacy when you are dead. A few weeks before our father went back to the hospital, Paul had called me. Our father had been writing strange checks. He wrote a check for $15,000 to a man he met in a coffee shop, for example, supposedly to help him start some kind of business. Luckily, the checks were no good because there was no money in the checking account. Perhaps, the insults to which his doctors had referred had indeed done damage to his brain.

I asked Paul now, as we pulled out unlabeled folders and made piles of paper, whether he thought this crazy behavior was the result of the illness and the treatments, or if it was just our father being himself. "How could we tell?" Paul responded. We found it hard to tell because we had always found it hard to know what went on in our father's head. Often, he seemed angry or bitter for reasons that were not clear to us; other times, he seemed to have the emotional depth of a Hallmark card. Neither of us thought to connect the way he was to what he might have experienced during the war or to his grief for the one true story he was never permitted to bring to the world. Only near the end of his life did he communicate that having that film taken from him overshadowed for him all his accomplishments in early television as a producer and director.

I was my father's executor, and I had to figure out what estate he left and what debts he owed. I knew it would not be simple. He never told me much about his finances, and much of what he did say over the years about money was inconsistent. We lived in nice apartments, but we were about to go to the poorhouse. When I was in college, I fought for financial aid because school officials complained that my father would not send them the necessary documents or, when he did, the papers made no sense. I investigated being legally declared an emancipated minor before the college relented and allowed me scholarships based on my own income since I was not receiving support from home.

After hours of sorting, the only clear thing was that our father had no organizing system at all. TV scripts from the 1950s were mixed with newspaper clippings from the 1970s; birthday cards I sent him years ago were stuck in folders with recent medical bills. This was going to take days or weeks, not hours.

We sat down in the living room. "Listen," Paul said, "I have to tell you. He said something to me at the end."

I looked up, puzzled. "Something? What do you mean?"

"So, he asked me . . . Well, what it comes down to is . . . His last wish was that his ashes be scattered at Ground Zero in Hiroshima."

My first thought was "Oh, shit." I remembered a Yiddish phrase I once learned from my father, though he hated to hear me use Yiddish, *hab mein ebben tsuris*. Indeed, I already had enough trouble of my own, and now I had inherited a headache from him. Remembering my years of conflict with my father starting as a teenager and continuing through his opposition to my marriage to a

Black man and disinterest in my public interest law work, I wondered what I really owed him now that he was dead.

I did not say any of this out loud. Instead, I said, "What do you think we should do?" But neither of us knew.

I went back home to Arlington, Virginia, and Paul finished sorting through the piles and closing the apartment. He shipped the results to me in boxes. In one box, I found manila envelopes labeled "Hiroshima." Opening them and thumbing through the papers inside, I caught my first glimpses into my father's memories.

When I first saw how thick the stack was, my heart raced. He had done it after all. Here would be a description of the atom-bombed cities and a chronology of his efforts to get the films released. I found instead bits and pieces of family history, fragments of horror, comical stories of his hopeless misfit with the military, and side glimpses of history, all scrambled together.

Slowly in this mix, I found breadcrumbs that would lead me to a man I had never met, the man my father was before the bomb.

CHAPTER FOUR:

The gift of the enemy

WASHINGTON, D.C. (1985)/HIROSHIMA, JAPAN (1983) —
Not long before my father's death in 1985, I started a job as director
of a non-profit center for abused children. When I interviewed for
the job, the board asked me why they should believe I cared about
Black children in the District of Columbia. I pointed out that my
daughter and stepdaughter were among those Black children. I cared
deeply about advocating for children trapped in damaged families.
I failed to understand, however, that advocacy required more than
caring and more than a committed staff. We had to have rent, and
supplies, and support. I proved terrible at fundraising and too inex-
perienced to realize that the job was untenable without a good fund-
raiser. The money ran out. With it, so did my job.

In 1983, I gave birth to my daughter, and then watched with
guilt as my ailing father embarked on his last trip by himself, revisiting his memories. Within two years after that, I lost not only my
father, but also my mother and grandmother. Even my cat died suddenly, as if life just could not persist near me. My husband suffered
a sort of breakdown and disappeared entirely leaving all his posses-
sions behind. (I called hospitals, morgues, extended family, and anyone I could think of but knew nothing of his safety or whereabouts
for eight years. Eventually, he stabilized, and we were on good terms
for many years, but in the 1980s, I was left entirely alone with a young
child to raise.) I decided to buy a first house of my own (my family
were typical New York City renters) to have a fresh start. In order

to take title in my own name, I had to obtain a divorce "in absentia," because the other party had willfully disappeared. So, when the center lost its funding, I found myself a single parent with a mortgage and no income. Worn out by grief and anxiety, I reflected about what to do next. A spiritual workshop introduced me to the idea of the "gift of the enemy." The leader suggested that we should examine whatever seemed to be our biggest obstacle or our worst problem and ask how it hid a blessing.

My worst problem then seemed to be feeling frozen in place, paralyzed, and emptied of plans. I could not think how to move forward as a public interest lawyer when I felt I had failed to save the children's center. I remembered my father's years of unemployment in Los Angeles. After clashing with network bigwigs, he had been squeezed out as a television producer. For months, he put on a suit and picked up his briefcase and headed out the door as if he still had an office to go to. The police stopped him several times for the suspicious activity of wandering around Beverly Hills on foot. I hated the idea that I too had arrived at the point where I did not know who I was without a job.

It occurred to me at last that the gift of unemployment was freedom, and the time to use it. Once I was working again and my daughter started grade school, travel would be much harder. I decided this might be my opportunity to discharge what had grown to feel like a haunting obligation to my father. I started planning to follow his footsteps in Japan.

I did not have much in the way of actual plans. I had tickets to Tokyo for my daughter and myself with an open return. I had a letter of encouragement from my church. I knew only two people in Japan.

The first person was a Japanese student, Masahiko Sumiya, who had stayed with us to improve his English before starting on a business degree. The program representative who introduced us when I first picked him up for a two-week home stay told my daughter he was her new big brother. She was immediately convinced, and Masa has been family ever since. He spent breaks from his studies at Western Maryland College at our house, and we proudly attended his graduation. Masa, who had taught me a few words in Japanese, was going to be home in Tokyo that summer. He invited us to visit his family and to travel with him and his American college roommate, who was also going to visit him the summer of 1987.

The second connection I had was to Tsutomo Iwakura. Mr. Iwakura's group was known as the Hiroshima-Nagasaki Publishing Committee (now incorporated into the Japan Peace Museum in Tokyo). The group was created in 1977 with the goal of fostering a commitment to peace among the Japanese people and bringing the world a real understanding of the effects of the use of nuclear weapons on human beings. (Indeed, the original umbrella group was called the Committee of Japanese Citizens to Send Gift Copies of a Photographic and Pictorial Record of the Atomic Bombing to Our Children and Fellow Human Beings of the World.) They compiled graphic photographs of the aftermath of war in Japan generally, and of the atom-bombed cities in particular. They published *HIROSHIMA-NAGASAKI: A Pictorial Record of the Atomic Destruction*, an extraordinary and vivid collection of images, and gave a copy to each delegate at the 1978 Special Session for Disarmament at the United Nations. They also mounted a photo exhibition there for the session opening — shocking photographs of human damage.

✳   ✳   ✳

AFTER RETURNING HOME FROM HIS CANCER TREATment in the hospital in 1978, my father's strength fluctuated. The picture windows of his apartment at Kips Bay overlooked trees budding in the sidewalk boxes. City sidewalks glittered with mica in the late May sun. My father read about the exhibition with photographs from Hiroshima and Nagasaki taking place only blocks away.

One day, he felt well enough to pick up his cane and try to walk there. Although he was only in his early 60s, he already had the unsteady gait of an old man. Entering the display room at the United Nations, he walked back into his own past.

He gazed at the photographs that were shockingly alien to other visitors and shockingly familiar to him. One image stopped him completely. He leaned forward on his cane and peered closer to be sure. The blown-up picture showed a young boy of sixteen whose back was a bubbling raw mass of burns. He knew that boy. He remembered wincing when he turned on bright lights to film the same boy in a Nagasaki hospital. He felt that the heat of the lamps must add to the pain.

My father approached the exhibitor, a pleasant but intense Japanese gentleman, and explained that he had filmed this boy. The man seemed fascinated to hear about the many thousands of feet of color movie footage portraying some of the same scenes and people in the photographs on display. He was amazed to hear that my father had never been able to see the film after it was developed. My father explained that, whenever he tried to get access to the film, he was told it was too sensitive, too highly classified and, in any case, of no interest to the public.

My father had always wanted to make a public documentary from the footage to convey the human aftereffects of nuclear war. He believed in movies. He was sure that living color would communicate more than data or words, or even still photographs, could. Something more immediate, more human, more visceral. The Army was emphatically not interested in this plan. The footage was treated as top secret and used only to make military training films. After he left the Army and went into early television, my father kept returning to this project. I remember bursts of excitement around the dinner table that he had met this or that person who had top secret clearances and would help him get to his footage, and crushing letdowns as nothing came of it yet again. I never quite understood the reason for either the excitement or the letdown.

After hearing this tale from my father, Mr. Iwakura became determined to learn what had really happened to this film. He later told my father that the U.S. government reported that the film had been declassified in 1962 by operation of law. (Federal law requires review and release of classified material after certain periods of time.) Mr. Iwakura was advised that the film had been shipped to the National Archives in Washington. Almost 90,000 feet of raw footage identified as #342 USAF were now filed there. According to what Mr. Iwakura was told, it was merely an "accident" that the official card on the film that my father saw years earlier when he went to Norton Air Base in search of his footage was still marked "Classified." The many times my father sought help to get access to it and was told that was impossible were all "mistakes." My father did not find this credible, but he was amazed to hear that the footage was now accessible and so close by.

Having discovered where the film was, Mr. Iwakura's next goal was to obtain and view it. The National Archives charged a copying fee by foot for film. He launched a grassroots movement known as the Ten-Feet Campaign. The campaign called for each Japanese person to donate the sum of ¥3,000 (about $12 then) to roughly cover the cost of copying 10 feet of film. Hundreds of thousands of individuals are said to have participated in this unique fund-raising effort, which raised enough money (reportedly about $500,000) to purchase a complete copy of the footage and to produce documentaries from it. Along with the film, they obtained copies of the caption cards identifying many of the patients in the hospital footage. Mr. Iwakura's group translated the cards into Japanese and undertook to locate as many of the surviving patients as possible.

In Hiroshima, the search was led by Dr. Hideaki Nagai, director of the YMCA International Institute for Peace. It was Dr. Nagai who contacted Numata-sensei and persuaded her to appear in a short documentary that the Ten-Feet Campaign group produced with snippets of the film footage. My father saw Mr. Iwakura again in 1982 when the fruit of the Ten-Feet Campaign came to New York City. The two short films produced by the group, *Prophecy* and *Lost Generation*, were screened during the Second Special Session on Disarmament of the United Nations. This time, Numata-sensei accompanied Mr. Iwakura.

My father and Numata-sensei met face to face for the first time in thirty-six years at that film screening. She had not forgotten his face. He recognized her at once. Both were struck speechless. They gazed silently at each other for several minutes. She noticed that his hair had thinned; he seemed so much older and weaker. He was amazed to see her still alive and full of energy.

His face was lined and sad, and he kept saying how sorry he was, Numata-sensei told me later. She assured him that she did not hate him or have any bad feelings toward him for filming her. It was true that, for a long time, she had hated America. Had America not dropped the bomb, her life and her body would have been so different. She did not like being photographed at the time. But now, she insisted it was good that his film had preserved a true record. And, in time, she had realized that war leaves victims in every land. Now, she said, she hates war, but does not hate any human being.

Numata-sensei listened to my father speak to a group gathered to view the documentaries. He spoke about his experiences in Japan and the hopes he had had for the footage. For the first time, she understood his motives and feelings when he was photographing her. He told her that he felt that he was *hibakusha*, too, and she agreed.

My father brought his mother, nearing ninety, to hear his talk and see the films. He introduced her to Numata-sensei. He was eager for Nanny to hear Numata-sensei's story. My grandmother saw bits of the scenes her son had filmed so many years before. She listened to the survivors tell of the horrors they remembered. Only then did she finally understand why the son who came home to her was not the one she had sent off to war.

* * *

THE NEXT YEAR (1983), MR. IWAKURA ARRANGED FOR MY parents to travel to Japan. For as long as I could remember, my father talked about what a wonderful culture Japan had and how much he wanted to go back. He made us learn to eat with chopsticks. He introduced us to his favorite Japanese food, *sukiyaki*. He taught me a few words of Japanese. But he never traveled there. Now, at last, he would get to share the happy parts of his memories from postwar Japan with his wife, and she would also understand the pain inside him.

One day in April 1983, as plans for the trip developed, my mother walked home from her job in a photography studio. She felt tired by the time she reached the lobby of their building and sat down on a cold marble bench across from the elevator bank. She died as she sat.

My father refused to have an autopsy done. She had been a model once, and he could not bear the idea of her being cut up. He kept looking vaguely into the corners of rooms as if he might spot her lurking. He was supposed to die first.

Ten days later, I gave birth to my daughter. At 92, Nanny made my father bring her to Washington, D.C., to help me as my mother would have done. My father brought an orange rubber tiger toy for the baby. He would balance the baby on his lap and make the toy squeak. He smiled vacantly at her and murmured about how much her grandmother would have loved her. Nanny meanwhile told me to drink wine to make the milk come in and not to wrap the baby too tight. She was always practical.

My brother and I worried about my father's health, but, in the end, he decided to go through with his plans alone. I thought of going along to care for him but, in the end, I could not bring my new baby on a trip to Japan. On November 28, 1983, he left JFK airport and flew to Narita. Iwakura-san and his organization planned a full itinerary of public events and press coverage for my father's visits to Nagasaki and Hiroshima. Unfortunately, his illness drained him quickly of strength and left him sometimes unable to complete the schedule.

Numata-sensei saw my father for the last time during that visit. She told me later that he was amazed at how beautiful a city Hiroshima had become. And that he was also disappointed in a way that it had become much like any other city, with so little left to serve as a reminder to the world of what had been perpetrated there.

Figure 5: View of modern Hiroshima downtown from Hiroshima International Hotel. (Photo taken by Herbert Sussan on December 4, 1983)

My father was happiest about the chance to meet more of the survivors whom he had not seen since they were propped before his cameras, reluctantly showing their terrible injuries to a strange American soldier. He was astounded by the mere fact of their survival. He described the experience of these reunions as if mythic figures from Olympus materialized before him against all odds and, surprisingly, had familiar faces.

Figure 6: Herbert Sussan in front of Cenotaph in Hiroshima with Dr. Nagai (to his left) and five of the Ten-Feet Campaign hibakusha (Nishida-san, Kikkawa-san, Fukami-san, Numata-sensei, and Shibaki-san) dated December 1983. (Photo from Herbert Sussan's collection, photographer unknown)

Figure 7: Herbert Sussan looking down at modern Nagasaki from Glover Park in 1983. (Photo from Herbert Sussan's collection, photographer unknown)

My father's long-imagined return to Japan was at once unbelievable, exhausting, and frustrating. He was not a young man anymore, nor a well man, and his spirit was weighed down. These realities could not have been more painfully clear to him than when revisiting places he had not seen since he was young, healthy, and open-hearted. The reunions with survivors were inevitably emotional, but he had not anticipated how public they would be. In fact, the Ten-Feet Campaign had generated so much publicity that he was a minor celebrity.

When he laid armfuls of flowers in Peace Park, scattering the ubiquitous pigeons, the gesture was filmed by television crews from many international networks. He wrote to Paul about children "who recognize me from Japanese TV coverage and ask for my autograph and adults I meet [who] make me feel like a legend in these parts." American television was conspicuously absent.

Figure 8: Herbert Sussan signing autographs for students in Hiroshima, December 1983. (Photo from Herbert Sussan's collection, photographer unknown)

His return visit to Japan received considerable media attention, especially in Hiroshima, in the wake of the Ten-Feet Campaign. He had talked about showing my mother the scenes of the experiences that so shaped him, but now he had no one with whom to share his emotions. Despite his raw heartbreak and the strains of traveling on his own health, it was an enormous blessing that one of the dreams of his life, giving his terrible memories some meaning by speaking out publicly against nuclear war, came true for him before he died.

Figure 9: Herbert Sussan meeting with hibakusha and Ten-Feet Campaign leaders in 1983. (Photo provided by The Chugoku Shimbum and used with permission)

Figure 10: Herbert Sussan - a moment alone in Hiroshima in 1983. (Photo provided by The Chugoku Shimbum and used with permission)

* * *

WHEN I DECIDED TO GO TO JAPAN MYSELF ALMOST FOUR years later, I was carrying neither terrible memories nor longstanding dreams. I did not know whether I would be there for a few weeks or for many months. I rented my house out and arranged for a neighbor to manage it for me until I came back. The one mission I knew I had was to fulfill my father's last request to scatter his ashes at Ground Zero.

My own life was feeling unmoored. The losses of mother, grandmother, father, marriage, and job in such a short time seemed to have cut too many anchoring cables. Somehow, the solution seemed to be to cut the rest and sail off into uncharted waters. The idea of this trip encapsulated a mix of escape, vacation, and pilgrimage.

I talked to the Japanese Embassy. Getting a visa was no problem but the idea of scattering human ashes anywhere in Japan was anathema to Japanese culture and against the law, they told me. I decided I would not bring his ashes with me and would figure out after I was in Japan what I should do about them.

At the time, we attended a Presbyterian Church in Arlington and my minister there supported my sense of a call to go to Japan and seek how to memorialize my father and his wish to see the films used to educate people on the reality of nuclear war. The church "commissioned" me in a symbolic gesture to carry out this call. The commissioning letter offered me some credibility with various Christian centers that I would visit. Masa would meet us at the airport, and we would stay a few days with his family. We would use our rail pass to travel to Nagasaki at the southern end of Kyushu and then back north to Hiroshima in the south of the island of Honshu, following the route of my father's crew. I wanted to be in Hiroshima for the annual ceremony on August 6. That was the extent of my advance planning. That, and I hoped to meet some of the *hibakusha* that my father had told me about after his trip.

CHAPTER FIVE:

Irashaimase! Welcome to Japan!

TOKYO, JAPAN (1987) — I THOUGHT I MIGHT ALSO FIND satisfying answers to a lot of questions I was asked as a pacifist, or asked myself, when the subject of Hiroshima came up. What about Pearl Harbor? What about Hitler? What about Nanking? What if a man were about to rape your child, would you still be nonviolent and let it happen? What about stopping a murderer? What about killing one person to save thousands?

And, too what is so different about nuclear weapons? Isn't an atom bomb simply a more efficient means of eliminating a city with no different end result than the firebombing of Dresden or Tokyo? Is the real evil all strategic bombing — targeting civilian morale directly to undercut military support? The London Blitz was a terrible thing too. But hasn't every war in history devastated civilians? Was there ever really a pristine combat of honorable soldiers crossing arms to determine the right? Does it matter if the civilian dead were targeted deliberately or were just collateral damage?

My father pointed out one difference in how the atomic bombs were used in Japan. There were eleven cities he knew of that were firebombed and, in those cases, leaflets were dropped beforehand, and the goal of both the warning and the bombing was to destroy morale. Bombing raids sought to disrupt shipping or manufacturing to bring Japan to surrender without a land invasion. But no warning was given of either atomic bombing and, he was convinced, surrender was inevitable and imminent. Japanese industry had already been destroyed and starvation was widespread. He believed the atomic bombings were unnecessary. But I never knew if he would have condemned the atomic bombing as strongly had he thought them essential to victory.

The U.S. Government's narrative after the bombings carefully built up the idea of their necessity and reportedly inflated the likelihood of invasion and loss of life in alternative scenarios. Many authors have debunked much of the narrative from now-declassified primary sources, but that debate is not one to which I can contribute anything novel. My struggle is not to refight what was done in 1945 but to cry out to do differently with what we now know. What does our understanding of the long-lasting effects of nuclear weapons and their proliferation teach us? Can we learn from it?

Is the wrong in the fact of killing, period, regardless of the weapon or the victim? Quakers think of every person as carrying "that of God," so that in some way destroying any person is like erasing one spark of God from the world. But is it different if a government sanctioned the killing . . . or ordered it? So many questions to which I found few decisive answers. At least not answers that would be useful to persuade others operating from different viewpoints.

War technology seems to have proceeded along a systematic path over the centuries. From hatchet to missile. From arrow to cannon. From less to more damage per strike. From tomahawk to Tomahawk, allowing more and more deadly strikes from further and further away from the enemy. Perhaps the glory has been seeping away with every foot of distance between the warrior and the ones to be wounded. Nuclear weapons seem to take us to the end of this path — total destruction from a single strike with no need to view the consequences. What comes after the end of the path?

I suppose, in short, I hoped for a lot from visiting Japan bearing all these questions in my heart.

The purpose of this trip was not easy to explain in advance, even to myself and especially to my four-year-old daughter, Kendra. When she asked why we were going to Japan, I first said we would get to visit Masa in Tokyo. She was excited to see her "big brother" again. "Yay! He's very strong. He lets me hang from his arms!" Then, I explained, "we are going to visit Nagasaki and Hiroshima." "What are they?" she asked me. "They are cities. They are in Japan too. Those are the places I told you about where Pempah [her pet name for my father] took a lot of pictures of what happened when atom bombs exploded there many years ago." And then this —

Will atom bombs explode on us there?

No, no. No, atom bombs will not explode there. The cities are safe now. That happened a long time ago, before even I was born.

I offered up a silent prayer that my answer was true, and that no children in any city anywhere would ever again face an atom bomb exploding on them.

* * *

WE WAVED GOODBYE TO FRIENDS AT THE AIRPORT ON July 5, 1987. We had a three-day layover in Kauai. Kendra was fascinated by hotel sinks made like giant shells and swimming pools with fake waterfalls. Though we watched exquisite sunsets over pristine beaches, as required of any right-thinking tourist, I was far too wired for lazing about. We ran all over the island. Luaus, helicopter viewing tours, natural waterspouts, hotel shows, botanical gardens.

We visited a Japanese Buddhist temple. In the courtyard, as the night darkened, a bonfire drew us into its yellow warmth. Japanese women in colorful cotton kimonos moved in a circle taking slow steps forward and back with stately hand gestures in time to haunting music. I could believe that spirits of the dead might be conjured, beckoned back. In a center ring, many little children, some girls even younger than Kendra, copied the women's movements, or just hopped and swayed to the sounds of the music or their own hearts. We sampled sushi and Okinawan doughnuts from surrounding food booths. A few men and a few *haole* women joined the round as the evening lengthened. Deep-throated drums kept the beat while loudspeakers broadcast songs, which I was told represented regions or hometowns in Japan. After a while, I recognized many matching kimonos and learned that they proclaimed membership in the ten temples on Kauai.

By the time we were in Japan a few days later, my daughter too would be wearing summer *yukata* and we would be joining in such summer *O-Bon* dances as if they were familiar events. The annual *O-Bon* holiday embodies the deep roots of family and clan in Japan. Far-flung relatives return to their ancestral homes to try to bring peace and comfort to the souls of deceased ancestors. They clean graves and prepare offerings. I was taken aback by the ordinariness of what was thought to appeal to the dead – rice, candy, cigarettes, everyday things, as if a dead parent or child were merely out of the room and might be hungry when they got back. After the welcoming dances of reunion, the holiday ends by floating lanterns as boats to carry the dead back to their own realm, where they can do no harm to the living out of jealousy or anger.

From Kauai, we were on to Tokyo. My back hurt and my eyes ached after hours of inventing games and reading stories during the long flight. Kendra fell asleep at last. I never could sleep sitting up, but I closed my eyes, trying to imagine what was waiting for me in Japan. I thought about my father who had arrived in Japan knowing even less about what awaited him.

* * *

AMONG MY GRANDMOTHER'S PAPERS, I FOUND THREE little essays my father wrote as a schoolboy, for which he got A grades. One deals with the League of Nations punishing Italy after its invasion of Ethiopia. The second discusses the character of Madame Defarge as a "real hard-boiled revolutionist" in Dickens's *Tale of Two Cities*. The briefest essay read as follows:

> Although I do not know what life is, and when I shall depart from it, I have been with it through all sorts of incidents. It will be hard for me to leave life, but I will not say good night, but I will say good morning as I enter a new life.

As I flew toward the land of the Rising Sun, I wondered whether my father got to say good morning to a new life.

* * *

I GATHERED ALL THE TOYS, LEFTOVER SNACKS, AND CARry-on bags to disembark at last. After waiting in a long line to get through customs and explaining to immigration why I did not have a departure date, I was dazed and exhausted. Seeing Masa was a tremendous relief. He shepherded us to his car for the two-hour drive to Tokyo itself.

His parents lived in a district called Sumida-ku. On the ground level of their building was a bay for trucks to load and unload products from their confectionary company. To one side, an open staircase led to the upper floors; the second floor held small offices and a meeting room for the family business; the third floor was the family's apartment. We took off our shoes on the third-floor landing before stepping through the front door. Here I first experienced the entryway of a Japanese home. I had worried that I would not know when to take my shoes off, but the row of shoes left just before a large step up and the row of slippers waiting above provided hints. I knew about taking shoes off before entering a home, but Masa had to catch my arm to prevent me continuing in the slippers onto the elevated tatami room in the center of the apartment. One never walks on tatami in anything but socks. What's more, one changes into different slippers (usually rubber) on entering a bathroom or kitchen. After our long stay in Japan, it became so second-nature to slide in and out of various footwear that I did not even have to look down as I did it. In the early days, however, I was constantly tying and untying running shoes and worrying about whether I had the wrong things on my feet.

Their apartment was cozy and comfortable and crowded with multigenerational family members. I realized after a while that our arrival had displaced Masa's grandmother from her bedroom. Framed photographs of a distinguished elderly gentleman, who proved to be Masa's late grandfather, perched along a ledge at the top of the wall. A massive dark-wood cabinet served as a personal shrine, with more pictures, and candles, and offerings of rice balls and fruit.

Futons were spread out for us on the tatami floor. Japanese futons differ from the thick heavy versions that have become popular for sofa beds in the United States. These futons were only an inch thick and folded easily into thirds to be put away in a closet in the morning, along with the sheets and blankets and small hard pillows. Somehow, despite the lack of padding, futons on tatami turned out to be conducive to deep sleep.

I was offered a bath in the Japanese-style tub, the *o-furo*. A bathroom in Japan serves that function alone. The toilet, in a separate room, was itself a bit of a wonder with a miniscule sink built on top of the tank and a panel of control buttons worthy of an aircraft. I was afraid to push anything in case by accident it turned into an ejection seat and sent me flying. The room for baths was altogether different. The whole room was tiled with a big drain in the floor. In the middle of the wall were handheld shower heads on hoses. The prospective bather was to squat naked on a tiny plastic stool, scrub thoroughly and shampoo, and rinse soap off, all before thinking of stepping into the tub.

Luckily, Masa had explained this beforehand too. The worst thing a guest could do would be to step into the hot tub still grimy or even soapy. The family took turns soaking in the water, politely letting the guests enjoy the first round. The water felt like it was boiling at first touch, but I grew to love soaking in the heat and letting go of stress. I still love my hot tub.

Every object in Masa's family home was well-made and comfortable. Nothing was ostentatious or super-sized. I could not imagine a well-to-do American businessman, president of his own successful company, living in a third-floor walk-up apartment above his offices without central heating or air conditioning (rare in Japan) and with a kitchen barely big enough for two people to enter, much less work in, at one time (normal in Japan). Every member of the family ran up and down stairs helping in the office at all hours. A monitor would ding-dong whenever someone came into the building. Clearly, the business remained a family affair, and practicality, not ostentation, reigned. Of course, the well-to-do American businessman could probably never afford the cost of a three-story building smack in Tokyo, especially then, at the peak of Japan's housing bubble.

Masa's father took us all out to the first of many wonderful dinners he would host for us over the years. We enjoyed sashimi, broiled yellow snapper, and shrimp tempura (by which time my daughter was asleep on a bed of cushions). The chef came out and sat down with us after we ate. He drank beer freely while generously sharing his opinions that, among other things: America is still the greatest country; intelligent American women are conservative, but intelligent Japanese women are too radical (this after Masa's father informed him that I was a lawyer, a fact that throughout my stay was greeted with incredulity); and our dinner was delicious but he would make an even better one if we came back. We also learned the story of his life. He came from a rich family, dropped out of college, and worked as a journalist before being called to cooking. The tale sounded like an American kid trying to find himself rather than the lockstep obedience to family I expected. He was perfectly right that the meal had been delicious, though.

After some time getting oriented, Kendra and I moved to a weekly "mansion" that Masa helped us locate. *Mansion*, pronounced "Ma –ng – shi – on" in Japanese, means almost the opposite of the English sense of the word. The building is designed mainly for businessmen to travel inexpensively, so rooms are much cheaper than in a hotel and rent by the week. Our room was barely the size of a walk-in closet. A Murphy bed pulled down from one wall and a table folded down from the opposite wall, but not both at the same time. On a third wall was a kitchenette that would fit in a Winnebago. Finally, the bathroom was so tiny that the small sink and the deep square tub next to it shared a single rotating faucet. Kendra loved the dollhouse quality of it and happily watched cartoons on the little TV while making up her own dialogue in place of the incomprehensible Japanese chatter.

I amazed Masa's parents by setting out on my own with my daughter to explore the city. I didn't grow up in Manhattan for nothing. We were never lost as long I was underground riding the various subway lines. To my surprise, I found many of the Japanese place names recognizable from my brief Chinese studies in high school. I might not remember what most of the characters meant (and their pronunciation was completely different in Japanese), but I could confidently tell them apart and identify the one I was looking for.

Aboveground was a different story. I could not get anywhere from a subway station without detailed directions. For one thing, you seldom saw street signs, even if you could read them; in any case, the name of the street was not part of the address. Furthermore, the buildings were not numbered in any obvious order. Locations were specified by a neighborhood and a house number, mostly assigned in the order local buildings were constructed. This system was great for community identity but opaque to outsiders, which could be said of a lot of Japanese systems.

The saving grace was the reliable presence of the neighborhood *kouban*, a tiny open kiosk staffed by police. Every subway station had a *kouban* within a few blocks. The wall of each *kouban* was covered by a huge map of the neighborhood showing every building. I never went anywhere with my little girl without a slip of paper with our destination written in Japanese. The white-gloved policemen would study my slip of paper and solemnly show me the route on the map, while I tried to memorize the corners and turns. At that point I could understand only a little Japanese but, if I got lost, I would show a passerby my slip and then concentrate on understanding the first two instructions (so many blocks and then a right or a left) ignoring other words. After that, I could always ambush another innocent bystander for the next stage. Besides, even if we never found the goal I chose from the guidebook, wherever we did go was new and interesting. Back was always easy. *Eki*, station, was one of my earliest words, and everybody was happy to point us toward the nearest subway station.

We did a great deal of walking. The main roads were wide enough, but the side streets were incredibly narrow and filled way past capacity. Trucks, cars, and motorcycles zoomed by, dodging around parked vehicles halfway up on sidewalks. The vehicles seemed scaled down to seventy-five percent of their American size, making me feel even more outsized. People poured down the busy sidewalks. Where construction, parked cars, or some other obstacle blocked them, pedestrians too joined the street scene. I was reminded of New Yorkers squeezing around hot dog stands and delivery trucks in a steady stream, like parted columns of ants all determined to get to the food stash.

Bicyclists seemed to be either suicidal or homicidal. The suicidal barreled down the narrow streets dodging the cars and swerving around random disturbances in the flow. The homicidal maneuvered fearlessly down the even narrower sidewalks, through pedestrians, potted plants, old men flinging out buckets of water, and parked bicycles, all left unchained. Amazingly, despite this seeming insanity, in all my visits to Japan, I never saw an accident or its aftermath.

Department stores had miniature amusement parks on their roofs, and the general air of safety meant that kids were left there to enjoy themselves while parents shopped. The top floor usually had restaurants from casual to fancy, and in the basements were counters offering fresh and packaged food to go. I wandered around taking in the smells and sights, as I tried to find recognizable dishes that we could take back for dinners.

Eating was our entertainment in those first weeks in Japan. All the restaurants had lifelike plastic displays of the items they offered set out in the windows. I could order by taking the waitress outside and pointing. Kendra enjoyed looking at all the faux food so much that I bought plastic sushi for her to play with at home. Relatively inexpensive coffee shops in department stores universally offered a kid's *o-bento* lunch in a happy-faced car or a "Hello-Kitty" character platter. Kendra always wanted the Hello Kitty regardless of what food items were in it – and she continues to love Hello Kitty to this day.

Within days, Kendra could say *Arigato, Sumimasen,* and *Sayoonara* — Thank you, Excuse me, and Goodbye. Even that much Japanese always drew applause and cries of "*Joozu! Joozu!*" or "So clever!" But the very first word she mastered was the one that we heard from virtually every child, schoolgirl, woman, or granny who saw her: "*Kawa-i-i-i-i!!!*" meaning "Cute!!!!" I sometimes tired of this universal response to her as if she were an exotic pet, but the oohing and aahing never failed to thrill Kendra. She had finally arrived among people sensible enough to share her four-year-old opinion that she was the center of the universe.

Whenever we entered a store or restaurant, we were greeted by a chorus of "*Irashaimase!*" (Welcome! Welcome!). The shouted welcomes were a bit startling but, after a while, they did make me feel as if we were the very customers they had been waiting for all day. I have been disappointed in later years that most establishments replaced this custom with a tape-recorded greeting when you open the door. I hope it reflects that Japanese women are finding better employment options than standing around department store entry-ways wearing cute uniforms and white gloves just to bow and repeat that word.

Kendra loved Ueno Park in Tokyo, with its zoo, tiny carnival rides, and big ponds. I was surprised, though, to find men sleeping on many of the park benches. With all the talk of Japan, Inc., in those days, I never expected homelessness in Japan, but I saw it in every city I visited. Along Peace Boulevard in Hiroshima, I saw makeshift plastic tarps covering the belongings of homeless men. The homeless in Japan did not seem to panhandle or frighten passersby, as was the common perception of them back in the United States. Instead, they seemed to seek invisibility and to be embarrassed before other people. In Ueno Park, too, ragged men pulled huge carts of cleaning supplies or trash as if they were horses and diminutive old women with cotton work clothes and pyramidal sunhats bent over old-fashioned bundle brooms sweeping all the paths. They looked like peasants straight out of the Shogun TV series. Poverty did not disappear with the post-war prosperity, despite American images of the time of Japan, Inc.

Even late at night, riding the subways was perfectly safe, if not quite esthetic, especially on Friday and Saturday. My image of the staid stoic Japanese character was challenged by the sight of totally wasted men in suits sprawled snoring or bent over retching in the subways. One of the few releases for the *salariman*, and pretty much obligatory for advancement, was the after-work gathering at a bar to drink beer and sake and smoke like a chimney with co-workers. No one bothered us, but it was not a healthy atmosphere for a four-year-old girl, so I learned to avoid the subway on weekend nights.

On a Hato Bus tour, we visited the controversial Yasukuni Shrine (where the Japanese dead from WWII are honored despite protest from anti-militarist groups) and the Imperial Palace (intentionally left unbombed in the War), as well as other tourist destinations. We passed the Meiji Building where my father once had an office. The guide wore a bright yellow uniform, sported ever-present white gloves, and carried a little flag. She was enchanted by Kendra, and the feeling was mutual. Kendra proudly held her hand as the guide gave little speeches to the tour group at each stop. For months afterward, Kendra told everyone she met with great assurance that she would be a tour guide when she grew up.

I tried to imagine what the city could have been like when my father arrived more than forty years earlier, but so much had changed. We came to Tokyo as tourists to a friendly welcome. How different my father's journey to Tokyo had been and how much more uncertain his welcome as an enemy soldier entering a war-weary land. And yet, something in Japanese life called out to both of us.

CHAPTER SIX:

Wizards behind the curtains

HOLLYWOOD, CALIFORNIA (1939) — AFTER A TAXI TOOK him from the end of his long train journey to his new college, my father, Herb, saw exactly the paradise he always imagined. USC was "a small sun-drenched city of its own," with low buildings scattered about a campus rich in palm trees, wisteria, and bougainvillea, alien flora to a New York City kid. "It all reminded me of the setting of a Mickey Rooney and Judy Garland movie," he said, "and then I realized that it had been."

The atmosphere was far different from his four-story redbrick high school building, where students were packed into classrooms in two daily shifts. USC had a student body of only 5,000, a fraction of NYU's, and about the same as his high school. But USC spread across a grassy expanse such as he had never seen at his New York schools.

A student "buddy" met him at the train. Herb eagerly followed this new friend, anxious to get a first look at the cinematography department. They trekked around campus, traipsing through classrooms, offices, and tennis courts. At last, beyond the rest of the buildings, his buddy pointed to a cluster of five nondescript wooden shacks. This, he was stunned to discover, constituted the cinema department. Where were the big studios? The glamorous soundstages? Could he really learn the secrets of making movies in such an unimpressive setting?

The answer was yes. The little encampment served merely as a home base from which to explore the alchemy by which movies were formed. The real education was drawn from the college's unique surroundings. Students fanned out across Hollywood to hear lectures by the likes of David Selznick and Cecil B. DeMille. They learned the secrets, the history, the art, and the magic from the masters of filmmaking. Classes visited all of Hollywood's closely guarded precincts.

Hollywood in those days *was* a magic kingdom. The studio heads, governing like autocrats, kept the curtains drawn and the wizards concealed behind them. Movie stars were managed like thoroughbreds. A star might be gay, alcoholic, or otherwise present a problem, but the studio made certain no paparazzi got close enough to let the news reach the public. Audiences knew little about how films got made. No one had video cameras or cell phones. Home movies shot in eight-millimeter film had only recently become affordable enough for the average family to consider, and the results tended to be jumpy and primitive, in black and white, and without sound. Studying cinematography then was like being initiated into a high mystery.

* * *

ON THE THIN THREAD OF A CONTACT FROM HAVING been a script runner for a radio station in New York, Herb got up enough nerve to call Irving Reis and wangled his first behind-the-scenes look at the industry he wanted so badly to enter. He got invited to watch the shooting of *The Big Street* at RKO Studios. He described it this way in his oral history:

> I marched up to the guard, trying to look as if I entered studios every day, and announced, "Mr. Sussan to see Irving Reis on Stage 7." He picked up a clipboard and ran his eyes down a list. My heart pounded. But, after an eternity, he nodded. "OK.

> You're cleared for Stage 7, two stages down and two
> to your right." I was 18.

> The guard had been working this gate for over 20
> years. He knew everybody in the business, and he
> knew exactly what I was. But, as I stepped through,
> he smiled gently and added, "*Mister* Sussan." I
> grinned back and swung proudly into the studio,
> gawking at the size of those huge, stucco-white
> boxes called stages.

When he found Stage 7, a red light was flashing and a sign
in big letters warned "DO NOT ENTER WHEN RED LIGHT IS
FLASHING." How awkward and frustrated he must have felt sweating under the California sun, young and out-of-place. He watched
technicians rush by carrying cans of exposed film under their arms
to the processing labs. He looked about for anyone he might recognize from the movies. Finally, the red light shut off.

> Just as I started to open the door, it sprang open.
> The door was nearly a foot and a half thick and
> soundproof. Out of it poured a group of people in
> incongruous formal attire. Apparently, they were
> all out for a smoke during a break in the shooting.
> I slipped past and found myself in an enormous
> nightclub. Tables clustered in descending tiers
> around a circular dance floor in the middle of which
> I spotted Irving Reis beside a huge crane camera.
> On the bandstand was Ozzie Nelson, along with his
> orchestra and his wife, Harriet Hilliard. Hundreds
> of extras in full evening dress milled about, waiting

to serve as patrons. A wide staircase swept up to the
top of the set.

The film was adapted from a Damon Runyon tale about a crippled young girl, beloved by the staff of a nightclub. They had all chipped in and paid for surgery so she could walk again. In the scene being shot, she was to be wheeled to the top of the long staircase and, rising out of her wheelchair, to walk down the stairs to the cheers of customers and staff alike. The young girl who came down the stairs when filming resumed was Lucille Ball.

[It was the kind of classic Hollywood ending that my father loved but never quite managed in his own life. He told this story sometimes when my brother and I were trying to watch *I Love Lucy*. I imagined a gangly redhead mugging for the camera as she hopped out of the wheelchair and bounded down the stairs. It never occurred to me that the scene could be anything but comedy. I giggled at the thought of Lucy as a sentimental young girl in a melodramatic scene. I used to laugh at many of my father's Hollywood reveries. I never understood what they meant to him. Irving Reis had given him a glimpse of a special world, full of excitement, passion, and applause. He never found any other world as intoxicating or rewarding.]

Herb had to live in a more prosaic reality most of the time. Although his mother sent him a small monthly allowance, he scrimped by dining on ten-cent packages of Kraft Macaroni and Cheese and was always short of cash in college. He scrounged a job at the college radio station directing educational and patriotic radio dramas. The college production facilities were shared with a local radio station, KRKD. His excitement at making shows for broadcast was dampened only slightly by KRKD's practice of interrupting any program, even a broadcast reading of the Gettysburg Address, to announce the results of horse races. He did find it unsettling to hear: "Fourscore and seven years ago . . . the winner in the first race at Caliente was Red Rose paying 5 dollars and 40 cents . . . our forefathers brought forth . . . ." As he later learned, the station was owned by a group of powerful bookies who saw its main job as getting them the race outcomes fast. Their money helped pay the college station's costs.

Gambling, in fact, became Herb's cash flow solution too. He discovered poker casinos at the farthest stop of the Adams streetcar line in Anaheim. The casinos were housed in long, low wooden buildings with oversized parking lots. Not one boasted a window; not one clock could be found in any of them. Inside the casinos, normal time stopped, to be replaced by an intense smoky immediacy.

> The first time I got up enough courage to peep in the door, I was astonished to find 50 tables, with eight players at each. The room was crowded with housewives and waitresses, laborers and mechanics, old folks, and hookers. Attractive young women in short skirts moved among the tables selling chips to players and collecting rental charges every half-hour, which vanished into the canvas pockets of the money belts around their waists. Two tough-looking men sat on a raised platform overseeing the "collection time" and settling any arguments. I didn't see another student there, and the players were all deadly serious about their poker. No one was sociable; everyone was playing to win. I set myself a goal of $20 to $40, enough for the next week or so at school.

You chose your stakes: 25 cents, 50 cents, or one dollar. You placed your ante in a circle before you. You paid your "rental" for your seat. Already you had to win just to stay even.

I always played the lowest stakes game: five-card draw poker with 25-cent stakes. After I succeeded that first night among the poker pros, I took the streetcar every Saturday morning and sat at the table as long as it took to win my goal. Sometimes it took until Monday morning, and I rode back just in time for my first class.

[This explained the origins of his lifelong success as a gambler. He did not play for the sake of playing, to have fun, or to make a killing; he simply played to get the job done with the least possible risk. He taught me to play blackjack when I was little. He told me once that, if I ever went to a casino, I should take a fixed amount of money, a stake, with which to place bets. "If you run out, go home and count it as the cost of an evening out," he said. "If you win, pocket the excess, and play only the original stake after that until it runs out, then go home with the winnings. Never get greedy and when you win what you need, go home. Never get addicted to the thrills." Mostly I ignored my father's advice and never liked gambling, but I notice I have gone to many risky places over the years, but am always over-insured, which may be the same mindset.]

In addition to his gambling talents, Herb discovered a gift for persuasion. He once organized a network radio program on a zero budget. He heard that Mutual Broadcasting Network was adding a South American chain and proposed an orchestral salute to Latin music. He figured he could draw talented young vocalists and performers from USC programs.

The network asked him who was going to pay the orchestra. He had not considered this and had no money for musicians. He answered, "Well, if I get the program together, will you give me the airtime?" They said, "Sure!" assuming no musicians would work without pay.

Then Herb set to work finding people at USC from different countries in South America. He asked each one to try to convince the folks of their nationality in the musicians' union to get permission for union musicians to do this program without pay. And, in the end, he got it cleared by telling the musicians' union that the actors had agreed to work for free. He twinkled at his own cleverness whenever he told this story because, he said, the musicians' union had never made such a concession in the history of Hollywood.

Next, he had to get the actors' union to agree to this deal. He talked to a classmate who was dying to become a radio announcer. The kid's father was a union official. The kid went to his dad and said, "Look, Herb is gonna put me on the show, but he can't do the program and I can't get on the air, unless your people approve it."

And so it went. When Herb got one group to agree, he would go to the next. When any group balked, he would say, "Well, if I can convince those guys to do it, then will you do it too?"

No one ever thought anyone else would agree. So, they would get rid of him by saying, "Yeah, sure, kid. You get them to do it and we'll do it. But it ain't happening." In the end, he got all the clearances he needed.

> People kept asking me how much I got paid. Well,
> I was 20 years old, and I was standing in this stu
> dio in Hollywood, this enormous, big studio that

could hold an orchestra, and when I put my hand out everything started. I was staggered to look out at a studio with 70, 80 people on stage all looking toward me for cues.

It does something to anybody in that position for the first time, gives them a secure feeling. The strength, the feeling of power that you got doing that was amazing, and I really resented it when people came to me and started saying, "How much are you getting paid?" I thought I should pay them. It went on for several months until finally somebody said, "What are we doing?"

[My father seemed to view this escapade as brilliant strategy. I used to see it as evidence that he was a cheat, tricking people into agreeing to do something they would have refused to do had they been given the full picture. What strikes me now about what he accomplished was how unlikely it was for someone so young to manage so many adults, all show business pros, so effectively. Was it his persistence alone? Or did he have some special charisma or charm to lure them onboard? What had happened to that verve and enthusiasm by the time I knew him?]

Popular stunts at USC included driving around in a convertible with one kid wearing a studio mask of President Roosevelt and waving a long cigarette holder in his well-known gesture. The students loved the joke, but the administration did not. The university administration was thought to be hostile to Roosevelt and to fear that he would take the country into war. USC president Rufus B. von Kleismid opposed talk of any American involvement, on the grounds that the United States had not been attacked and should not interfere in German affairs. [My father repeatedly told me that he got into USC under a "Jewish quota." He blamed his failure to get a degree in the end on the influence of the "Nazi dean and president."]

Herb was so caught up in the "excitement and fantasy of filmmaking that [he] scarcely noticed the ominous developments in the world outside." The hottest topics on campus were whether USC would make the Rose Bowl again and who would be the Homecoming Queen. Herb had so many distractions that he barely managed to show up for his classes.

He studied editing and camera work and literature and play-writing. He took a course on the use of music in cinema from Boris Morros, who had once served as violinist to the court of the Czar and now composed Hollywood soundtracks. Morros reminded Herb of his own Russian-speaking papa, who had also been a fine violinist. Morros always wore garishly colorful shirts and plaid suits, making him the butt of student jokes. His influence later helped Herb obtain his wartime assignment to military film work. [My father was shocked when it was revealed, after Morros's death in the 1960s, that he had been an important double agent for the CIA. But then, my father's capacity to be shocked by government secrecy and deception never seemed to fade, even long after the point when I thought distrust was the only sensible stance.]

One thing Herb did not do while he was at USC was pass his courses. He failed playwriting, for example, despite writing a play for the course that was produced and staged that semester. He had not bothered to turn in an assigned paper. [He did not tell me about any of his own misbehavior when I was young, but, apparently, he did not need a German-leaning administration to flunk out. He confessed much later that he basically poured himself into the experiences he loved and left undone those assignments for which he cared little. Maybe we were related after all.]

On December 7, 1941, he woke up to find that the Japanese Navy had attacked Pearl Harbor, Hawaii. Japan and America were not at war before that attack, although much of the world was. By the end of that day, America was in the war. That was the ultimate reason Herb never graduated.

From the Japanese point of view, "Operation Hawaii" was a great tactical victory. America was clearly poised for war in the Pacific, and now the threat of its naval power had been blasted before it could harm Japan. Japan did send a formal declaration of war, but it was delivered too late and was worded too ambiguously for Americans to consider it fair warning. The American people were outraged and galvanized.

Nothing was the same after that, for the country, for the university, or for Herb.

CHAPTER SEVEN:

A funny place to be stationed

HOLLYWOOD, CALIFORNIA (1941) — AFTER PEARL
Harbor, patriotic fervor swept through USC, as it did through the
whole country. Every male student talked of nothing but where
he could best serve. "No one questioned that we would all enlist.
There was no such thing as an anti-war movement at college. We
were young. We were strong. Our President told us that our country
needed us. In 1941, we never questioned the word of our President."

By the time America entered the Second World War, any
doubts were well stifled, and the young flocked to enlist. Herb had
tried to enlist before Pearl Harbor. He wanted to join a Navy film
unit led by John Ford, but he flunked the physical. He was too overweight by the Navy's standards, and besides, he had had an automo-
bile accident the year before that left a vertebra in his back damaged.

After being rejected by the film unit, he forgot about enlisting
and trudged back to school to try to finish his overdue coursework.
By then, the atmosphere at USC was changing. Rumors spread that
the Japanese Navy was on its way to the West Coast from Hawaii.
Students passed on the story of a Japanese sub that surfaced not
far away and lobbed a shell into an oilfield on the outskirts of Los
Angeles. A far-off war among Europeans had suddenly washed up
on their own beach. Eyes turned in suspicion to Japanese classmates
who had been buddies only weeks before. Within a day of the attack,
the FBI, under Los Angeles director J. Edgar Hoover, was arresting
dozens, and soon hundreds, of Japanese residents, immigrant and

native-born alike. Their names were on lists compiled well in advance of all those with suspicious associations or dubious travel histories or reportedly inadequate loyalties. Most of them had seemed like ordinary neighbors, but now anyone with Asian features was suspect.

One of Herb's close friends in college was Sumo Watanabe, whose father worked at the Japanese consulate in Los Angeles. She was in class one day, and then, "without time for explanations or farewells, she was gone." Not long after, most of the *nisei* students (second-generation Japanese Americans), few of whom had ever seen Japan, vanished to what Herb later called "American versions of concentration camps" and "an infamy of America's own."

After that, the military wanted all available manpower, and Herb was drafted after all. He was placed in the Army Air Corps, though on "limited service" because of the back injury. After basic training, he was sent to Lowry Field in Denver, which had a military photography school. Suddenly, he was teaching filmmaking instead studying it! An old sanatorium had recently been converted to create classrooms alongside an airfield. The school taught aerial photography, foot photography (for ground missions), and filmmaking. Students were sent out on location in the hills around Denver to practice by shooting ghost towns and landscapes.

In Denver, Herb heard that the Army Air Corps had formed the First Motion Picture Unit in Culver City, California. He was eager to serve by doing what he loved — making movies. He applied for a transfer but was turned down. He was told he had no chance of getting that plum assignment.

Meanwhile, he was coming to hate Lowry Field. The facility, which had accommodated only 600 trainees before Pearl Harbor, was scaling up to train 57,000 men annually in 1942. No one had space to themselves; new construction was going on all around.

The photography school ran 24 hours a day in three shifts. He was assigned to the midnight to 8 a.m. shift, even though he never could sleep in the daytime. He felt that his "entire life was upside down and not just from being in the service." He swore that he simply never slept for weeks on end.

The mountain winter had been gathering force around him. One night, Herb decided it was simply impossible. "And I just could not do it anymore." He walked straight out of his barracks and onto the shoveled path. Snow loomed deep on either side. In the dusk, nothing but glittering snow was visible in any direction. The snow blanket muffled the usual noises of a round-the-clock training base. On impulse, he swerved off the path and headed straight into the snow, plowing into fluffy white cliffs. Then he stopped, turned, and toppled backward. He just lay down in the snow.

Surprisingly, this escapade achieved its apparent purpose. He came down with a fever. He heard that, if you got really sick, the Army shipped you home for a month rather than have you lie around the military hospital taking up space. For good measure, Herb added an imaginary pain in the side. He landed in a ward for appendectomies and hernias, attended by a surgeon from the Mayo Clinic who was in the Army now. The doctor was not fooled.

> He examined me and said "Look, I don't think you really need an appendectomy. You want it out?" I said, "Yes."

> The doctor decided that the appendix might as well come out, "because if you go overseas, there may not be good attention and then it's serious. You don't have appendicitis now. You have a potential for appendicitis. I know you are not in extreme

pain. But I am willing to do it." They had us on the tables in the morning lined up one after another.

So, I went in and had that surgery, and I went home to my mother for a month's furlough.

Nanny nursed him back to health with her chicken soup and piroshkies, served with lots of rest and plenty of advice. Herb was almost as eager to get back to base as he had been to leave it.

When he returned to Lowry Field, the much-coveted order for transfer to Culver City was waiting for him. He was warned that he would probably be trained for combat film work overseas. The Motion Picture Unit prepared cameramen to record all sorts of combat conditions. The permanent cohort at Culver City was limited to experienced professionals. Herb did not care as long as he left the snow behind. He was on the next flight back to LA.

From the airport, Herb took the inevitable cab to the gate of the former Hal Roach Studios in Burbank. These studios once produced great silent film comedies with such performers as Laurel and Hardy, Our Gang, Buster Keaton, and The Keystone Cops. The driver glanced at him sideways and remarked, "Funny place to be stationed! Who do you know?" Herb had not known anyone in that sense, as far as he was aware. Years later, he would hear that his old professor Boris Morros pulled strings for him behind the scenes.

As Herb stood handing his orders to the guards, two open convertibles drove out of the gate filled with admirals and generals, "none of them in proper hats." He gasped to the guard about the "carloads of brass all out of uniform," but the man laughed, explaining that they were merely "a bunch of actors on a late lunch break."

Jack Warner was the original mastermind of the First Motion Picture Unit, proposed as a practical way for him to show patriotism without losing his staff. He persuaded Washington to let him form a professional unit to turn out training films for the Army, since lots of men had to be trained up fast. Warner got the rank of colonel and several hundred Hollywood people had found a way to hide out for the whole war. Somehow, however, word leaked that the erstwhile soldiers were also making Warner Brothers' movies on the side.

The real Army arrived in Burbank unexpectedly and ordered all the men in the studio who were in the service to report to an enormous sound stage on Sunset Boulevard. The men were upset when they learned they would be sleeping on cots there that night and eating a dinner called "mess." They were used to sleeping at home and eating well.

The next day, Colonel Warner was relieved of his command. The Army Air Corps really did need training films, however, so they leased the entire Hal Roach Studios instead, for the duration of the war. Paul Mantz, a well-known stunt pilot, was appointed the new Commanding Officer. This choice sent waves of relief through the men. If Warner had been like a father, Mantz was like an old friend.

The guard who greeted Herb on his first day may have been blasé about fake generals, but he was dubious about Herb. He figured this young fellow belonged up the hill where the combat photographers trained, but his orders were for the studio itself. Scratching his head, the guard sent Herb to see the adjutant who should be able to sort it out.

Herb headed for one of two single-story wooden structures serving as temporary barracks, the one with a sign reading "Squadron Commander." Inside he found himself facing an officer at a desk.

> I was astonished to see a face familiar from the movies: Lt. Ronald Reagan, Squadron Commander.
> He said, "I think you're looking for the Adjutant.

Right through there." The Adjutant took a look at my service record and asked, "How the hell did you get transferred here, Sergeant?" He glanced down again at the papers and mused, "Well, we've got a bit of a problem. They thought you could be used in a combat film unit, but you are listed as 'limited service.' I can't assign you to combat training." At that moment, Lt. Reagan came in and the Adjutant turned to him. "Lieutenant, this man was transferred here for combat training, but he's limited service. I can't send him up the hill. He knows a bit about film work, took cinema three years at USC. I can use him here. What do you think?"

Lt. Reagan had the Table of Operations (T.O.) on a shelf, which dictated which officers of what ranks and how many enlisted men of each rank were allowed in the unit. They decided one more was allowed. "If he fits in the T.O., it's all right with me," pronounced the Lieutenant after a look at my record.

I breathed a sigh of relief.

Herb was shown to his cot in the other barracks. The interior of this building was undivided and boasted two rows of twenty bunks separated by seven-foot-high, olive-green lockers. A matching footlocker lay at the foot of each bunk. The room was spotless, if barren. Most of the beds had no linen, and the place seemed barely inhabited. When he asked where the rest of the men slept, Herb was told that the men who used the barracks were either on temporary duty on a movie or were "regular Army." Over time, Herb came to understand the arrangement.

In fact, most of the other "enlisted men" had only altered their lives to the extent necessary to report to Hal Roach Studios instead of Warner Brothers every morning. Their expensive cars filled the parking lot; they returned nightly to their comfortable homes with swimming pools; their uniforms were custom tailored in Beverly Hills. It was the best-dressed air force in the world.

Their military salaries were a fraction of their regular studio income, but their lifestyles did not seem to suffer. They were almost all privates. They had one goal — not to be promoted. A promotion would mean "shipping out," which was a terror to them.

This is not to say that legitimate work was not being done by the unit. Their films helped train an air force in record time. They carried the world of make believe all the way into the military. And they did their job well.

Still, it wasn't like combat. Nobody was getting killed. The only way you could get killed was to have a light fall on you or some horrendous thing of that sort.

Herb served as company clerk, taking sick call, and organizing film crews. One Friday evening, George Montgomery was desperate because he needed the weekend off to go to Las Vegas. He and Dinah

Shore had made plans to get married, but Lt. Reagan had left the post. Herb's talent at forgery saved that romantic adventure when he made them a weekend pass in Reagan's name. If there was an award for the best-liked man on post, Lt. Reagan would surely have won it. He was an all-round "nice guy." He was also a terrific basketball player, popular for games.

> I vividly remember his daily morning ritual. First, he would sit at the desk and, with meticulous care, insert his contact lenses. In those days, contacts were uncommon. I realized that he too must be on limited service, because of his eyes.

> Next, he called me over to a map of the war fronts in Europe and the Far East. He carefully moved colored pins to show where the air forces had struck or the armies had moved. Reagan fought the war very effectively on his map, and I could see his pleasure on the day that he defeated Germany and moved his yellow pins to the Pacific.

[My father once said that world affairs might have been very different if Reagan had been sent to Hiroshima. But Reagan, unlike my father, never left the studio and the "world of unreality" for the real war.]

Herb himself admitted to enjoying the pleasant safety of Hollywood, but something about the city in the 1940s troubled him.

> The races lived in complete separation: Blacks in the Watts area; Asians in Chinatown; and Jews in Boyle Heights. No country club accepted Jews. As a result, prominent Jews in the movie industry built

the Hillcrest Country Club across from the 20th Century Fox Studios. (Ironically, years later, oil was struck on the 8th hole of the club's golf course and its membership became perhaps the most valuable in the area.)

One time the base got advance notice that General Hap Arnold, commanding general of the Army Air Corp, had decided to inspect this peculiar Army installation. Panic ensued until a plan emerged that took advantage of the strengths of the personnel available.

So, there was a script written, and everything that was going to happen was rehearsed on the stages. The two guards at the gate were two actors who were assigned there. They looked perfect as guards.

The generals walked through, and everything happened according to the script that was rehearsed. In the middle of the day, General Arnold stood in the middle of a wide-open area and all the men were brought out. He said, "I know that all of you people would like to be in combat." And they were all scared to death.

"But," he said, "you're doing an important job here, and I think you ought to stay here." And they were all relieved.

There was some real sweating, but it had been a good show.

Of course, Herb was bound to love returning to movie work and working with the Hollywood establishment. After a year and a half, though, a feeling nagged at him that he was not contributing enough to the war effort.

> I couldn't stand it anymore, and I mean it sincerely, I just couldn't stand being involved in a war that went on and on, and I was sitting in a movie studio. I thought it was wrong. Which really is foolish, I suppose, from a practical point of view, but I thought it was wrong.

He applied to Officer Candidates School, expecting rejection. To his surprise, he was accepted, He assumed that, by that time, nobody else was left waiting for admission. So, saying goodbye to Hollywood and all his movie friends, he shipped out to Miami.

CHAPTER EIGHT:

An officer and a gentleman

MIAMI BEACH (1943) — OFFICER CANDIDATES SCHOOL (OCS) sprawled over all the four- and five-story beachfront hotels in Miami Beach. The setting was gorgeous: pastel colors everywhere; palm trees against the clear blue ocean; beaches not yet overdeveloped and overpopulated.

All that loveliness did not relieve Herb's misery, however. He was convinced that every man there was single-mindedly dedicated to making him drop out. He was not, and he would have been the first to admit it, the model of the modern Air Force lieutenant.

To begin with, he was not the right sort of physical specimen, displaying the results of the love of food his mother had instilled [and which he passed on to me]. After being kept inside so much as a boy, he never acquired much enthusiasm for exercise of any kind. [Certainly, I never knew him to participate in any activity more strenuous than walking a few blocks to a deli or pastry shop. He never came along when my mother took us rock-climbing on the granite boulders in Central Park or skating at Wollman's ice rink. I cannot imagine him ever climbing into a canoe or mounting a bike. Not that I have done either often.]

In addition to not looking the part, he did not know how to act the part. Unlike most fellow trainees, he had never participated in ROTC. As a result, he constantly tripped over things that he was expected to have already mastered, from military courtesy to unit leadership.

But Herb's biggest problem trying to make it at OCS was the ridiculous place from which he arrived at the school. He was told the minute he got there, and over and over after that, that "nobody from Hollywood will ever get through OCS." He was inclined to think this might be true, but finally he was told it one time too many. He got mad and resolved that he would get through if only to spite them all.

The price was high, at least to his way of thinking. In three or four months of officer training, he did not see "anything of any pleasure in Miami Beach." What's more, he lost sixty pounds. Between him and success still loomed one ominous last trial — the jungle obstacle course. He was convinced that would break him.

[He was probably right about that. I certainly never knew him to get closer to nature than a sidewalk tree box. I do not think he would have had much luck tackling a jungle. As I say, I inherited his body type and his endless battle against weight. In shape or out, neither one of us was made for gymnastics, agility, or speed. At best, we are more like pack mules, capable of a certain plodding persistence. Both of us were also city-born and city-bred and unable to make sense of a compass or map.]

Fortunately, Herb had a gift for finding ways to navigate his world without overreaching physically. He found an easier approach. The graduation ceremony involved a show to be put on by the graduates. Herb undertook to write the show, called "Stars without Bars." He recruited a musician and a composer, both also from Hollywood and as eager as Herb to edge past the remaining barriers out of OCS. The last month of training was to be spent in bivouac in the countryside. While the rest of the corps marched the twenty-five miles from Miami Beach, the self-styled show producers passed them, riding in a truck with a piano. Then, they settled into a tent with the piano and got down to business.

When it came to lyrics, Herb believed the only way to write them right was to write them lying down. One day, he was lying down in the proper writing position and coming up with clever, if dirty, lyrics. The musician was diddling on the piano with the composer leaning over him. Outside, the sweaty air may have been filled with the shouts and stomps of men training in earnest, but these three creative artists lounged in the tent's shade trying to top each other with a good zinger.

Suddenly, the tent flap whipped open. A colonel marched in, trailing heat and dust. He glanced around and shouted: "What the devil is going on in here?!" Herb leapt up from the bed to his feet. The musician sprang to attention, the piano bench surely crashing behind him as he saluted. Herb answered: "Sir, we are writing a show, sir!"

Drawing a slow breath, the colonel took in the situation. His outrage fixed on the cot, obviously recently abandoned. He glared at Herb, who was no doubt disheveled. "All right, Mister." he finally said. "Continue writing your show. But do it walking, not lying down!" Between writing on his feet and then overseeing rehearsals, Herb managed to slide through OCS without ever going through the dreaded obstacle course.

His mother came down from New York for his graduation. He got permission to meet her at the train station, but she walked right by him. "She didn't recognize me at all. I felt so wonderful at that time. That was the last time I looked that good, and I had become an officer."

Figure 11: Herbert Sussan, portrait on OCS graduation. (Photo from collection of author's grandmother, photographer unknown but likely military photo)

*   *   *

IN 1944, THE NEWLY MINTED LIEUTENANT HERBERT Sussan of the U.S. Army Air Corps was sent to the School for Information and Education – which meant propaganda – then housed at Washington and Lee University in Lexington, Virginia. He learned how to give speeches; to "inspire American troops on why they fight." He inspired himself too, convinced that Americans had good reasons for everything they were doing. [That confidence was crushed later when he saw Nagasaki and Hiroshima. He called it "a shattering feeling . . . such a schizoid kind of feeling."]

His next posting taught him something about the limits in America itself of the freedom for which he believed the troops were fighting. At Will Rogers Field in Oklahoma City, Herb was put in charge of the dining rooms, theaters, and officers' clubs. Thousands of soldiers and officers passed through the base; they needed to be fed and entertained to keep up morale. Even keeping to a small fee for officers to join the club, money poured in. Any money unspent at the end of the year would go back to the federal coffers in Washington. The obvious solution, at least to Herb, to the problem of too many bored men and too much money was to serve great food and put on great shows. He went at it. They served steak dinners for sixty cents and threw parties with music by Harry James's orchestra flown in from Hollywood.

In Oklahoma, he ran headfirst into a culture strange to a New Yorker. The base was strictly segregated. Black troops were housed in dirty shacks left behind by the workers who built the base, while white troops lived on the main base, some distance away. Separate buses were run to carry Black and White troops to separate areas of the city for recreation. This all struck him as "unfair and wrong." He decided that Black troops should be able to see the same musical shows and hear the same Hollywood orchestras, but all he could arrange was that the contracts would all require an extra performance at the Black club after the white club. "The acts weren't pleased with it. Everybody at the Black base still resented that it had to be done that way, and I resented it myself. It would have been much easier to put it on in one place."

Herb was reminded of the lecture that impressed him most back at Washington and Lee. A Jewish dentist, whose name he forgot, spoke to the troops, while standing by the proud statue of Robert E. Lee in the chapel. He asked all the Catholics in the hall to stand up. Then, he asked the Jews . . . and the redheads . . . and he kept going until the whole audience was standing. Herb took the point – everybody was, in some way, a minority. The message had not arrived in Oklahoma.

Between shows, Herb gave pep talks to as many as 15,000 men a week as they passed through on their way to combat assignments. After a while, however, the audience changed. Men started to come back from combat. What could he say to them, Herb asked himself, when he had never seen war as they had? These men had fought mostly in the Pacific which they made clear was "a horrendous place to serve," and they were deeply disillusioned. Herb stopped giving talks about "why we fight" or about the strategies for victory. All these soldiers wanted to hear was reports of what was happening to the men they had left behind.

Herb found it "almost impossible" to imagine himself in their shoes, and it ate away at him. The same guilty itch that drove him out of Hollywood was bothering him again:

> I had been in the military [all this time] and I felt like a fool. I was in the air force doing exactly what I wanted to do all the time. I was in motion pictures; I was in entertainment; or I was in something else of that sort.

> There was something going on out there, and I would like to have felt that I was some part of it. I didn't know what part; I didn't really even know how to fire a gun at that point so I wasn't going to do that. But I thought intellectually that I had something to learn, and I had something to say.

The normal feeling was, "Look how smart I am – I never went overseas," which is what all these fellows in Hollywood had to say, but I felt sorry for them.

So, I wanted to go overseas.

That was an easy wish to fulfill as the war dragged on, and he quickly got orders to ship out to Europe. He was excited about the prospect. He knew from his sophisticated father that Europe was a "civilized place." As he was packing clothes for Northern weather in the fall of 1944, however, the Allied victory in Europe came within reach, while the Pacific Theater of Operations had the more pressing need for troops.

His orders changed. And Herb met his war.

CHAPTER NINE:

Dinner table battles

NEW YORK CITY (1968) — MY WAR IS VIETNAM, OR AT least the fight against the Vietnam war. My father and I fight it over the dinner table.

"I have a right to an opinion, too! I think the government is just telling any lie to make people keep supporting this war." I lean forward and spit the words out. "Why should a bunch of old men send kids to kill people who never did a thing to us?"

My father sits stiff-backed in his cast-iron chair, the biggest one, the only one with arms on it. He speaks in a voice that sounds calm but contemptuous to me. "You don't have enough experience to have an opinion about this! You are just parroting what you hear from a bunch of hippie drug addicts."

The more rational and superior he seems, the more overheated and impotent I feel. "You don't care about my friends that may have to go to Vietnam and might get killed for no reason!" Near tears, I spill some of my No-Cal root beer banging the glass down onto the table too hard. I feel my face reddening and am furious with myself for not being able to hide my feelings.

Our dining table consists of a thick heavy slab of marble with crevasses and variegated colors sprinkled with mica that looks like glitter, all of it sealed in a coating impervious to heat, stains or anything else. My father said the coating was designed to seal spacecraft. No matter what, the surface is always smooth and cool.

It is impervious to my glare. I stare down at our dining room table because I feel too flustered and angry to trust myself to look at my father. From the head of the table, he gazes directly at my mother. She says nothing, but I feel disapproval of me radiating between them. I know she will never be on my side in this argument even though she has no sympathy for the war. My younger brother sits on the opposite side of the table from me, picking at his plate of meat-loaf, garlic bread and green beans.

My father answers me: "In a war, the government has to keep some secrets. The enemy is always listening too. You should show some trust and respect for our leaders and our country. Nobody wants young men to die, but sometimes it is necessary to fight for something important."

"Why should I trust a bunch of liars? If our country is doing something terrible, isn't our job to make it stop? You of all people should know better than to say we should just trust the government!"

I look at my plate. I cannot believe his hypocrisy. My father has whispered about his secret films that the government is hiding. It is all he says about World War II or his part in it. He tells us that the footage should have been shown to the American people and that he could have produced a movie from it that would have shown why atomic weapons should never be used or even made. I have over-heard him nagging friends who are supposed to be able to get access and complaining about the suppression of the film as top secret. As far as I am concerned, he is either being naïve or dishonest to tell me to just trust the government.

"You don't understand how important it is to stop the spread of Communism. If Vietnam falls to the Communists, who knows where it will end! The Communists killed my aunt in Russia, just because she was Jewish. What do you think will happen if we don't stop them there and some day they come here!?"

I vaguely know that Nanny has an old letter with spidery Russian writing that I tried to read when I was studying Russian in school. I never made much sense of it, but Nanny told me it was from her sister Sonya who died in Stalin's camps, accused of smuggling.

"There aren't any Cossacks coming for the silverware under Nanny's bed, and the Commies aren't coming here either. It is just a way of scaring us into going along with a pointless evil war!"

I tease my grandmother sometimes about keeping her silverware hidden under her bed. She told me once about a pogrom when she was young. She saw a "parade," and ran off to follow it, and so was separated from her parents when the rampage began. She finally made it home through familiar streets turned suddenly terrifying. Her family was mostly merchants. Her grandfather lay on the back of a warm stove tending a samovar with tea he sold the Russian way, in glasses with sugared rims. Her mother had a maid, a young Gentile. While the pogrom riots raged, the maid brought them bread since no Jew dared go out. All this seemed so long ago and far away, though, that I could not comprehend why my grandmother might still worry about long dead Cossacks in a vanished world. Any more than I could understand my father's paranoia about distant Communists.

"What if this war goes on and on?" I continue. "In four years, they can make Paul go. Will that be okay with you too? Or then will you stop calling the guys who leave this country rather than fight a war they don't believe in cowards or traitors? I bet when it's your own kid you will be the first to want him to get out of here!" My brother's eyes roll in disgust. He has heard this all before. At least it was me they were yelling at and not him, this time.

"Leave the table this instant and go to your room! As long as you live in my house, you will talk to me with some respect!" I stand up, the chair scraping loudly against the wood floor, and my paper napkin falls unnoticed to the floor.

"Okay, I am leaving. And I will leave your house too! I don't need this bullshit, and I don't need you! Then I will be free to think for myself!"

"You can't leave this house. You are only sixteen, an infant in the eyes of the law. Your job is to get an education. I have not been paying for your schooling for you to waste it. Someday you will regret your attitude and wish you listened to what I am trying to tell you. Get to your room and do some thinking!"

I slam my door and fling myself on to my bed – its frilly canopy out of synch with the posters all over the walls. Martin Luther King, Jr. looks down from one; another warns that "You can't hug a child with nuclear arms." I turn up my transistor radio and catch a recent Beatles tune: "Hey Jude, don't make it bad. Take a sad song and make it better." My face is still hot; it is not fair that I blush so easily.

Some tears squeeze past my pride, but I yank up one of the books lying on the unmade bedspread. I dive into another world where I feel safe and not stupid. When I read, nothing in this world touches me, and I can easily understand everything going on. In books, effective retorts come to the heroines when they need them, not hours later. In books, plots unspool, and people change. In my life, the same arguments replay over and over, and I never make myself understood.

I will be out of this house for good by next September, one way or the other, I vow to myself. If I do not get into college somewhere, I will get a job and my own place somehow. Meanwhile I know how to be somewhere else even while I am still here. Every book opens into a different universe. My mother always says that they could drop the bomb when I am reading and I would not even look up.

*   *   *

LESS THAN A YEAR LATER, MY PARENTS RENTED A CAR – real New Yorkers never own cars – and drove me to Bryn Mawr. They poked around the dorm and got misty-eyed walking on campus. I could not wait for them to leave. I was sixteen and finally free.

Bryn Mawr's campus could be a screen set for a classic college of green lawns and Gothic stone buildings. I was completely uninterested in the scenery. I had not even particularly wanted to go to Bryn Mawr. The dean of my high school was a Mawter and would not sign off on any other applications unless I applied there. I was, according to her, plainly a Bryn Mawr type of girl. I think she meant I was book smart and socially (as well as musically) tone deaf. She was right.

Not surprisingly, I quickly joined the anti-war movement at college. Bryn Mawr was no hotbed of left-wing action, but the Quaker approach of speaking truth to power suited me. The more deeply involved I became in antiwar and civil rights groups, however, the more conflict erupted between me and my parents. I was perfectly clear that my parents were on the wrong side of the famous generation gap, especially my father.

He was full of fears that made no sense to me. He was afraid of the Communists. But he was also afraid that *we* would be suspected of being Communists. Of course, I had no comprehension that he had been through the McCarthy hearings and saw the devastating effects the witch hunts had on the television industry – and especially on Jewish artists in it. He hated that I studied Russian in school. My father's parents were Russian Jews, but they vowed never to speak Russian at home so "the boy" should be a real American. I thought this loss of heritage was a shame and tried to undo it. To practice, I found an international newsstand where I could buy *Izvestia*. My father did not want it in the house. He was even more paranoid when I talked the school librarian into teaching me some Chinese. Of all the languages in the world, I had to pick those two.

* * *

AS A YOUNG GIRL, I HAD DISCOVERED STRANGE PIC-tures on a high shelf in the closet. I was told not to touch them. Three bound books, like large scrapbooks, with black and white photographs of exotic people and bombed ruins. The books and other loose snapshots were stashed in a closet wherever we lived. I once asked to take them to school for show and tell. My father screamed at me.

"They'll arrest me for showing obscenities to minors. Don't ever touch those pictures!" He never explained.

I blushed. I did not know exactly what obscenities were, but I knew that they were shameful. Some pictures I had seen when I pried into the closet were frightening and upsetting, but there wasn't anything about sex in them, so how could they be obscene? They were all old pictures of sick people or ladies in kimonos or smashed buildings. I knew I had done something dangerous and awful, but I did not know what. I worried that "they," the vague powerful authorities, might come for my parents. I stayed away from my father's "dirty" secrets for decades afterward.

* * *

IN THE EARLY 1980s, WHILE THE TEN-FEET CAMPAIGN was making the story of my father's films widely known in Japan, a few American journalists like Greg Mitchell took an interest in my father. I got a call one day from a friend who said to turn on National Public Radio right away. When I did, I heard my father's voice explaining again about how the films were kept classified by the government for so many years, hidden from the American people. He talked about what he saw and filmed. I was confused and annoyed.

He had not told me much of what he now told the world. He had not come to a single anti-war demonstration. He did not go door-to-door arguing for peace. He did not sit through planning meetings, or edit newsletters, or debate strategy. He never came to Washington for lobbying days. So how did he get to be some kind of hero of the peace movement? The thought irritated me. The old dinner battles echoed jealously in my head. Surely just having seen the worst of war, through no will of one's own, is not enough to qualify a person as a peacemaker.

I did not understand until much later that heroism for peace may consist less in doing and more in seeing and bearing faithful witness. The courage of a messenger may not involve marching, or giving speeches, or phoning Congressmen. Sometimes, the call is simply not to do what comes too naturally to many of us – not to avert the eyes, not to turn away, not to close the heart. Why did he see the suffering and human pain where most of his compatriots saw only well-earned victory?

By the time I thought that might apply to my father, he had been dead for decades. In my college days, I had a much simpler view of him – he was a hypocrite because he made TV shows and movies but made no effort to end war.

My war was about marches and demonstrations. He did not talk about his war. And he was right that someday I would wish I had listened to him better.

CHAPTER TEN:

Before the noise dies away

PACIFIC THEATER (1944-45) — HERB FOUND HIMSELF ON a troop ship crisscrossing the Pacific for 38 days on its way to Manila. The ship, as he remembered it, had 36 officers and more than 5,000 enlisted men. Naturally, the situation screamed captive audience to Herb. In no time, he ferreted out the men with talent and mounted performances designed simply to ensure that the troops spent at least thirty minutes on deck every day as command wanted. In between shows, he and a buddy, John Cosgrove, who had Broadway experience, formed a bridge-playing team and proceeded to fleece their shipmates.

The only stop they made en route was Kwajalein Atoll, in the Marshall Islands near Bikini which, ironically, would later become famous as a place to test atomic bombs. That was not what the Navy was using the area for when Herb arrived. The Navy had set up a special way station on a nearby island called Maug Maug. Maug Maug looked "like a Dorothy Lamour set, with a white beach, palm trees and one big shack," and nothing else "except Quonset huts full of beer, Quonset huts full of Irish whisky, and Quonset huts full of Havana cigars." The point was to get as wasted as possible as fast as possible and forget how bad the war was for as long as possible. When the men were totally tanked, they were thrown all together on a big barge to take them back to their ships.

That was Herb's introduction to military R&R, and also the first time in his life that he ever smoked a cigar. From then on, he was rarely without a cigar, sometimes chewing on it unlit. It became a sort of trademark prop for him.

"When the ship arrived at Subic Bay in Manila, the war went live. The city was shattered. Methodical bombing had reduced the streets, shops, and houses to rubble and ruins." This was Herb's first view of a bombed city. It was not his last, but it set the image in his mind of what to expect of a city that had been bombed. Theoretically, the Allies had taken Manila back, but Japanese fighters were still there, hiding during the day.

His first night on the island, he shared a tent with his bridge-playing buddy. They had no choice but to sleep right on the ground having no sleeping bags. In the middle of the night, their tent was raked by machine-gun fire. It was the first time Herb had been shot at. All he ever had to say about it was: "Fortunately we weren't hit. Some people were."

Things were better in the daylight. He hated the Army grub, but Filipina women came in from the villages carrying big baskets of fruit on their heads to trade with the soldiers. He lived on that fresh fruit, savoring its exotic flavors, for days.

He discovered Radio Manila at the Army Air Corps headquarters. The station broadcast all over the Philippines and was headed by a colonel who had been an executive vice-president at CBS in New York. The colonel was eager to take Herb and John on staff. The commanding officer at headquarters had different ideas. He had been waiting for months for officers to fill vacancies in Air Force combat units. The quarrel about where the two of them would go next lasted quite a while.

> So, John kept yelling and shouting, and I stopped shouting. John Cosgrove stayed and a year later he sent me a post card from a place called Mindanao.

He was sitting under a tree with two young ladies giving him coconuts and drinks and fanning him. He had got his way. He was on a little island and had a boat and had to supply all these little islands where they had outpost bases with radios, books, and so forth. He loved the war from then on.

They sent me out to a combat group.

Herb was assigned to the 345th Bomb Group of the 5th Air Force, based on Leyte. They were known as the "Air Apaches," and the squadrons had nicknames like the "Black Panthers" and "Bats Outta Hell." He was a Johnny-come-lately to the B-25 group, which already had the longest service record in the Pacific. He was not a fighter pilot. He was not much of a fighter at all. The young colonel in charge was at a loss for what use he could possibly make of this officer with no visible skills. Finally, he told Herb, "Do whatever you want."

Herb took charge of recreation and post supplies. He accompanied the group when they were sent to Ie Shima, a small island off the coast of Okinawa where Ernie Pyle, the war correspondent, famously died and is buried. They arrived in huge landing ships, carrying tanks on the inside and men on the outside. The minute they came into the port, a panic started. Shouts rang out: "Put the plank down and let us off! Let us ashore!"

Herb was astounded until one of the officers told him what had happened to the group when they arrived in the Philippines. The port commander had made them wait overnight aboard ship before disembarking. Kamikazes hit the ships that night and killed several hundred trapped men. Here, they were much closer to Japan. Now they could see Okinawa, where each cave was bitterly fought over. No wonder they were frantic to get off those ships.

A few months after Herb joined them, the bombing group was called together. They were finally in one place long enough for the many decorations members of the unit had earned in combat to catch up with them. The 345th is recorded as having flown 10,609 sorties by the time the war ended, losing 177 planes and 588 men. By military practice, group decorations went to each man then in the group. Herb was abashed. "There was nothing I could do. So, I ended up with decorations that, as far as I was concerned, I never earned."

The 345th flew daily combat missions from Ie Shima, with high fatalities. B-25s were dangerous to fly even when they were not under enemy attack. These bombers were nothing like civilian aircraft; they were accident-prone, flying low to dodge radar and carrying heavy armaments.

> When I started flying, I realized it was like a piece of tin; nothing like an airplane today. You can hardly visualize it. It would shake like the whole thing was going to come apart and it had nothing between the outside, the tin and you. It was a very scary thing to ride in. At least I thought so.

[This description helped me understand why my father was always proud of his leather bomber jacket. I knew he was not a pilot or a bombardier, so I thought it was just an affectation, but after flying in a tin can in a war zone, you are entitled to treasure such a souvenir.]

Figure 12: Herbert Sussan in flight jacket in front of plane. (Photo from Herbert Sussan's collection, photographer and date unknown)

By this point, Herb found himself drawn into preparations for the upcoming invasion of Japan. Army engineers bulldozed the island: "every tree, every twig, every bush, everything was flattened and wiped clean." Airstrips were being built, as were hospitals for the casualties the Army expected. The base was regularly bombed to slow down progress. They all knew what was coming.

One eerie day, the noise died away, and the hustle stopped in its tracks. The news came in that their commander-in-chief, President Roosevelt, had died on April 11, 1945.

Even in combat, it was as if the world stood still. Nobody could do anything. People all took it as an individual personal loss. Everything stopped on Okinawa and on our island. As far as we could tell, the Japanese stopped too. That night we were not bombed. That night we did not raid any place. People walked around stunned; people walked around shaken.

Harry S Truman was sworn in as President the same evening. And the war went on.

Preparations continued for an invasion. Airfields on Okinawa were lengthened to accommodate longer-range bombing forays to reach the home islands. Troops were massing. Then, in August 1945, all activity came to a sudden halt again. The talk was of a "special bomb" that had been dropped on Japan.

Nobody understood the significance of it, really, when we first heard about it. There had been no inkling among the military, and everything had simply continued for the invasion.

The air raids stopped. The kamikaze pilots disappeared from the skies over Ie Shima. We had been bombed every day because we were so close to Japan, but now they stopped bombing us and we stopped our raids.

Then we heard the Japanese had surrendered.

CHAPTER ELEVEN:

What you don't need if you are not going to fight a war

IE SHIMA, JAPAN (1945) — THE MEN OF THE 345TH LINED the runway on Ie Shima, absolutely silent. Their long service and high losses had earned them the honor of facing the surrendering enemy. In the distance, they saw white dots grow bigger against a blue sky. Soon, two planes, newly painted all white for this role, landed and disgorged the Japanese delegates. These diplomats would negotiate the logistics of Japan's surrender. Ie Shima was a way station on their journey to meet with General MacArthur in the Philippines.

The soldiers were battle-scarred and filled with hatred, fueled by all they had suffered. The war was personal to them. They had been whispering that the Japanese delegates might not survive the flight. After all, the crews of these planes surely shared their feelings.

Nevertheless, the Japanese arrived. Here they came, stiffly disembarking onto the deck, blinking in the sunlight. "Japs" — portrayed in war propaganda with big teeth, crazed barbarism and suicidal persistence — suddenly still and somber. The enemy dressed in diplomatic attire. They looked as alien as extraterrestrials to the roughly 27,000 American fighters, rigidly at attention, staring at them. For many in the bomb group, this was their first close-up look at their former targets.

> To us, they were weird looking in formal clothes and top hats. We all knew we were watching history

in the making. We had had no idea what it would be like. Nobody moved. You could hear a pin drop. It felt like you were not really living at the moment; it felt like you were looking at a saint in a motion picture. At least that is how it felt to me, and that is how it is staged. I recorded the event on film and later put out a special newspaper to commemorate it.

After that, the troops on Ie Shima discovered that the end of the war had different meanings to different people, beyond winning or losing. There were celebrations, filled with jubilation that no invasion was going to be necessary after all. Those who had been in combat for many months would be heading home. And yet, the absence of war hit some as a loss.

That night, several men in our group committed suicide. The pilots who flew these planes into combat had a clear task; they knew how to do it; they identified with what they were doing; and they understood why they were doing it. It seems clear to me that some of them simply had no objective after four years in the Pacific and found going home to God-knows-what almost impossible.

A group of tough men from the Negro company that unloaded supplies from ships and carried them to shore to the depots decided to drink aircraft transmission fluid as their way to celebrate the end of the war. Seven or eight of them died and about ten or twelve went blind. It was the strangest thing in the world to see these giants of men — and they were giants — after what happened to them.

The end of the war had taken away structure, expectation, and raison d'être of all they had been doing there for so long. Some men could not handle the sudden change.

[How much does the persistence of war in history have to do with its ability to meet such real needs for a sense of purpose, for structure, for recognition, for bonding in a common mission with a common enemy? No wonder protesting for peace is such an uphill struggle. The song that says, "War! What is it good for? Absolutely nothing!" is not as dead-on truthful as I assumed.]

*   *   *

HERB WAS LEFT BEHIND WITH A SKELETON FORCE ON IE Shima, as his few months in the Pacific did not qualify him to go straight back to the States. He was given the assignment of wiping out the base that they had been frantically building just days before.

"So how do I do that?" he asked his superiors.

"You dump all the planes off the cliff. You dump all the trucks off the cliff."

"What if the people come back here? They can use the trucks."

"Somebody else will give them trucks."

And that is how he spent the next several weeks. The experience was both disillusioning and educational.

We dumped airplanes off the island's cliffs and into the sea. We dumped wonderful trucks off the cliff. We dumped Jeeps off the cliff. All the equipment we had. This terrible waste seemed typical to me of the military way of doing things.

You have to understand: when there is a war, there is no accountability. That was the first time I understood it.

Everything went off the cliff. What else are they going to do with it? It was combat equipment. If you're not going to fight a war, you don't need it.

It's just like the atomic bombs. If you're not going to fight a war, you don't need them. It's exactly the same.

The war was over. Herb was about to meet the enemy on their own turf.

CHAPTER TWELVE:

We have met the enemy, and are they us?

TOKYO, JAPAN (1945) — AFTER IE SHIMA WAS CLEARED, Herb's next assignment was to accompany a general's furniture on a flight to the new headquarters in Japan. Herb put on a sidearm for the first time. He wanted to look military to face the arrogant soldiers and combative population he had heard about.

Herb flew into an air base called Tachatawa, about 15 minutes by car from Tokyo. Tachatawa was where the kamikaze pilots who had attacked them at Ie Shima had been stationed. He realized that most of them must be dead by now. Their old officers' quarters now housed American officers. And each officer had a private maid who cleaned up his room. Herb watched with interest as the Japanese maids arrived every morning and slipped away to change into their cleaning outfits. His maid was so fastidious she even cleaned the inside of the pot-bellied stoves daily. Every evening, the maid would change back into a kimono and bow to welcome him back home. He understood that these young Japanese women must have provided the same service for the kamikaze pilots just weeks before. They knew exactly where things were and how to do the job. Yet they were unfailingly friendly and polite. He found this confusing.

One day, his maid invited him to visit her parents' home. He was curious, and he accepted.

[Hearing this amazes me. Surely such invitations were not routine, although he does not explain how he came to be welcomed in this way. His height, his pallid skin, his round blue eyes must have been as exotic and peculiar to her as they would later be to those who remembered him from Nagasaki and Hiroshima. I do not know what she and her family may have experienced during the war, but he was their enemy. Was he so innocuous or even appealing in demeanor? Or did they sense the possible advantages of a connection with the new power?]

Herb was scared at first. The town had an unwelcoming closed air. On the surface, no hostility was shown to the conquerors, but he knew that hard feelings must smolder somewhere under the banked fire. The American commanders offered their explanation — that the Emperor had told his people to accept surrender, and they obeyed.

> The Japanese, from my impression, were prepared to fight door by door. I think the only thing that saved all the Americans was that the Emperor, who was not only a political figure and a royal figure but also a god-like figure, decided they would surrender. There was no question how important the Emperor was to the people. I was amazed at that whole phenomenon, this simple business of acquiescence. I decided it was part of the Japanese character and totally foreign for most practical purposes to Americans.

Still, Herb concluded that, while they resented losing the war, most people had not asked for the war. They had lost so much from it. Over and over, he heard from ordinary Japanese, *"Tojo baka, Tojo baka."* General Hideki Tojo, the war minister who had fostered Japanese militarism, was being called "crazy." Herb was startled by the absence of visible antagonism against the Americans, but still he was sure enormous hatred must lurk somewhere, hidden from him. So, he went on his visit with some trepidation but much curiosity.

He had never been inside a Japanese home. He now encountered Japanese customs up close. [He was always as clumsy and oversized as I am, so I can picture him easily: sitting on the ledge in the *genkan* entryway to untie his military shoes; shoving his big stockinged feet into small slippers; bowing to the host and hostess; trying not to bang his head on the low ceilings; awkwardly sitting cross-legged on the tatami with its faint smell of fresh hay; wrapping his too big fingers around a too small cup with no handle to sip steaming tea. Wherever his eyes roamed, they would have found no familiar object to orient him.]

As his hosts served him dinner, Herb's feelings shifted unexpectedly. Over the rice and miso, offered with the best of whatever bits of vegetables or fish they could find to serve an important guest, the family opened a window for him to a different world.

> And I liked what I saw. I didn't want to admit it to myself, because after all, directly as a result of these people, I had lost five and a half years of my life.

* * *

HERB WAS PUT IN CHARGE OF OVERSEEING THE INVENtory of a dozen military post exchanges in the area and of arranging entertainment for the American forces. In a little plane so ramshackle that his feet hung in an open area below, he hopped from base to base inspecting the establishment of the new PXs to serve the occupiers who were pouring in. He discovered the job was coveted because of the opportunities for those working the PX to make money in ways that raised "some ethical concerns." A carton of cigarettes was selling on the black market for $150 when it cost 60 cents at the post exchange. A nickel candy bar could bring ten or fifteen dollars outside. Herb was astounded, but he explained that something held him back:

> I am sure some people got very rich. But I just didn't have the ability to do it . . . I felt that, if I did anything wrong, it wouldn't work. Nobody believes this or believed it in Japan at the time, but I was in charge of 12 PXs and didn't make one penny out of it.

He also staged a variety show for the officers at the air base. The performers were Japanese, brought in from Tokyo. He discovered in organizing this event the nature of the power of a conquering army.

> I have to explain something that is very hard for people to understand. We occupied Japan. That meant we could have or do anything we wanted. The Japanese government had to pay for everything. So, if we said, "We want this thing here," they had to bring it here. I thought this show would be interesting, so we got it and put it on. They were very good.

> Just before the show went on, I went into the dressing room. I was amazed to see the men and women performers all dressing and undressing together. That was one of the customs I learned about. There was a different approach to nudity than we had. I found it interesting. Finally, before I left Japan, I adjusted to it totally, but then it was interesting to me to see how the mores of one country and another differed. Very few people did adjust to it. Including

the chaplain, who didn't adjust to it at all and made us build separate dressing rooms.

Another experience that captured how different the Japanese worldview was from his American attitudes came when he was taken to a shop in Kyoto. A sign on the door said: "Founded 1125." The craftsmen inside the studio were making lacquerware. In the back, an elderly man was working on an especially exquisite screen. The lacquer seemed to have great depth. His son worked beside him.

"That's beautiful," Herb said. "Who is it for?"

"We're making it for the Emperor."

Herb gasped, and the old man explained further. "We've worked on it for 98 years so far. This is the fifth generation working on it."

"Well, when will you finish it?" Herb asked. The answer was: "I'm not certain. I'm not certain yet."

Herb was stunned by this embodiment of the stoicism and fatalism of Japanese philosophy. He decided the Japanese, unlike Americans, could accept time passing without the need to get immediate results. He also imagined how such tolerance of frustration and loss would have played out if an invasion had been necessary and the Japanese had been ordered to fight it. It could only have been terrible.

Figure 13: Herbert Sussan with three traditionally garbed Japanese women in front of torii gate. (Photo credit to U.S. Army; labelled by Daniel McGovern as "Sussan + Geishas in Kyoto 1946)

CHAPTER THIRTEEN:

Finding my father's voice

WASHINGTON, D.C. (2007) – BY THE TIME HE DIED, MY father had long seemed to me an angry and bitter man. Only a hypocrite could hate nuclear weapons but approve of the Vietnam War and support civil rights but not want his daughter to marry a Black man. Only a hypocrite could claim to be dedicated to making a movie to stop nuclear war, but never make it. He talked about his past mostly with resentment. He had been disappointed, cheated even, by someone – the government, the television industry, various business partners, his wife, his kids. He had a sign he taped to the wall with his favorite saying, "No more coulda, woulda, shoulda," but, despite the reminder, he seemed to spend all his time thinking about how things could or would or should have been.

Once I found his oral history at Columbia, though, I discovered an entirely different man. The man who came through in the tale on the tapes was an eager, ambitious, open-hearted young man with a knack for finding himself in the middle of amazing experiences. He seemed so warm and kind. I wish I had met him. My brother's reaction when he read some of the material was the same as mine: "I like this guy, Herb Sussan. Amazing!"

My father did not tell me that his young assistant was using a tape recorder. He did not tell me that her recordings were compiled into an oral history. He did not tell me that he had declined or neglected to sign a release for his oral history to be made public. If I had not discovered it or had not been authorized to open it as his executor, the tapes would have remained sealed. My father failed to tell me a lot of things.

In trying to frame this story, I had to wrestle with why he left so many gaps and silences between us. I had to wonder what right I had to open up things he had left covered. But I realized he was from a generation that taught men they should be strong and stoic. And many veterans do not talk about their wars. Perhaps the silence was not intentional withholding but an attempt to protect loved ones from remembered horrors, or simply an inability to talk about emotions. An older me could hear his story with more compassion than I once was capable of.

I came back from Hiroshima determined to share the story of my father and the *hibakusha* with the world. I set about trying to find out how to write a book. Words are my professional tools and my stock in trade as a lawyer and a judge, but I use them like bricks to build sturdy workmanlike walls of argument. The story I had to tell demanded a different sort of writing. I tried to learn how to do it, attending writers' residences, workshops, and critiquing groups. I studied memoirs and guidebooks on writing creative nonfiction. In the process, I began to understand how it was possible for my father to have cared deeply about getting access to the footage of Hiroshima and Nagasaki and yet have accomplished nothing for years at a time. The book I tried to pull together out of his notes and my own encounters in Hiroshima has taken me thirty years.

In retrospect, I see value in the delay. Had I finished the book soon after returning from Japan, I would not have heard my father's full story in his own voice as I did in the oral history. Had I completed it sooner, I would not have been able to look back across his life with the perspective of having lived longer now than he ever did.

And his voice and my growth allowed different, older memories to return. I started to recapture flashes of the humor and earnestness that still hung about my father when I was quite little. He chanted a made-up ditty that went "Soooo—sahhhnnn is a funny old man!" followed by a string of ridiculous sound effects that could fit in on a Spike Jones recording. He repeated over and over that in Japan we would be little Sussan-sans and laughed afresh every time. I had completely forgotten his laugh.

We would sit on the arms of a huge overstuffed chair each year as he read us *The Night before Christmas*. He would walk through the door with his hands behind his back or in his pockets after a trip, and we would jump and tug on his arms, crying "What did you bring me? Did you bring me a present?" Once, he brought me back a beautiful soft white stuffed cat that I adored and kept with me all the time even when the fur rubbed through and the stuffing peeked out. I would once have sworn he never played with me as a child, but I would have been wrong.

He made imaginary frames from his two hands and pretended to film me dancing, so that I felt like a star. He pretended to direct the world — cuing the Chicago Fire or the San Francisco earthquake at FreedomLand amusement park where we went in the summers or waving his arm imperiously to cut a scene when my brother was crying.

Figure 14: Herbert Sussan in his classic pose using his hands to frame a scene. (Photographer, date, and place unknown, but likely during his 1983 return to Japan)

I forgot all of this until after I listened to his oral history. I can't be sure that the shadow that consumed the father of my early childhood and turned him into the man I remembered in later years was entirely the product of Hiroshima and Nagasaki, any more than I can be sure that the cancer that consumed his body grew from the time he spent there. Many choices are made in a lifetime; such complicated effects as depression and cancer have multiple causes. Nevertheless, I am convinced that what he saw and heard in the atom-bombed cities and his inability to convey those experiences in film lay at the core of what poisoned him.

After the discovery of the oral history, this book became a dialogue. Not his story alone, not my story alone, but the bigger picture of what the bomb meant to, and did to, both of us over the years — first to drive my father and me apart, and then to bring us together across the barriers of years, generations, continents, and even death.

I did not write this book to win old arguments. I might have done that if I had finished the book when I started it in my thirties, which may be another reason I was meant to wait despite my frustration with my own slowness. I did not finish this book now because I finally got answers to the questions that have plagued me for so long – either the personal ones about why my father acted the ways he did or the public ones about why my own country alone has used nuclear weapons or about why wars never end.

The years have given me instead better questions. Questions about where the impulse comes from to create a collective "them," whenever we feel threatened and how that urge leads us to see "them" as less human. Questions about how we can better love each other just as we are, flawed and vulnerable and damaged, and about how we can better love our country and our world.

I became convinced too that the stories my father preserved on tape and the memories he left on my heart were meant to be shared, even if he had not found the way to do that before he died. And that the stories contain the seeds of answers.

I left home young, but I took a long time growing up. Author Louise Erdrich has written that when "we are young, the words are scattered all around us." She goes on to say, "As they are assembled by experience, so also are we, sentence by sentence until the story takes shape."

CHAPTER FOURTEEN:

Strategic Bombing Survey and an imperial engine

TOKYO, JAPAN (1945-46) — SOMETIME IN NOVEMBER 1945, Herb got a call from an old acquaintance, Lt. Daniel McGovern, a distinctive figure, lean and more than six and a half feet tall. McGovern trained as a combat cameraman in Culver City and knew Herb from his days with Reagan there. McGovern had become a respected Army cameraman doing aerial filming in Europe. He wanted Herb to join a special unit being put together for the U.S. Strategic Bombing Survey under the direct orders of President Truman to make a photographic record of the results of the strategic bombing of Japan.

RESTRICTED

GENERAL HEADQUARTERS
UNITED STATES ARMY FORCES, PACIFIC   1-19
AGPD-A

Advance Echelon
APO 500
1 Jan 46

AG 210.453   AGPD

SUBJECT: Order.

TO   : Off, civ and EM concerned, US Strategic Bombing Survey APO 234.

1. Fol-named off, civ and EM now on dy Pacific Hq US Strategic Bombing Survey APO 181 WP o/a 5 Jan 46 to Ube, Hiroshima, Okayama, Kobe, Osaka, Kyoto, Nagoya, Shizuoka, Toyama, Akita, Aomori, Sendai and Hitaichi, Honshu; Nagasaki, Kagoshima, Oita and Yawata, Kyushu; Tokushima, Niihama and Imabari, Shikoki on TDY of approximately thirty-eight (38) days for purpose carrying out instructions. Upon compl will ret present sta. Tvl by mil acft is dir for accomplishment of an urgent mission directly related to the emerg. Rail, govt mtr and water transportation auth. TDN. Transportation Corps will furnish necessary transportation. Alws of 50 pounds personal baggage auth each individual while traveling by air.

1ST LT DANIEL A MCGOVERN 02044851 AC
1ST LT ROBERT H WILDERMUTH 0470775 AC
2D LT HERBERT S SUSSAN 0588154 AC
Mr. Dan B Dyer, Civilian
Mr. Ernest M Hall, Civilian
S Sgt Olaf A Bolm 39530683
S Sgt Michio Shimomura 36979913
Sgt Benjamin R Potts 12064413
Cpl Wallace G Hoover 16160372
Cpl Henry Wischhoefer Jr 19146065
Cpl Raymond V Wizbowski 36868306

2. Above-named off and civ are accredited representatives of the US Strategic Bombing Survey and have been directed by the Chairman, US Strategic Bombing Survey, to inspect plants, buildings, installations, structures, and their contents; examin copy or microfilm books, documents or correspondence and papers, including official reports and records; take photographs, interview military and civilian personnel, when necessary in the accomplishment of this mission.

By command of General MacARTHUR:

B. T. Doyle
B. T. DOYLE
1st Lt AGD
Asst Adj Gen

DISTRIBUTION:
11 off, civ and EM concerned (thru USSBS) (10 ea)   AGPO, Manila (8)
Pacific Hq USSBS APO 181 (1)   AGPD-A (10) AGPE, Manila (8)
Chairman, USSBS APO 234 (1)   AG Records (24)

RESTRICTED

Figure 15: Orders for SBS crew, listing crew members and cities to be visited for "accomplishment of urgent mission."

SBS had had experts in every aspect of Japanese life, military and civilian, tasked with documenting the effects of strategic air attacks on Japan. A similar project had been undertaken in Germany under President Roosevelt's orders. Since the SBS itself had already left Japan to write its reports in Washington, Herb concluded that the concept of doing any filming was an afterthought, maybe McGovern's idea. Herb was excited about the plan and settled in Tokyo to prepare.

Herb bunked in the former Tokyo Electric Company building. When he arrived, he was escorted to a dining room on the top floor. Glass windows on all sides gave a wonderful view of all of Tokyo. A hundred tables filled the room with the finest china and linens that could be found in post-war Japan. Beautiful waitresses in full traditional garb seemed to Herb to float among the tables without touching the ground. The maître d'hôte and busboys wore full formal dress, as if in the best French restaurant in New York. The lunch that day was a buffet with dozens of dishes on long tables. It was a far cry from the combat rations with dehydrated food and chlorine-flavored Coke water of a few months before. It was also a far cry from how the Japanese people lived at that time. Outside, the Ginza was a row of closed stores, and the black market flourished.

Down in a large room on the second floor of the fourteen-story building, another officer showed Herb a shocking sight. With no explanation, the man pointed to a large table on which lay hundreds of parts of some sort of mechanical instrument and asked if Herb knew what it was.

"I haven't the vaguest idea," Herb replied.

The man said quietly, "The Norden bombsight. The Japanese were just about finished putting one together when the war ended."

The Army Air Corps considered the Norden bombsight, an automated targeting system, one of the U.S.'s principal secret weapons making possible effective strategic bombing of targets. If any mission failed, Herb had been told, the crew was admonished to destroy the bombsight first even at the risk of capture. Floaters were removed from aircraft to ensure they would sink along with the bombsight, even if the crew had less chance to escape. No one believed it could be duplicated; no one believed it had ever been captured; yet here it lay. Herb could not help wondering what the outcome of the war would have been if the Japanese had had the bombsight one year earlier.

Herb's team operated out of two rooms in the Meiji Building. From their fifth-floor window, they looked across a moat and medieval battlements, past a classic Japanese arched bridge, into the grounds of the Imperial Palace itself. General MacArthur shared the same view from his office two blocks down the street in the Dai Ichi Insurance Building. Dai Ichi, appropriately enough, means "Number One" in Japanese.

The devastating effects of firebombing were visible everywhere else in Tokyo. Only the Imperial Palace and the street with these two brick office buildings had been left untouched. The United States had not wanted to kill the Emperor, fearing that might harden resistance. The rumor Herb heard was that MacArthur had been planning to use the Dai Ichi building as his occupation headquarters even before the surrender, so it had not been attacked either.

Herb marveled at General MacArthur's authority. He thought the General had the air of a monarch surveying the country he ruled. Yet, from that pinnacle of power, the General had decreed the freedom of all Japanese to vote in elections and to form their own government. He created democracy by fiat.

Herb felt he was witnessing the birth of this democracy when he looked out his office window one morning. Thousands of people surged near a platform across from the Palace. A ten-foot tall sign was hoisted behind a small group of speakers. The noise and disorder suggested a riot. Herb hurried downstairs. He could not understand a word of what was said, but he vibrated with the sense of excitement galvanizing the crowd. He was watching one of the first democratic political rallies in Japan.

Before he left Tokyo, Herb met this imperial democrat in person. He was called to General MacArthur's office. The exchange that followed made him understand why the higher-ranking officers had sent a second lieutenant to the meeting. The Supreme Commander asked Herb, while his crew was out taking these films of various Japanese cities, to also cover just how well MacArthur's occupation was going.

> If we did that film on the side for him, he would very much appreciate that. I can tell you that General MacArthur did not offer it to me as simply a suggestion. It was an order.

This put Herb in a delicate position. MacArthur was more than just a formidable figure. He was already almost a myth — a man to whom no one said no. At the same time, the orders from Washington were specific, and the time allowed to complete those orders was short. He was going to have to turn down the additional assignment. In the end, Herb told General MacArthur that, in order for the crew to do the work he requested, the General would have to contact Washington. If Washington agreed, the crew would do everything in their power to cover what the General wanted them to, which was essentially to make a public relations film for the occupation. The matter was never raised again.

Meanwhile, Herb was rounding up cameras, generators, and cans of film. He simply requisitioned all the color film in the Pacific Theater — and got it. Kodak had started only shortly before making the Kodachrome film that they would use. The SBS set the itinerary and identified the cities to be recorded. A special train was requisitioned for the unit from Japanese government railroad stock for travel to 22 cities on a 38-day timetable. They were to head directly to Nagasaki and work their way back northeast.

Herb was eager to set out on this adventure. This jaunt seemed like a terrific way to top off his time in the service. Just one thing bothered him. Where was the script to plan what they would shoot?

* * *

BY EARLY JANUARY 1946, THE TRAIN STOOD ON THE SIDings at Yokohama, ready to roll with supplies for the eleven crew members who would carry all they needed to live on board. One car held their sleeping compartments; another was a lounge where they could work, and meet, and relax; another, a dining car. Most important was the cold car, stocked with ice, to keep perishables. When they set out, it was largely filled with their precious color film, plus cigarettes and candy bars which served at the time as the principal trading items in Japan. Finally, the train would also haul two Jeeps and gasoline for them, to give the crew mobility in each city.

All that was missing was an engine. After the long war, most train engines were not working for lack of parts to maintain them. Herb had run into the same problem finding operational cameras and equipment from the Japanese movie studios. Anything unessential had been sacrificed to the war effort. At last, an engine was located. On its side, Herb spied a sixteen-petaled polished brass chrysanthemum. Herb found the Yokohama stationmaster and pointed at the golden flower on the black metal. Through an interpreter, the stationmaster explained that this was the symbol of the Emperor of Japan. The crew set out to survey the destruction of Japan drawn by one of the Emperor's own engines.

As the train passed through the crowded railroad yard around Yokohama, the men broke out their first beers. All around, freight cars were loaded with American supplies for the occupation troops, intended to make Japan as much like home for them as possible. Herb gazed out the window at them and wondered at this plenty amid the desperate poverty he saw among the defeated Japanese.

> Poverty was horrendous in Japan after the war. People lived in wooden shacks built out of remnants of homes left after the bombings. Food was sparse and high-priced. Everywhere the black market prevailed. Yet wherever American boys went, there had to be Coca-Colas, Babe Ruths, cigarettes and beer. I saw the seemingly endless crates being loaded on to boxcars . . . and remembered Ie Shima, where equally endless rows of 500 lb. bombs were stacked next to our camp. Better, I thought, mountains of candy bars and Cokes than hills of dynamite.

The train quickly left behind any signs of the Tokyo fire bombings. The tracks ran through picturesque country. Every inch of tillable land along the railroad track was under cultivation. Tidy plots squeezed between houses; craggy hillsides were green and immaculately terraced. The engine chugged and the wheels clacked as they rolled southward. Peasant figures from ancient paintings trudged behind oxen in the watery rice fields. The serenity seemed timeless.

The rail line soon ran alongside the waters of the Inland Sea. While villages nestled in the valleys among these rice paddies had remained intact, most of the coastal towns of significant size had been bombed. The engineer slowed the train as it passed each station. The shells and outlines of destroyed houses were visible from the train windows. The large patches of burnt rubble and grey cinders contrasted starkly with the inviting countryside.

Herb noticed the imperial seal on a door at one small station and sought an explanation. Dr. Earnest Hall, a crewmember, was a former professor of English at Tokyo University and an expert on Japanese culture. Dr. Hall explained that every station in the country had a private waiting room for the Emperor's use alone. Though he might never come, each station was suitably prepared.

The crew of the train pulled by the Imperial engine lived like royalty themselves.

> On our train, we enjoyed dinners of all the steak, vegetables, potatoes, and ice cream we could eat. At the start of our trip, that menu didn't seem unusual to any of us. Most of the world outside was starving, but we ate like kings. Beer flowed freely; my pipe was full of tobacco. I was 24 years old, and a private train was carrying me on a tour of Japan. I was ebullient; my spirits were soaring. I loved to make films, and here I was to be paid for doing it.

> What could be better?

CHAPTER FIFTEEN:

Where Nagasaki used to be

NAGASAKI, JAPAN (1946) — THE TRAIN HAD ALREADY become the world of normality; a break in the steady puffing of the engine and clattering of metal on track was enough to rouse Herb abruptly from a sound sleep. Dawn light filtered into the sleeping car. It was too early, and something was not right.

He raised the shade by his bunk and peered out. The land was gone. The train was sailing along with nothing but water beneath. The rippling water absorbed and muffled the usual train sounds. He seemed to be on a spirit train leaving the world behind. It was some time before he learned the explanation:

> We were crossing the narrow single track over the Shimonoseki Straits between the largest island of Honshu and the southern island of Kyushu. I was looking out on the "wrong" side, so I missed an amazing sight which we later filmed on our way back north. A great graveyard of ships, all half-sunk and protruding out of the sea, spread out for a mile. Giant battleships, aircraft carriers, and freighters of Japan and other Axis countries, had been caught by a hundred B-29s while attempting to escape, and had been bombed in precision raids.
>
> A perfectly legitimate military assault: still, its result displayed again the monstrous wastes of war.

As the train passed the haunted, half-drowned vessels, the mood began to shift. The sense of holiday receded as they rolled toward their first scheduled stop — Nagasaki. Dr. Hall lectured about the city and passed around a pre-war guidebook.

Nagasaki had been a city of some 200,000 inhabitants, spread across the Urakami Valley and extending up the surrounding steep hills. For many years, Nagasaki had been the only port open to foreign trade, starting in the 1500s, despite recurrent spates of expulsion of foreigners and suspicion of their strange ways. Dutch and Portuguese traders, based on the tiny island of Dejima in Nagasaki Bay, had made it the most Westernized city in Japan in those early days. Shipbuilding blossomed where the world's sailors made port, and industry in general had thrived. Christianity survived underground in Nagasaki for over 300 years, despite severe persecution. Those crypto-Christians who were discovered died martyrs. Nevertheless, crypto-Christians were present when an American, Commodore Matthew Perry, arrived in 1853 to force the reopening of Japan to foreign trade. It was not uncommon in Nagasaki to find, in a shop or a home, a figure of Buddha that could be opened in a secret way to reveal hidden inside a crucifix.

The guidebook had promised spectacular beauty. The scenery through which they rode seemed to bear this out. The narrow tracks ran through striking mountain passes and among trees brilliant with reddish browns and yellows.

What most captivated Herb as they rode across Kyushu, however, was not the natural beauty, but the story of the legendary romance of Madame Butterfly recounted by Dr. Hall. The tale was set in the Glover Mansion high on one of Nagasaki's hillsides. In 1904, Puccini debuted his opera about the affair between the American naval officer Lt. Pinkerton and his Japanese "wife." Pinkerton finds a charming young geisha and takes up housekeeping with her while stationed in Nagasaki. He is warned that she loves him deeply, but he cheerfully leaves for a better assignment with a casual promise to return. She bears his child and waits faithfully, watching the ships entering the harbor, awaiting her true love. When he does show up, he is accompanied by his American bride who is "generously" willing to take Butterfly's child to raise. Butterfly commits suicide in at least some versions. Some scholars believed the unlikely claim by John Luther Long, whose story appeared in the January 1898 *Century Magazine,* that his sister met Tom Glover, and heard that he was the son of a real-life Butterfly. Hence, the Glover connection.

The day they were to reach Nagasaki dawned particularly bright and sunny. The romantic tale of Butterfly and her love had distracted the crew for a short time from their mission to create a record "in living color" of the tremendous effectiveness of the strategic bombing of Japan. They gathered in the lounge car of their train to hear a final briefing on Nagasaki's history and geography. Lt. Robert Wildemuth busily polished his brass buckle to a high shine. Harry Mimura methodically checked his Kodak Cine-Special camera. Mimura was a Hollywood cameraman who had been visiting Tokyo when Pearl Harbor was attacked; he was stranded in Japan for the duration of the war. Sgt. Michio Shimomura and Cpl. Raymond Wizbowski played gin rummy, smacking down cards and leaning back in their chairs. Shimomura was a *nisei* interpreter who bitterly blamed Japan for causing the wartime internment of this family in America. Wizbowski was an enlisted man who had been a combat cameraman.

Off in a corner, Dan Dyer slouched deep in thought over his target maps. Herb saw him then as a rather "mysterious individual in civilian clothes," but later became convinced that Dyer was actually a member of the Strategic Vulnerability Section of the Defense Intelligence Agency, involved in planning and targeting of bombing raids on Japan. He concluded that Dyer –

> was making this trip to document his success in terms of the destruction of the targets he had chosen. He was actually, though unofficially, the ranking member of the team. He was a civilian, but the military is run by a civilian head. Then it was the Secretary of War, who is now called Secretary of Defense, but then it was called what it was — Secretary of War. I became the person in charge of production on the train, but Dyer could call for particular sequences to be done.

Herb learned that Dyer carried target maps and was carefully evaluating the corresponding effects of the bombing choices.

Ando-san, the cook, moved among them with a carafe, offering seconds of coffee and filling the car with its cozy smell. Herb sat at another table by himself. He was pecking away at his typewriter, starting a log he planned to keep for the entire trip.

Figure 16: Herbert Sussan working at typewriter on the crew's train in 1946 (Photo credit to U.S. Army).

At last, Dr. Hall ended his remarks on Nagasaki with: "And that's where we dropped the big one."

Early in the afternoon, with the sun still high, the train passed slowly through a ravine to enter the northern part of the Urakami Valley on the single useable track.

> The houseboy came over to me and said, "We're arriving there." My nose was pressed to the glass of the train windows. We entered the city of Nagasaki . . . but there was no city.

> Silence permeated the railroad car. No one moved. I was transfixed, thunderstruck by a monstrosity beyond words. All of us were absolutely stunned.

Some of the men on the train were pretty hard military. They were cameramen that had been in tough military situations. But nobody had seen anything of this sort. And nobody could believe it was one bomb. Dan Dyer broke the stillness to point out a pole not far from the track. He said it marked ground zero.

The total and complete destruction that confronted us is beyond description. Everything outside was gray or a strange color of burnt rust. There was no true color anywhere in sight. Nothing to free my eyes from the endless blocks of rubble in the valley and shattered buildings on the hillsides. The train slowed down, almost crept, on the track which was apparently intact. For the next five miles, the ruins and the rubble were broken only by a religious torii gate left miraculously still standing.

Then we saw the shattered cathedral, which astounded me. I had had no idea there was a cathedral in Japan.

Roof tiles of the traditional Japanese homes covered the ground as far as the eye could see. Their ceramic surfaces were blistered from the heat of the blast or the raging firestorm that followed and consumed any building that survived the first blast.

Not one living creature of any kind could be seen amid the destruction. Evidently, everyone and everything in this part of the city had been killed, injured, or had fled. All this from one bomb.

I silently thanked the Lord that we were inside the train and the rest of this world was outside.

The train with its stunned occupants inched forward. Hundreds of twisted steel girders, heat-blistered and pushed over in one direction, loomed eerily outside the windows. Enough rocks to stock an enormous quarry. A circle of death fringed by green hills. They rolled by elementary and high schools pushed aside as if by a giant hand. Herb was certain that none of the students could have survived the falling ceilings, splintered glass, or dreadful heat that destroyed the interiors. He was amazed to learn later that a few had, though with some of the most horrendous scars he was to see during their stay.

Herb continued to peer out train windows. At last, the train slowed to a halt. What he saw was absence. Not the ruins of a bombed city but mere rubble, vacancy, the lack of movement, the impossibility of life.

That was the first inkling Herb had of what had happened at Nagasaki. He had been given no preparation on the effects of the atomic bomb. He had no idea how it differed from a conventional bomb. He was not told of any special dangers it posed nor of any special precautions to take; they carried no radiation equipment or Geiger counters. He never imagined his government would send them into a location that would be injurious to their health with no warning, no military operation under way, and the war over.

CHAPTER SIXTEEN:

Calling in the Marines

NAGASAKI, JAPAN (1946) — THE AMERICANS SAT GAZING out of the train windows at what was left of Nagasaki Station. A single platform remained next to the siding. On that platform stood the first living people they had seen since entering the atomic wasteland.

A short man in a uniform with polished buttons stood rigidly in front. Two uniformed assistants flanked him. Behind them, eight women in nondescript baggy clothes stood roughly at attention, carrying mops, brooms, and rags. In perfect unison, the entire entourage bowed to the train.

Harry Mimura left the train and walked slowly onto the platform. Solemnly, he returned their bow. Herb watched from inside the train as Harry exchanged words with the obvious leader.

After more bows, Harry returned on board. Behind him, the group on the platform leapt into action. The women scattered around and under the cars of the train.

Harry explained that the proud man in charge was the stationmaster, while the women were the lowest rank in the railroad service whose job was to clean the toilets on the trains. Then Harry paused, obviously finding it difficult to continue.

"The stationmaster welcomes all of us to Nagasaki," Harry finally said. "He apologizes because he no longer has a station . . .."

Figure 17: SBS crew's train at the siding in Nagasaki in January 1946. (Photo credit to U.S. Army; date and place identified by Daniel McGovern)

* * *

THE DAY WAS COLD, THE AIR CLEAR AND BRISK. YET, NO breezes stirred, intensifying the overwhelming stillness that hung over the city. The world seemed to have stopped as the group waited by the train at the Nagasaki Station. Suddenly, a Jeep roared around a turn and up the station ramp to stop alongside the lounge car. Two Marine MPs jumped out and saluted, in a manner to which Herb had grown unaccustomed. The sergeant announced, "Colonel Blackwell sends his compliments and asks how long your unit will be here and what you plan to do. Please report to his office."

Herb rushed back to his compartment to grab their special orders. In all the languages of the Allies (English, Russian, French, and Chinese), as well as Japanese, the orders stated that the group had permission to enter any building, interrogate anyone, acquire any needed food or material, and to demand cooperation of military and civilian personnel, by order of President Truman and the Joint Chiefs of Staff. Along with the orders, he shoved into his briefcase the War Department pass that named him as a representative of the Strategic Bombing Survey "established pursuant to Presidential directive by the Secretary of War of the United States." With these impressive documents in hand, he felt ready to offload a Jeep from their train and follow the Marines to their headquarters at the harbor.

The muddy road carried them away from the center of destruction toward the wharves, about six miles from the hypocenter of the atom bomb explosion. In this direction, he at last saw Japanese people moving about. The convoy passed the Marine encampment, composed of a great number of tents connected by wooden walks. Rainstorms had preceded their arrival, and the entire bivouac area was a field of mud. Above, the hills were dotted with former tourist hotels, apparently undamaged — pretty, pastel-colored villas.

The commanding colonel presided from the former harbormaster's office, with a panoramic view of the harbor where American ships were unloading the ever-popular Coke, candy, cigarettes, and food. Nagasaki harbor, like the railroads, had not been targeted, again with an apparent view to the later convenience of the occupation.

The colonel wore what struck Herb as a commando uniform complete with combat wings. He sat bolt upright behind an oversized, heavy mahogany desk. Herb saluted, identified himself, and handed over his documents. The colonel glanced at the orders and then back up at the young man in front of him. "At ease," he barked. "Sit down."

A barrage of questions followed, aimed at determining how soon he could be rid of this nosy crew. "Colonel, I don't know how long we'll be. I've never seen anything like this. It's going to take longer than we expected."

"What do you want from me?" Herb told him they needed to replenish food supplies and get gas for the Jeeps. "Lieutenant, we are ordered to provide anything you need; we will do so. Just bring the requisition form to the sergeant and he'll see to it."

Thanking him, Herb rose to leave, but hesitated. He told the Colonel that he had passed a number of tents in the mud, and noticed that, on top of the hills, the hotels stood dry. "Why don't you use the hotels to house the men?" he asked.

Nagasaki was an occupied city, and it was occupied by the United States Marine Corps. These Marines had seen combat in the Pacific, fighting island by island, in jungles, beaches and caves. They surely deserved to enjoy the lovely hillside villas, Herb thought.

"Lieutenant, these men are Marines. They like to live in the mud." He pushed a buzzer on his desk, and the sergeant opened the door. Herb was dismissed. He followed the sergeant back to the Jeeps. Herb's face must have shown the effects of the Colonel's last comments.

"Hardnosed, huh, Lieutenant?" The sergeant smiled. "Sure is," Herb answered. "He does it by the book. Told me Marines don't like houses, they like mud."

Just then, a navy landing craft discharged a dozen seamen at the dock, followed soon after by a second group. Two Marine trucks pulled up, and the men crowded onto them. They were loud and boisterous, obviously off duty. Herb could not imagine what recreation they could find in this devastated shell of a city.

"What the devil do they do here?" Herb asked the sergeant. "Go look at the effects of the bomb?" The trucks moved off in the opposite direction; the sergeant offered to show him. Curious, Herb jumped in the Jeep. They sped up one of the hills. They passed a truck parked in front of one of the villas that was visible from below. The men were piling out, acting as if they were on the way to a party. Over the door of the three-story wooden house was a large sign with just the number "1." The other truck stopped at the next house, marked "2." The houses continued up the hill until number "10."

The sergeant anticipated Herb's naïve questions. "These are all brothels, set up to take care of the Navy men docked here. They bring them up in trucks every day. Once they go in, whatever happens, they make them take mercuric oxide [a painful prophylactic procedure of those days] before they can get back in the trucks."

So that was the reason the Marines were not billeted there instead of in the mud.

CHAPTER SEVENTEEN:

Why is this reaction different from all other reactions

WASHINGTON, D.C. (2020) – MY FATHER LOOKED AT Nagasaki and saw something beyond military success, something that portended ill for his own people too, for people everywhere. He described his sense of the place this way:

> It is just almost impossible to verbally convey the feeling of walking through miles and miles of shattered tops of what had been little homes, with nobody, nobody in the area. You can never antici- pate seeing such ruins in your whole life, let alone to have endured it. It is certainly beyond any ability I have to describe, because more than seeing it, it is something that you feel. At least I felt it.

He felt appalled, horrified, but he soon saw that was not a common response. He thought that the Marines "acted as if this was just another town that had been taken in the long and bloody trek from Australia through the Pacific."

I continue to be fascinated by my father's response to the death and destruction around him. He seems to have reacted differently than most other Americans at the time, seeing the defeat for human- ity beyond the victory for the United States. A hideous war was over. The perfidy of Pearl Harbor, the vicious fighting in the Pacific, the atrocities against prisoners of war were all fresh in the minds of the occupying troops—and in my father's. Why was he not simply filled with a sense of triumph or at least relief?

A delegation of Russian naval officers arrived one day on its own train. They looked about the ruins briefly and fixated on a single point of interest. They were fascinated by the street *benjos*. These open urinals consisted of a hole at ground level over which to relieve oneself. Those that were not buried under debris survived the bombing. The idea of such toilets amused the Russians, who took many photographs. Allied sailors too came as tourists and casually picked up burnt roof tiles or melted glass as souvenirs. Nurses had their snapshots taken, smiling, in the ruins of destroyed homes, and then stopped for a quick beer on the train.

Reveling in being alive is not so strange a reaction to overwhelming evidence of mortality. My father was not immune from that feeling. After all, he enjoyed hearty meals with steaks and chickens and cold beer and ice cream requisitioned from military stores and kept in the train's freezer. One evening, during a thunderstorm, he found shelter in the arms of a warm, breathing woman. She was a British captain whose parents had died in the blitzkrieg of London.

Yet, he seems to have found the lightheartness and triumphalism somehow especially inappropriate after he saw Nagasaki. Life was worth celebrating, but death deserved respect. The ghosts of the dead city haunted him without regard to whether they were ghosts of the enemy.

My father was a Jewish soldier in an army that had defeated the Nazis. He was within sight of Okinawa when World War II ended. His tent was machine-gunned in Manila. He crossed the Pacific in troop ships risking enemy sub attacks. Kamikaze planes dive-bombed his base in Ie Shima until the day of the surrender. He would have participated in any invasion of the home islands. He had every reason to celebrate Japan's defeat and to view the Japanese with hatred.

Yet he explained his film crew's work in Nagasaki this way:

> We were the only people with adequate facilities
> and equipment to make a record of this holocaust. I
> felt that if we did not capture this horror on film, no
> one would ever really understand the dimensions of
> what had happened.

I try to imagine what I might have felt or done if I had been delivered so dramatically from the relief of victory to the sight of the hard consequences. Would I have wept, or closed my heart and mind to the costs of my own survival, or felt called to bear witness? Would these sights have made me hate all war, or just thank God that my country had the bomb first? Or both?

Figure 18: Herbert Sussan holding camera – specific place and date unknown.
(Photo credit to U.S. Army)

CHAPTER EIGHTEEN:

Tiny green shoots

NAGASAKI, JAPAN (1946) — THE SUN SHINING THROUGH the train windows woke Herb near dawn the next morning. He listened to the intense and complete silence of the place. The lack of sound was a presence in its own right, not merely the absence of the steam engine's chug or the rattling of the wheels. He stepped out into the morning dew dampening a dead city of rubble. As the sun climbed higher, the valley was illuminated with a white starkness that eerily highlighted the graveyard of broken roof tiles.

He climbed back into his Jeep and set out before breakfast, driving alone toward the hypocenter. His leather flight jacket could not keep out the morning chill creeping into his flesh. He stopped near the marked hypocenter and circled the bare wooden pole, looking in all directions and taking pictures on each side.

Not another soul was in sight. He could see for miles, with nothing to block his line of vision. He saw past the train frozen in the freight yard to the naked girders at the Mitsubishi works. In the direction of the V-shaped gap in the hills through which the train tracks entered the valley, the only standing object was a section of the remaining wall of the Nagasaki prison, precariously balanced at a 45-degree angle. Behind it, the prison, the guards, and the prisoners were gone. They had all received death sentences.

He saw the outline of a medical school and hospital that had been filled with doctors, students, and patients at the moment of the explosion. Later, he was told that a surgical demonstration had been under way in the amphitheater at the moment of the explosion. No one survived the operation.

Nearby was the crushed but unmistakable outline of the cathedral. Inside the ruins, he saw a teenaged girl in a lovely kimono lifting a chalice for the Mass to her lips. The solemnity of the ritual in the ruins took away his breath. Abruptly, the scene vanished, and he realized it was all in his imagination; there was nothing here but a jumble of blocks and broken statues frozen in time. He wept.

> I felt an urgent need to get back to the station and the safety of our train. I couldn't take any more. Tears welled up in my eyes. I just could not accept the inhumanity of it. I knew the other men on the train would not find tears very masculine. I was glad that I was alone. I blew my nose and started back to the Jeep.

Then a movement caught his eye. Herb spotted an elderly man in baggy, worn-out clothing coming down the road. He carried a large watering can in one hand and a rake over his shoulder. Herb felt that the old eyes sparkled and the wrinkled mouth formed a slight smile; he wondered what the man could be doing in this devastated area. The stooped old man bowed to him. Herb nodded and stepped back. The man carefully raked a small section of land where the rubble of roof tiles had been pushed aside. Then the man silently gestured at Herb to come closer and pointed down at the earth.

Looking down, Herb saw tiny green shoots pushing up through the soil. Sparingly and precisely, the elderly gardener fed water to each of the shoots. He was tending a vegetable garden ten feet from ground zero . . . and it was growing. Already life had begun to reassert itself.

After that, Herb found a sense of clarity about the purpose of his presence in this scene. He had seen firebombed cities before, but he was sure that day that Nagasaki was more than just another bombed city.

> My feeling was that we were there — we were there at that moment — and hopefully that moment would never be repeated on earth. And that while we were there, we'd better cover everything we possibly could photographically, and with motion pictures so that people throughout the world could see what had actually happened. We had no expertise in what we were doing. We had really been thrown into this situation, and all that we tried to do was cover whatever we thought we were reacting to.

> For instance, the idea that whatever the force that was used there might have been, it had been hot enough to burn steel and blister stone just stunned me. It was beyond any concept that I could understand. So, we photographed these things when we saw them. I was astounded at the directional effect of what had occurred, and these enormous waves of force that had pushed everything aside. That existed no place else where a bomb had been dropped. A bomb was an explosion. This was nothing like it.

> I could not change or alter any of what had happened. I could not escape the role that I now felt I had to accept, however reluctantly or even fearfully. I was scared and I don't mind saying so. I thought

that anyone who was not afraid of this weapon or who wanted to hide the facts about it had to be blind or demented.

We had military duties in our filming, but surely I could arrange to capture enough of the human tragedy, as well as the physical facts, to make a difference. My personal mission became to get the truth by visual means, which I was sure would be the most effective.

Figure 19: Nagasaki in 1946 from "Japan in Defeat." (Photo credit to U.S. Army)

Figure 20: Nagasaki in 1946 from "Japan in Defeat." (Photo credit to U.S. Army)

Figure 21: Nagasaki in 1946 from "Japan in Defeat." (Photo credit to U.S. Army)

[My father did find words later in writing the "Japan in Defeat" report to describe what he learned about what happened in Nagasaki from the survivors, health care workers and others to whom they spoke, as well as their own observations:

> The congregation at the cathedral was buried beneath tons of red brick and innumerable stone religious statues. Within the gutted circular amphi-theater, corpses of the student doctors, bodies shattered and horribly burned, covered the white, tile floor. The Steel and Arms Works was a twisted mass of steel girders, leaning away from the blast as if shoved sideways by the wrathful hand of a giant. Out of the maelstrom of blast, fire, and debris at the high school, stunned students moved under the rubble, faces and hands seared forever by flash burn. Guards and prisoners perished side by side as the overhead blast brought down the ceilings and walls upon them. In the valley itself, only charred bodies, shattered tile roofs, and wooden partitions remained of the populated areas. Even as the first miraculously saved townspeople ventured forth from the undestroyed sections of Nagasaki on the opposite side of the mountains, the smell of death enveloped the once-alive Valley of Urakami.]

CHAPTER NINETEEN:

Two requests

NAGASAKI, JAPAN (1946) — A LOUD VOICE WAS SHOUTing out names. Herb drove back up to the train just in time to hear the loud voice start commands for exercises. Lt. Wildermuth, the most "regular" of Army officers, had the five enlisted men in the crew out on the platform. The two Japanese staff gazed on in amazement, and the civilians in the crew peered out the train windows at the sight. Herb "found it incredible that morning calisthenics should go on in the midst of this holocaust."

Herb drove straight to Marine headquarters and borrowed a telephone line to contact the officer in charge, Daniel McGovern, in Tokyo. He had two requests. The first was that Lt. Wildermuth be relieved of duty. The second was for open-ended orders to allow them to stay longer and document not only technical results but the stories and treatment of those who witnessed and survived the bombing.

> I claimed that such documentation would serve a military purpose, but deep down I lied. What I really felt was that living evidence would move people, would present a graphic picture, would make a case for eliminating these inhuman weapons.

> Still, I saw then that I would have to walk a difficult path between appearing to serve intelligence needs while filming material that would make the truth of what this bomb was clear to the world.

The first request was accepted immediately, but McGovern hesitated about the second. All the Strategic Bombing Survey experts had returned to Washington to write their reports, and they wanted the film as soon as possible. Herb pressed and finally McGovern agreed to ask, warning that a positive response was not likely. Within a week, though, not only was Lt. Wildermuth transferred, but the project's orders were rewritten to extend "as long as required to complete our mission."

The next order of business was to devise a plan for the task ahead. Herb talked to the taciturn Dan Dyer, who now disclosed that he had been in Nagasaki before on a brief observation trip. Dyer had specific ideas of what he wanted to document for the War Department. His primary interest was to measure precise distances from the hypocenter and film exact technical details at one mile, two miles, and so on. Herb by contrast wanted more on film than ruin and rubble. He wanted to record the human story and the effects on the human victims. Finally, they came to an agreement. Dyer could use the combat cameramen for his plans; Herb would have the civilian cameraman, Harry Mimura, to accompany him.

Harry Mimura proved a fortunate choice. He spoke both English and Japanese fluently. Herb sensed from the beginning that Harry shared his deeper purpose. They liked each other. [They stayed in touch for years. I remember Harry Mimura visiting our apartment in New York City once when I was a kid. He seemed to me just an old man, but I was at an age when all grownups seemed old and boring. By the time I got interested in my father's story and visited Japan, I was sad to learn that Mimura, like my father, was dead.]

They headed for Omura Naval Hospital, set up in the town to handle the worst burn cases and run by two American military doctors. Herb nicknamed them Dr. Gillespie and Dr. Kildare since one was much older than the other. Japanese doctors were working there too, but Drs. Gillespie and Kildare were eager to treat patients with penicillin, which had been found to reduce mortality in casualties during the war. They had requisitioned all the penicillin they could get to help these terrible burns heal and to prevent infection. Penicillin was not available to the Japanese at all at that time. Herb wired Washington trying to help get more penicillin for the two doctors who claimed it could make a life or death difference in treating the burn cases.

Nevertheless, between when they scouted out the location and when they returned to the hospital with cameras to start filming, some beds had emptied as patients had died. What struck Herb was that these people had not suffered a direct hit (almost all of those who had had died at once). These people had been far enough away to come out alive and had had months to recover. Had this been an ordinary bomb, they should have been healing, even if with crippling injuries. Instead, many were growing sicker.

This burn hospital and other hospitals in Nagasaki they visited later were full of inexplicable cases. The after-effects were mysterious, and the mystery was depressing to the helpless doctors. Herb and Mimura decided to photograph all the burn victims they could find, figuring it would be valuable medically to know what had occurred and what treatment was being used. They hesitated a bit, though, about whether it was right to do this.

Dan Dyer, who was meticulously supervising the footage on structures and inanimate objects, had no such problems. The ruins were empty of people. They could offer no objections, standing only as mute testimony to the effectiveness of the bomb.

Herb had already been told that the survivors were being shunned by their own people, perhaps because of their dreadful scars, or for fear that others would "catch" whatever illness was happening to them, or simply because they, however accidentally, had escaped a death that claimed so many thousands of others. If they refused to be filmed, Herb thought the impact of what they suffered in Nagasaki might well be lost. He decided that, despite the breadth of his crew's orders, they would need cooperation before filming the survivors. Knowing that Japanese people deferred to authority, he sought assistance from the governor of the Nagasaki Prefecture.

The governor's office was beyond the circle of destruction, but the small houses and buildings nearby had missing windows and dark burns on their roofs. People were bustling about. Rebuilding was under way here, and small businesses had even begun to reopen. The Jeep pulled up at a three-story brick building, its upper windows replaced by slabs of wood. Inside, they entered wide double doors to the governor's office.

Figure 22: Crew in Jeep driving down center of unidentified town in 1946, with Herb in center. (Photo credit to U.S. Army)

Herb was in full uniform because he felt it crucial to proceed delicately. He was accompanied by Sgt. Shimomura as interpreter. Shimomura resented Japan for having started the war, putting *nisei* like himself in an awful position. This anger was not assuaged by anything he had seen on the trip. Shimomura was an excellent translator, but he had a bad habit.

> On our way to the governor's office, I had a talk with Sgt. Shimomura. While polite outwardly, he vented his feelings by prefacing his English translations with such gratuitous comments as: "The son-of-a-bitch says . . ." or "The little bastard wants to know . . ." I ordered him to play this one absolutely straight. He was amused but saluted and said, "Yes, sir," and smiled.

The governor stood to greet them from behind his large desk. Behind him a newly installed glass window looked out on the city. He was flanked by his own interpreter and another aide. After the required bows and introductions through the interpreters, everyone sat. Herb showed the governor the polylingual orders and explained that they had come to film the physical damage and medical effects of the bombing.

"What do you want the prefecture to do?" the governor asked. "You can see that we already have many problems." Sgt. Shimomura translated his remarks. "Our main problems here," he continued, "are the shortages of much-needed medical supplies and the starvation of thousands of survivors who cannot afford to buy food on the black market. What are you going to do about these problems?"

Herb replied that that a supply ship was bringing American medical supplies for the city. He admitted he had no answer for the long-term food supply problem but assured the governor that five trucks of American rice would arrive the next day . . . enough to feed thousands of people.

The governor responded, in perfect English, "You're right, Lieutenant. It won't solve the problem. But still, thanks for the kind gesture."

To Herb's obvious look of surprise, he said that he had lived in the States for years and graduated from Princeton University. Herb's instincts in warning off Sgt. Shimomura were right. The governor explained that he found it "wiser to deal with the occupation authorities in Japanese. Their remarks to each other are usually revealing."

[This story was one of the few about his time in the bombed cities that my father loved to tell when I was young. At least, the part where he cleverly warned an interpreter to play it straight and it turned out the interlocutor spoke perfect English. He did not mention that the interlocuter was overseeing a starving prefecture overlooking a crushed city.]

He ordered tea and continued, "I know Americans like to get right down to business. What exactly do you really want from me?" Herb explained he wanted to record the survivors, their keloid scars and other injuries, and their stories. He asked if the governor could arrange their cooperation by some method in exchange for help with supplies. The governor's answer sounded typically American.

"Alright, Lieutenant, you've got it. I don't have much choice anyhow, do I? And the rice will be here tomorrow, right?"

In the end, Herb had written authority from the governor before he began to shoot in the hospitals. And the rice did arrive.

> However, I was embarrassed to learn that, though
> it was grade-A rice, it was the bleached long-grain
> variety preferred by Americans, and unpalatable to

the Japanese [who generally favored white or brown short-grain varieties grown in Asia, despite having been reduced to scrounged grains and acorns during the war]. The intended goodwill gesture backfired. Still, it was better to have some rice than none, and eventually it was all eaten.

From that point on, Herb and Mimura spent a great deal of time in the hospitals. They had no doctors or medical experts on the team. They had had no idea what radiation did to the human body. They simply filmed the effects they saw and left it to other people to explain them.

CHAPTER TWENTY:

Facing the quiet survivors

NAGASAKI, JAPAN (1946) — HERB TOOK SPECIFIC CASE histories on all the people to determine where they were when the bomb dropped and what happened to them. [He was stung in later years by some Japanese critics who complained, after the films were finally made public after decades of U.S. government suppression, about the lack of oral interviews. He argued, "If you relate to the situation then, it wasn't easy to record sound, or to make motion pictures, and so on. But we did what we could do." The detailed case histories and sound files that were made have not been found.]

One of the distinctive effects of the extreme heat of the bomb and the burns it caused was that the Japanese developed severe keloid formations. These formations look like growths, making faces look melted, suddenly stopped in time. They saw person after person who had, in one tiny moment of horror when the bomb went off, been scarred forever. Minor happenstances, such as the angle of their body or the pattern on their clothing at that instant, determined the appearance and locations of permanent burns on the body.

And these were the people lucky enough to be still alive. Herb had no way to photograph the thousands of people who had died in past weeks. They heard about people who at first felt fine, who had been in a bomb shelter or far enough away to be unscarred, but who turned nauseous, slowly weakened, and finally died from some new sickness. Radiation sickness was mysterious to Herb.

They visited the Nagasaki Red Cross Hospital. The windows still had no glass but the white stucco building itself was intact. A doctor showed them the room where x-ray film had been stored. The films had all been exposed simultaneously by the wave of radiation.

Doctors pointed out to them a stark demonstration of the bomb's peculiar effects. A patient had lain in bed awaiting treatment at the instant of the explosion. The only evidence that remained moments afterward of the patient's existence was bloodstains. The blood had sprayed across one wall and strangely could be seen on the opposite wall as well. The bomb's blast wave had liquidated him, first spraying out all his blood in one direction and then imploding in a backlash to scatter blood in the other direction as well.

The doctors spoke of their frustration helplessly facing an endless stream of suffering patients after so many of their own personnel had been killed or injured by the blast. Their equipment had been destroyed; they had shortages of all kinds of supplies; they were operating out of improvised laboratories.

> It affected all my senses. I could smell the breakdown of most civic functions. I could touch the shoddy dressings and see the raw major wounds and burns on the bodies of the patients. I could hear the strange dulled silence despite the mob of patients and staff, jammed into every possible space. One difference of the new bomb was the sheer number of the casualties to be coped with at the same time. It was like a dozen busy emergency rooms of Bellevue Hospital in New York, except for the quiet.

In the corridors outside we passed nurses who had survived the blast but bore the scars of glass splinters which had sliced into their faces and bodies with great force. In one operating room, the surgeons were removing glass from patients, a line of whom was patiently waiting.

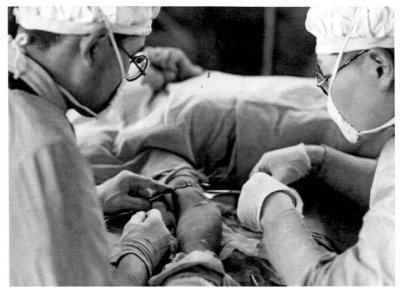

Figure 23: Surgeons at work. (Photo from "Japan in Defeat")

At the Red Cross Hospital, they met the victims face to face. Many outpatients too came into the hospital for filming as a result of the governor's help.

> What remains in my mind from that day is a collage of images which embedded themselves in my heart and my very body. Such sights were never before seen by men. I knew at once that I would never be able to forget them.

> Patients on crutches, missing legs, arms in slings, smashed hands, shattered limbs, burned flesh that did not heal, hideous cuts made by flying glass, children with open wounds around the edges of healed

keloid scars. I was struck by the grotesque accidents that determined the imprints of the bomb that the victim would carry for life.

A woman was burned where her clothing was black but spared where white cloth was and she would wear that pattern permanently. A boy had burns where his pants had holes in their knees. A woman was burned on one side of her face and her hand that was facing the blast at that second, and not on the other. A man who was driving a truck bore keloids illustrating his short-sleeved shirt and its V-neck opening. A young woman whose face looked as if melted wax had hardened was treated by a doctor who was burned on head and arms where he was not protected by the white of a doctor's smock.

Burned babies nursing from scarred breasts as both mother and child were treated by nurses in immaculate uniforms, themselves scarred. Like the blistered tiles, shattered tanks, smashed windows and even the burned concrete of the roads, these human beings were permanently printed with the effects of atomic war.

He filmed a woman who had been wearing a kimono in a checkered pattern at the time of the bombing. She had the squares burnt into her skin. He filmed a young boy who had been swimming in the river that fateful morning. The submerged half of his body escaped injury, but the side that was out of the water on that stroke was severely burned.

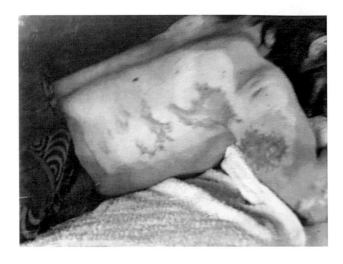

Figure 24: Burn patterns on woman's skin, 1946. (Photo from "Japan in Defeat")

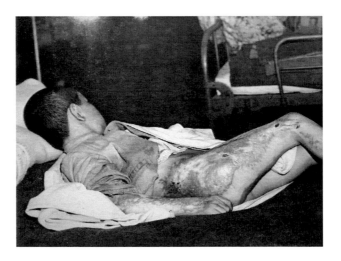

Figure 25: Boy with burned side, 1946. (Photo from "Japan in Defeat")

The third hospital they visited was Urakami Dai-Ichi Hospital (now St. Francis). Patients slept on pallets on the floor or in close-packed beds. They were separated only by the huddled encampments formed by their families – parents, children, wives, or sisters of the patients, each with a small iron brazier on which to prepare food for their kin. They brought the patients water or food when they were able, whispered to them, cared for all their needs, and comforted them as best they could. Herb was struck by how they tended their loved ones quietly, with none of the noise one might expect in an American medical ward. Japanese hospitals regularly required a family member to help nurse the patient and to arrange for the patient's meals. But many entire families stayed with these patients, day and night for months, because they had no other place to stay, no home to which to return.

This sight awoke Herb to the impact of the bomb even on those who had not been killed or injured. He was impressed that everyone patiently waited for doctors and nurses to reach them. No one pressed for special treatment. No anesthesia was available for the painful treatments he witnessed, yet he heard no loud cries or moans.

The worst case he saw in all the hospitals in Nagasaki was the teenaged boy who had been riding his bicycle as a messenger when the bomb went off. His entire back had been burned literally to the bone. He was bathed in as much penicillin as could be scrounged up. It seemed a miracle that he had lived at all, and the doctors frankly did not expect him to survive much longer. The hot lights were set up to make the visual record of what he was suffering. That was Sumiteru Taniguchi.

Figure 26: Taniguchi-san in 1946 from SBS footage. (Photo credit to U.S. Army)

[It was this photograph of the same Taniguchi-san that my father saw and recognized at the United Nations exhibition and that led to the Ten-Feet Campaign. He lived against all odds and became renowned in Japan as an anti-nuclear activist.]

CHAPTER TWENTY-ONE:

Wasurimono nain desho!
Don't leave anything behind!

NAGASAKI, JAPAN (1987) — TINY DANCERS, ALABASTER white, posed frozen in a perfect pas de deux. Only they heard the music. All around them was dusty darkness. But they were not alone. Beside them were their twins. The same beautiful couple lay crushed and broken, as if by the hand of a perverse child.

Kendra and I peered through the glass of a display cabinet in a dimly lit alcove in the A-bomb Museum in Nagasaki. This alcove commemorates the non-Japanese victims of the bomb, among whom were Dutch priests, German missionaries, Asian students, Korean workers, and Allied prisoners of war. It has the feeling of an afterthought. On a slip of paper is the explanation that the statuettes of the dancers were donated by one of the Dutch POWs who experienced the bomb in Nagasaki.

The frightening images and objects throughout the museum brought back memories of the forbidden pictures my father kept on the high shelf of the closet when I was a child. Signs in Japanese and English spelled out numbers and science. I found it hard to process the flood of bland data and awful images. The two pairs of tiny dancers spoke to me directly without needing more explanation. Beauty and cruelty, life and murder, posed side by side, they bore silent witness to everything of which man is capable.

We arrived in Nagasaki the night before on the Shinkansen, the "bullet train," so-called after its pointy nose and its great speed.

We sped overnight down the backbone of Japan from Tokyo to Nagasaki in hours, whereas my father's train trip along roughly the same route had taken days. Women with little carts passed up and down the aisles frequently, offering canned juices and *o-bento* box lunches at high prices. They bowed to the car as they entered and bowed again as they left, but I was not tempted to buy anything. Luckily (and because he knew better), Masa had gotten us frozen tangerines, boiled eggs, and roasted chestnuts from station vendors and instructed me to pick out *ekiben* (boxed meals) for us from the booths before boarding, where they were much cheaper.

Over the heads of the bowing women, an electronic ticker showed in Japanese and English our speed and our arrival times. At each station, a recorded announcement repeated the mantra: "*Wasurimono nain desho!*" Don't leave anything behind! It seemed so appropriate to my mission to recover memories and history that had been left untold for too long.

Only an hour out of Tokyo station, we began to pass rural vistas. We saw rocky cliffs with waves below, a wide lazy river, areas of cultivated fields, and towns with clusters of small houses with their traditional tile roofs interrupted by solar panels. Although I was exhausted from walking around Tokyo and rushing to make the train with our baggage, I sat up long after tucking Kendra in. Like my father, I have never been able to sleep sitting up. I watched placid towns and busy roads whiz by until it was too dark to see any more. We crossed from Honshu to the island of Kyushu over the bridge at Shimonoseki Straits, no longer the site of naval wreckage but instead considered a scenic attraction. The bullet train raced past, toward Fukuoka and beyond, without a break.

Our arrival in Nagasaki was inauspicious. We were over two hours late. I had thought Japanese trains were always on time, but this was an exception. Rain poured on us — from the sky, the roofs, the steps, the walls — like a universal waterfall. Nagasaki had no subway, and I had no idea how to find the youth hostel at which we planned to stay. I resorted to the New Yorker's solution and grabbed a cab at Nagasaki Station.

The door opened by a robot arm without the driver having to get out. All cabdrivers in Japan wore white cloth gloves. The car itself was spotless, and the driver exuded displeasure at the wet wiggling child kneeling on the cloth-covered seat. He insisted on leaving us at the bottom of a steep slope of wet cobblestones, indicating, as far as I could understand, that cars could not go any further and that I should walk uphill to arrive at my destination. We tried. Wearing a heavy backpack and holding Kendra's hand, I trudged carefully up the slippery cobblestones. We finally came to a *kouban*. I communicated our problem by signs, pointing at the hostel in a guidebook and repeating the few words I could muster. The guard took pity on us and called another cab, while various cars whizzed past us up the supposedly forbidden hill. The next driver took us at least ten blocks in a different direction but brought us safely to the right place in the end. I concluded that Japanese taxi drivers may be more polite and much more elegantly appointed than the New York variety, but they are no more reliable.

We left our shoes on the low shelves by the door and crept along in floppy plastic slippers to a small room with two bunk beds. I let the backpack drop and changed Kendra's clothes. We ate dinner at the hostel: rice scooped from a big electric cooker with a plastic paddle, miso soup in bowls lined up on trays, fried cheese and shrimp balls, various radish pickles, and a salad of shredded cabbage with a glob of mayonnaise. We had to scurry to be ready for bed before all the lights went out at 10 p.m. on the dot.

The next day the weather had cleared. Hostel rules required us to be out by 8 a.m., and we bustled off to see the rain-washed city. The hills in Nagasaki reminded me of San Francisco. We visited the Glover House and Gardens as I told Kendra the sad tale of Madame Butterfly. Paths wound around and up and up through courtyards, ponds, and plantings. Huge carp, patchworked in orange, white, and black, congregated hopefully wherever people stopped on the stepping-stones across the wide pools. One could more easily imagine this to be the site of a doomed love affair than a target for an atom bomb.

From the hillside, we had excellent views of Nagasaki Harbor. The port was an industrial and shipping center again, with huge cranes, big ships, and busy dockyards. Mitsubishi Industrial Works, where warships were built for the war, was part of the military activity justifying selecting Nagasaki as a secondary target for the second use of an atomic weapon. (Interestingly, the company's official history of the site skips any mention of the atomic bombing, skipping from the delivery of the battleship Musashi in 1942 to the Emperor's postwar visit in 1949. https://www.mhi.com/company/location/nagasakiw/history/ (accessed Jan. 23, 2020).) Kokura was the intended primary target that day but was spared because of weather conditions.

We went to see Urakami Cathedral, knowing how much its destruction had affected my father emotionally. The church was rebuilt in 1959, intentionally incorporating some of the surviving architectural details from the original building. Two towers housed bells that survived the bombing. The small one had to be recast, but the larger one had been found undamaged. Statues of Joseph and Mary, almost intact but visibly burnt, stood outside surrounded by other statues, left with their heads blown off, as sad sentinels. Inside the beautiful cathedral, no sign remained of anything but peace. The sunlight filtered through restored stained-glass windows. We prayed.

* * *

ON A LEDGE OVERLOOKING THE BAY, I MET THE REAL
boy who did not die, Sumiteru Taniguchi, the horribly burned bicycle messenger whose photograph triggered the connections leading
to the Ten-Feet Campaign. My father was wrong, Taniguchi-san told
me, to worry that his klieg lights added to the pain; in fact, their
warmth was welcome. But the pain was indeed so terrible that,
although he remembers being filmed, he could not think anything
about it at the time. In retrospect, he considered the film "crucial"
to explain the reality of what happened; otherwise, those who saw
him living on might disbelieve "the full horror of what occurred."
Seeing his own photograph from the film brought back even to him
the reality of the hard experiences he endured. He used the color
photograph from the SBS film on his business card so that those he
met would recognize at least a little of that horror.

Figure 27: Herbert Sussan greeting Taniguchi-san during 1983 return trip to Japan
with unidentified individuals looking on. (Photo from Herbert Sussan's collection,
photographer unknown)

Taniguchi-san lived a long life, despite doctors' predictions
and my father's expectation. He even went back to work for the post
office. He married and had two healthy children, and even grandchildren, by the time I met him in 1987. He was 88 when he died in 2017.

Beginning as early as the 1950s, he began speaking out, attending the **Second World Conference against Atomic & Hydrogen Bombs,** held in Nagasaki in 1956 (the first had been held in Hiroshima the year before after the United States first tested a hydrogen bomb). At the conference, Nihon Hidankyo (Japan Confederation of A- and H-Bomb Sufferers Organizations) was organized to bring together groups across Japan supporting *hibakusha* testifying against nuclear weapons. Taniguchi-san felt his children might blame him if he remained silent (and he reported that his children did not experience discrimination despite his outspokenness).

Taniguchi-san was lean and lanky with a drawn face. He showed me his scars, lifting his shirt as he had done so many times. He continued to hate showing them, but they are part of his *kataribe*, a way to teach the world the meaning of nuclear war. His skin still feels cold all the time, he told me, but if he bathes in hot water, the skin is so thin it can crack by touching a hard surface.

His chest and back were carved with empty spaces and strangely stretched skin. His scars are monumental and shocking, even when you think you know what to expect or have seen them before in photographs. Once seen, the scars are impossible to forget.

CHAPTER TWENTY-TWO:

Shadow images of bombs past

NAGASAKI, JAPAN (1946) — IN NAGASAKI, HERB'S CREW captured on film the phenomenon that came to be known as shadow images. Near the center of the explosion, everybody had been killed — many vaporized in the intense heat of the blast. Dark smudges, like strange shadows cast without the sun, marked the only remains of people who had been in the path of the incredible heat wave. These bodies, or indeed any other physical object, imprinted shadow shapes on the stone, steel, concrete, or whatever lay behind them. Herb was haunted for the rest of his life by the incomprehensible meaning of the shadow images. Someone had just disappeared from the face of the earth, leaving only a little residue that was gone long ago and these shadows.

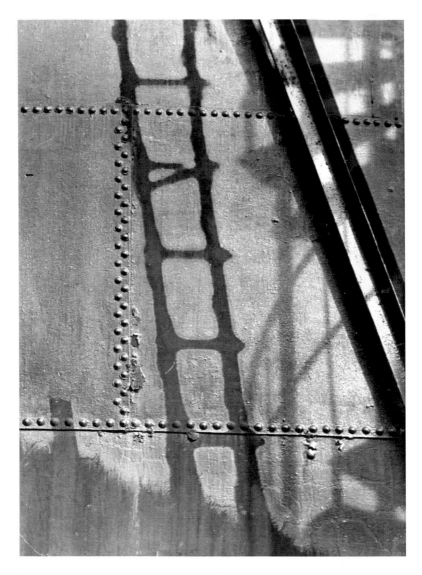

Figure 28: Shadow image of a no-longer-existent ladder in Nagasaki, 1946. (Photo from "Japan in Defeat")

Figure 29: Bridge in Hiroshima showing shadows of the railings on both sides – from the sun casting shadows to the left and permanent shadows from the bomb to the right, 1946. (Photo from "Japan in Defeat")

The eerie silhouettes were one way in which the atomic bombs differed from the effects of any other types of bombs. Radiation sickness was another, of course, and poisoned not only those present on the day of the explosion but also those who entered the city for weeks afterward. The unscathed perished, while some of the most severely injured survived, depending on each individual's exposure to this invisible killer. The difference that most struck Herb, however, was the idea that the entire destruction of the city came from a single bomb. Yes, there were other cities that had been wiped out in fire-bombing, but that took dozens of planes and thousands of bombs. People on the ground during such raids knew a bombing run was under way. But these people were totally unaware of the significance of the handful of planes passing above, and they were swept away instantaneously.

The destruction of the cathedral and the associated medical school disturbed Herb deeply. He could not fathom what made the United States drop such a bomb on the biggest Christian community in Japan. Despite being Jewish himself, he could not swallow the irony of the Christian West placing ground zero just above Japan's only cathedral. Now all that was left of the bravely built cathedral were some pillars, shattered walls, broken and burnt statues of the saints, and large chunks of smashed brick. What the shoguns could not squelch by forcing samurai to tread on the cross or the face of Jesus, the allies had reduced to rubble in an instant.

Figure 30: Herbert Sussan and Dan Dyer standing in remaining arched entrance to Urakami Cathedral, Nagasaki, January 1946. (Photo credit to U.S. Army; identification by Daniel McGovern's notes)

The crew learned that, shortly before they arrived in Nagasaki, a Mass had been celebrated in the cathedral ruins for the first time since the bombing. Herb asked the priest if the service could be reenacted to make a film record, and the priest agreed. The Mass was a scene of great beauty in the midst of horror. All the celebrants were clad in elaborate kimonos and silk veils. The sun shone into the gutted cathedral, shimmering through motes of dust in the air, so that it looked like rays of light coming directly from heaven.

They also filmed the first reopening of a primary school after the bombing. The sight of the children, all dressed neatly, filing into the ruined classroom catapulted Herb into another world. They bowed in respect, according to the prescribed manner, to the teachers who were there to greet them. He was awed by the ability of the Japanese, down to the youngest children, to rebuild their country and their lives after such devastation.

Figure 31: Herbert Sussan in Japanese classroom, date, and place unidentified but presumed to be Nagasaki in early 1946. (Photo credit to U.S. Army)

The church and school scenes were not military at all, of course. Herb and Harry Mimura had resolved to go beyond the hospitals to try to capture the human and cultural aspects of the aftermath. Herb "had a very strong feeling for the people" and struggled against Dyer's single-minded determination to focus on making a technical and military record.

One day, Herb accompanied Ando-san, the crew's cook and attendant, to the harbor depot to requisition food supplies from the Navy. Everyone in those days knew the food on Navy ships was the best in the service. Sailors traditionally were served fresh food, while the Marines were still living on the same K-rations and canned products they had eaten in combat. With their Presidential orders, Herb and his crew could have their choice of food without question.

As they drove, Herb became conscious of Japanese men eating their breakfasts, squatting with backs propped against the remains of small buildings along the way. They all seemed to be eating the same meal: a small tin box of rice. Some lucky few added tiny pieces of seaweed or vegetables to the chopstick-loads of rice. They gave the Jeep a perfunctory glance as it passed them, but no one begged or complained. Hunger was rampant everywhere in Japan at the time. Vegetables could be obtained only by a long trek to the countryside or from the black-market stalls set up in the ruins by farmers who carried produce into the city daily on tiny wooden carts. Meat or fish were often unobtainable. Embarrassed by the luxury of his own supplies, Herb marveled at the dignity with which those meager meals were consumed.

Herb continued to keep a daily log of everything they filmed. He confided to this journal as well his personal reactions to the people he met and sights he saw. Those reactions grew steadily more heart-wrenching and less orthodox.

CHAPTER TWENTY-THREE:

The ceremony of remembering

HIROSHIMA, JAPAN (1987) — HIROSHIMA MEANS "WIDE island." In fact, Hiroshima spreads across a river delta, with many bridges connecting sandy islands. Modern Hiroshima houses over a million people and fairly buzzes with life. Outside of Peace Park, little about the city would suggest the absolute destruction that once prevailed here. Office buildings, banks, restaurants, and department stores crowd along downtown streets. Crosswalks fill with shop girls in various black and white patterned outfits; schoolkids in uniforms form giggling clusters; and *salarimen* in suits bustle across the broad streets to the cheery melody of folk tunes alerting the blind when it is safe to cross the street.

The Shinkansen pulled into Hiroshima station in the early afternoon of August 5, 1987. I expected a small platform and planned to look for a taxi outside. Instead, I found myself in a large station with kiosks and stores and people bustling in all directions. I took Kendra's hand and went to the exit, but I found a large parking lot and bus stops with no taxis or taxi stand in sight. Only after wandering around back inside and asking in broken Japanese (*Takushii-wa doko?*) where to find the taxis, did I figure out that we had to go through a tunnel to the other, even larger side.

There I came upon a photo display that stopped me in my tracks. Poster-size black and white photographs that looked like enlargements from my father's secret closet stash, faces and bodies of survivors, stood in a long row. I stared at them for a long time before hoisting my backpack and heading for the taxis now in sight.

∗   ∗   ∗

BONG! YOU CAN FEEL THE VIBRATION IN YOUR BODY even when the sound can no longer be heard by the ears. And then it repeats. Bong! The sound is coming from a hanging temple bell struck by a beam of wood swung against it.

It is yet again a hot August morning in Hiroshima, the day after our arrival. The deep-toned temple bell slowly tolling out its call sits in front of the cenotaph in Hiroshima's Peace Park. Each year, the bell is brought out on a wheeled base from the Peace Memorial Hall for the annual memorial ceremony. It is rung only this one time each year.

People are streaming across the wide boulevard toward the Peace Museum. An enormous banner announcing the ceremony hangs the length of the building. The museum building is elevated, so people walk directly underneath to enter Peace Park, where the annual ceremony of remembrance is held. From more than a block away, I hear solemn strange music. The flags all fly at half-mast.

Japanese Boy Scouts in full dress uniform offer flower bouquets to the guests and assist the old and disabled to seats. A long slow procession of people approaches the cenotaph where a formal casket contains the roster of the victims of the bomb, to which new names of the dead are added at each ceremony.

Schoolchildren in crisp uniforms, bent old women, *salarimen* and government officials in suits, saffron-draped Buddhist monks, and entire family groups solemnly come forward. They place their flower bouquets reverently, bow their heads, and fold their hands in silent prayer. One after another, waiting tubs with water from

Hiroshima's rivers fill with bouquets and are whisked away and immediately replaced.

The words engraved on the cenotaph are translated as "Rest in peace, for we will not repeat the error." This phrase caused some controversy over the years. Who erred? Who vows never to repeat the error? Do the words imply some fault on the part of the people of Hiroshima? Do they mean that Americans would not make the same mistake again? In the end, the absence of a specific subject has seemed to make more and more sense. The important thing is not so much who to blame but how to prevent such a monstrous fate from visiting any people anywhere for any reason.

The old people are sober and sad and pray deeply. They fan themselves as they find seats. Young people seem a little unsure of themselves, looking sideways at each other to be sure how to behave. The monks strike resonant hand-held prayer drums. Many Westerners seem a bit ill at ease, perhaps worrying whether they are intruding or being blamed. Children and babies alternately gaze wide-eyed or burst into tears, overwhelmed by the unfamiliar people and sounds. The air is perfumed from the smoke of hundreds of incense sticks. Meanwhile, some people busily pose and photograph each other.

Kendra and I walk to Peace Park in a group with other guests, volunteers, and directors from the World Friendship Center (WFC), where we spent the night. When we finally inch up to the cenotaph, I too lay down my flowers and pray for peace.

Suddenly, I choke and find myself in tears. This ceremony seems more like my father's funeral than his own did. And I feel freer to mourn him here.

The orchestra plays a classical piece written about the tragedy of nuclear war. The mayor of Hiroshima reads a proclamation. The names added to the cenotaph this year are read. A moment of silence is observed at 8:15 a.m., the moment that morning when all clocks stopped in Hiroshima. At the pinnacle of the ceremony, hundreds of peace doves are released to fly into the blue sky.

They are ordinary pigeons. The Japanese word for the birds does not distinguish white doves from other pigeons. The "doves" were originally included in the ceremony based on an understanding that they symbolized a message of peace in Western cultures. The rest of the year the sanctified pigeons scratch out their living from the leavings of tourists in Peace Park and have begun to make themselves a nuisance. On their big day, however, none of that detracts from the poignancy of their soaring into the sky.

* * *

THIS PUBLIC CEREMONY IS THE SECOND REMEMBRANCE held that day. Hours earlier, a private ceremony took place at dawn in a quiet corner of Peace Park. Only *hibakusha*, peace activists, and a few guests attended this intimate ceremony. No pomp or music or speeches interrupted silent reflections. Those survivors who shun the public gathering assemble near the mound in which are interred the ashes of the unknown dead. I am unaware of this ceremony that first time I attend the anniversary, but I join it on future visits to Hiroshima.

By then, I have come to see myself as a second-generation *hibakusha*.

CHAPTER TWENTY-FOUR:

The sun always sees

HIROSHIMA, JAPAN (1987) — AFTER THE CEREMONY, WE returned to the World Friendship Center. WFC was founded in 1965 by Barbara Reynolds, a Quaker who became known as a Peace Pilgrim for her persistent struggle against nuclear weapons. WFC's mission is to offer inexpensive hospitality for visitors seeking to understand Hiroshima's unique role as a city of hope, as well as to host activities aimed at preserving the peace message from Hiroshima and building bridges of friendship between the Japanese people and the rest of the world. International directors come for two years to manage WFC, supported by dedicated local volunteers.

When we first stayed there, WFC was housed in a traditional-style Japanese home a short ride from the train station. During our first visit, the directors were Bill and Jeanne Chappell, a retired American couple who were members of the Church of the Brethren, one of the three historic peace churches along with the Mennonites and my own denomination, Quakers.

Beside the entrance, I saw the first of many peace poles with signs reading: "May peace prevail on earth." These signs are sometimes mounted directly on buildings but are more often placed on four- or six-sided wooden poles. The signs are produced in a huge variety of languages and are displayed all over Hiroshima, but I had never seen them in the United States before our time in Japan. A year later, however, when I took Kendra to her American kindergarten at the Quaker Sidwell Friends School, I was thrilled to find a familiar peace pole welcoming us near the entrance. (These days, I pass it on Sundays when I attend my Quaker meeting held on Sidwell's campus. Another greets me on return beside my front door with signs in English, Japanese, Russian (for my grandmother Nanny), and Portuguese (for my mother, who was born in Brazil). After September 11, 2001, I added a plaque in Arabic, only to have it defaced by a vandal – I have replaced it.

WFC sponsored "coffee house and friendship" nights, organized home stays with Japanese hosts, held English-language classes and discussion groups, and arranged opportunities for survivors of the atom bomb to speak locally and internationally. On August 6, 1987, WFC hosted *kataribe* for visitors from three *hibakusha*: Fumiko Sora, Michiko Yamoaka, and Chiyo Takeuchi. Sora-sensei taught English for many years but had dedicated herself to sharing her message of peace to visitors from all over the world. Yamaoka-san was one of the Hiroshima Maidens and still bore the scars on her face. She maintained deep ties with Sidwell Friends School from the time when Quakers offered refuge to the Maidens. All three women had been to the United States at various times as part of peace delegations, and I met them all many times while I was staying in Hiroshima. Yamaoka-san visited my home on a later trip to the Washington area. Takeuchi-sensei made the strongest impression on me that first day in Hiroshima, though.

Takeuchi-sensei was a heavy-set elderly woman squinting out from bright black eyes set deep in a face like a shriveled apple. She hunched over bits of origami paper and paper circles with simple faces painstakingly painted on. She was already in her eighties at that time, but her hands were quick and busy as she spoke to us. She was always engaged in the same repetitive task to which she felt called — creating paper-doll couples dressed in colorful kimonos.

Figure 32: Paper dolls for peace folded by Satoko Yamashita of the Friendly Association of Wishing Peace. (Photo by author)

Takeuchi-sensei had been a primary school teacher in the 1930s, but she gave up her profession when she was thirty-six while the war was raging. The principal of her school decided to require students to begin each day with a deep bow not only to the teacher but also to the picture of the Emperor. Children were to come to order in the manner of soldiers, barking their greetings and responses. Other teachers agreed with her that these practices were too militaristic, but at the meeting to discuss the issue, she alone spoke out. None of the other teachers backed her publicly. Education decrees demanded more and more military training and more and more deference to the Rising Sun war flag and the "Kimigayo" anthem, both associated with the warmongering party. She said that she held pacifist ideas even then.

This astonished me. I shared my father's assumptions about the universal blind acceptance of imperial orders in wartime Japan. We were both wrong.

Takeuchi-sensei was raised in the Shinshu school of Buddhism. Both her parents were religious. As a child, she once stole fruit from a neighbor's bush. When her mother questioned her, she admitted taking the fruit, but protested, "Nobody saw me do it." Her mother gently reproached her, saying "The sun always sees." This school of Buddhism believes in the "inner life." Takeuchi-sensei read widely and came to believe that each person has a full inner life. She learned to trust in her own inner life.

Her description of her Buddhist philosophy struck me as profoundly consistent with the Quaker concepts that there is "that of God in everyone" and that divine wisdom is accessible to all by deep listening to the "still, small voice within." She concluded that peace comes only from education in love. Love should be beyond all boundaries between individuals and groups. Love should never seek a return or expect repayment. She had come on her own path to the same ideas that Christians can find in first Corinthians. If only we all had ears to hear.

This thinking, and her love for children, drew her to become a teacher. She grieved that the Japanese government's policies forced her to leave the career she loved. She knew too that, if she simply stayed at home with her parents, the government would mobilize her for mandatory war work in some factory. Instead, she set up a business tutoring neighborhood children.

On August 5, 1945, some of her former pupils came to her home to visit her. She drew a little pond with small koi fish swimming in it. The picture was so peaceful and calm. One little boy said he wished he were a fish like that. "Because they have no war in their world," he explained. The next day, the war came to his world in the atomic bomb. The boy was terribly burned. He lived nearby, and all night she could hear him crying out, "*Itai! Itai!*" (It hurts! It hurts!). The next day he was dead. That is all that Takeuchi-sensei recounts of her exposure to the bomb, and it is typical of her that she tells not of her own suffering but of the suffering of one child among the many she loved.

One memory that stayed with her vividly from her early teaching years was of little blond, blue-eyed celluloid dolls sent from the United States as a gesture of friendship in 1927. One came to her primary school. She remembered how all the children begged to hold the doll and make it cry "Mama!" A note accompanied each doll that read: "Pretty Japanese girl, please play with me and be my good friend. May the United States of America and Japan always stay friends." The children had a song about the dolls that went: "When I first came to Japan's harbor, my eyes were full of tears. I was alone and could not understand Japanese. What could I do if I get lost?" The song ended with the words of the note. All the children wanted to be the doll's good friend.

The blue-eyed dolls were sent to Japan to arrive in time for *Hinamatsuri* (Doll Festival) on March 3, 1927. (Over three hundred dolls were sent to Hiroshima, but only four are known to have survived.) Each year on March 3rd, girls throughout Japan celebrate *Hinamatsuri* — *Matsuri* means festival and *hina* means princess. On *Hinamatsuri*, girls carefully arrange a special set of dolls (*hina-ningyo*) on a multi-level platform covered in red cloth. The dolls are miniature replicas of an ancient Heian imperial court, including the royal couple, ministers, musicians, and servants. The girls solemnly pour each other sweet rice drinks and offer each other little cakes using their absolute best manners. Families pass these dolls down through generations.

Those blue-eyed dolls came to Takeushi-san's mind when Barbara Reynolds was planning to return to the United States and asked her Japanese friends what she could take back with her to help American people understand the feelings of people in Hiroshima. Takeuchi-sensei thought of dolls. But remembering how the children at her primary school vied to hold the special doll, she thought it would be better for each American child to receive a doll of their own. She wanted to make dolls that would show the love of Hiroshima's people, rather than simply tell what was done to them or seek to get paid back for suffering. She wanted to put her own idea of the beauty of the human spirit in each doll. She knows that few people understand this when they see the folded paper dolls. She figures that most think, "Well, that's nice for some children to play with. They're pretty." But children, she believes, can feel the love that is carried in the little dolls.

Takeuchi-sensei was not alone in her doll-making project, as many volunteers joined in, moved by her vision. The paper dolls are dressed in paper robes of court like the imperial couple in *Hinamatsuri* sets. Each pair of male and female paper dolls is packaged carefully in plastic along with the following explanation of Takeuchi-sensei's project:

> Everybody can be the possessor of a loving heart.
> In all the world, there is no country that does not
> have dolls. This shows that many people have loving
> hearts. Children especially love dolls, but they don't
> have self-desire in their love of dolls.

The hearts of children that show love to dolls will grow up into hearts that have love toward human beings. Hearts that love human beings are hearts that seek true peace. From such hearts will come a wonderful flowering of peace like the bursting open of buds in spring.

These dolls have been folded with such simple loving thoughts. If these dolls could be our ambassadors and convey our thoughts to as many people as possible in foreign countries and could bring support, we would be very happy. Moreover, if we can make friends all over the world by sending dolls, world peace would not be just a dream.

Let's fold paper dolls

And cultivate a loving heart.

To convey our loving hearts,

Keep a dream of peace in our hearts,

Let's fold paper dolls and

Let's send paper dolls.

Friendly Association of Wishing Peace

Each flyer, in Japanese and English, is signed by one person with an address and city to make clear that the message is a personal one. That is Takeuchi-sensei's *kataribe*.

When I came back to the United States, I brought with me a stack of the doll packages that Takeuchi-sensei gave me and distributed them to friends' children and people who expressed interest in peace work. I kept several myself to remember the gentle but determined Takeuchi-sensei who has since passed away.

Folding paper dolls may seem too naïve a method to change the world. Nevertheless, if the message is not directed to the hearts of children, who else is likely to hear it?

CHAPTER TWENTY-FIVE:

A thousand paper cranes

HIROSHIMA, JAPAN (1987) — IN THE EVENING, WE returned to Peace Park, gathering near the Children's Monument with others from the WFC. The story of the monument begins with a young girl, Sadako Sasaki, who was exposed to the bomb at the age of two. When she was 12, she developed leukemia. She wanted desperately to get well and live. A folk tradition taught that, if you folded one thousand origami cranes, you might not die, because the cranes were symbols of long life and hope, or the gods would at least grant you one wish as a reward for your persistence. She fought the disease courageously and folded hundreds of cranes. Nevertheless, sadly, she died too soon, before she could finish her thousand cranes. Her friends finished the effort for her, and at her funeral she had the full thousand cranes. Or, others say, she finished her thousand and yet continued to fold more until her death, still hoping, or hoping to help others. Like so much about Hiroshima, her story has multiple versions, but the endings are all sad.

Children throughout Japan raised funds to build this monument to honor Sadako and the many other children who died because of the atomic bombs. Its form resembles a slender soaring mountain with open sides or perhaps a rocket. At the pinnacle, a girl stands with her arms outstretched holding the silhouette of a crane. Two other figures seem to fly upward on the sides of the monument. Inside the hollow form is a statute of Sadako.

The statue in the center of the monument was invisible that day, although I knew it must be there from photographs I had seen. Instead, the interior and base of the monument were completely buried in foothills made up of chains of hundreds of folded cranes. Pictures made by using folded cranes as colorful flattened tiles to create mosaic-like patterns were piled around it. On top were giant paper cranes in shiny metallic paper. The effect was of a volcano spilling out a kaleidoscope of colors. (Years later, this exuberant display would be domesticated by hanging the strands inside plastic display cases and keeping the area around the monument clear. The purpose is to gather the cranes safely and protect them from the weather. But I loved the wild diversity and spontaneous outpouring as it was when I first saw it.)

Figure 33: School children surrounding the monument with chains of folded cranes hanging inside and in piles visible between the girls' skirts. (Photo by author, late 1980s or early 1990s)

The WFC group sang peace songs and prayed together a bit in a circle to the side of the crowd. We all made colorful paper lanterns with supplies provided there – wooden frames and colorful wax paper for sides. August comes in the middle of the summer *O-bon* season in Japan, so throngs of atom bomb dead are believed to be visiting their living relatives or haunting their beloved city. Throughout Japan, at the end of *O-Bon*, lantern boats were traditionally set adrift to carry spirits back to their proper homes. In Hiroshima on the night of August 6th, the tradition arose to float lanterns in the river that borders Peace Park in the hope of bringing the souls of the atom-bombed to repose at last. Participants write the names of their own dead, or those whose stories they have heard, or their own prayers or wishes for peace on the lanterns.

On my lantern, on one side, I wrote "Pempah," my daughter's baby name for the grandfather who died when she was two. On the other side, I wrote: "May we thirst for peace, as they once thirsted here for water." As it grew dark, the candles in the lanterns were lit, placed in the water, and allowed to float off. When our turn came, our little group went gingerly down the wet stone steps of the old embankment to the water's edge and released our lanterns. The scene felt incongruously ancient and magical in the center of what was now a busy modern city.

Under a bridge on which my father had seen negative impressions of vaporized people, a flotilla of twinkling vessels bobbed away on the inky water bearing comfort to the dead and hopes that Hiroshima's horror would never be repeated.

I hoped his spirit was among those riding the lanterns to comfort.

CHAPTER TWENTY-SIX:

Playgrounds as fishing holes

HIROSHIMA, JAPAN (1987) — WE CAME TO JAPAN BECAUSE I felt a duty to my father's memory to see the places that loomed so large in the last years of his life. The ceremony in Hiroshima touched me deeply. After that, I needed to decide if I had accomplished what was needed. Should we head home? Should we sightsee? Or was there more that I was called to learn and carry out to be faithful to what I needed to do? Once we were in Hiroshima, I had felt oddly at home. Something about its island geography, its commercial bustle, its weather, and its people's style, more direct than elsewhere in Japan, echoed my New York hometown feelings, as it had for my father even when he saw it so soon after the bombing. I realized I needed to be in this place for more than a ceremony. At the same time, I wanted to escape the complicated feelings it triggered in me and to have some space to reflect on how I might find more understanding in a country still so foreign to me. We traveled on.

In Kyoto, I climbed endless stone steps to exquisite temples and watched staged geisha shows, but I most looked forward to visiting the famous Ryoan-ji rock garden. I had seen so many pictures of the stone islands in a raked gravel sea and imagined the peacefulness I would find. When I finally visited, the garden was much smaller than I envisioned it, tourists and their megaphoned guides jammed along the path, and street noise intruded from just beyond the low wall. The peacefulness is still there but you must lower your gaze and narrow your focus to find it. I realized that you must dig deep to find the Japan you are looking for, because if you only look at Japan on the surface, you may miss what matters most. I returned to Hiroshima to begin digging deeper.

One night, I had a dream that I removed earplugs from my ears and was horrified to find them covered with blood. Blood poured out of my ears. Frightened, I asked a nurse to examine me. She said this was the natural result of the high fever I had been running lately. I answered that I had not even realized I was sick. Reflecting on this strange dream, I finally recognized its meaning to me. My ears had indeed been filled with blood, death, and sorrow. Nagasaki had opened my eyes and my mind to the terrible damage done by the atomic bombs. Hiroshima opened my ears and my heart to the pain and sorrow that stalk all those touched by these weapons until peace comes. All of us. My heart had been burning despite my own efforts to push away and deny any pain. I needed to open my ears and my heart to hear the story that Hiroshima had to tell.

Before coming to Japan, I corresponded with an American woman, Ronni Alexander, who worked with Iwakura-san, the organizer of my father's 1983 visit, and served as interpreter during that visit. She wrote, in rather Japanese-style understatement, that living in Japan would present "a number of problems." The yen was strong compared to the dollar; the cost of living, especially in a Westernized manner, was extremely high; anything but a tourist visa would be hard to get. She summed it up this way: "I have lived in Japan for ten years and am very happy here, but many non-Japanese find it quite difficult. In any event, you should be prepared for a very different Japan than the one experienced by your father." The tone was discouraging, but the content was accurate. Still, I decided to press on.

During our first visit to Hiroshima for the memorial ceremony, I made a new friend, Michiko Tashiro (now Kitayama), whose daughter, Mirei was a bit older than Kendra. They had lived in the States and were fluent in English. Her then-husband, Akira Tashiro, was a reporter at *The Chugoku Shimbun*, the leading newspaper in that region. Talking to them helped me to get an inkling of what I was meant to be doing in Japan. I asked Michiko-san if she might help me find a place to stay longer in Hiroshima. Finding rooms or an apartment was a daunting proposition for a foreigner. Ms. Alexander's warnings about the obstacles I would face had only been reinforced by the various "bibles" for Western residents of Japan that I acquired and poured over (such as *Gaijin's Guide: Practical Help for Everyday Life in Japan* by Janet Ashby and Jean Pearce's *How to Get Things Done in Japan*, published by *The Japan Times*). I was lucky to have found a friend.

Michiko-san was the first of several close women friends I made in Japan. Foreign visitors have complained for years about how difficult it is to get behind the façade presented to the world by their polite but private Japanese friends. Japanese friends will show them sights, take them to events, or meet them at a restaurant, but the foreign visitors sense that they do not quite know these people. I met Americans who lived in Japan for ten years and had never seen the inside of a Japanese home. Many explanations have been offered for this phenomenon from the cultural (a populous island nation had to develop ways to live in invisible bubbles of privacy amid the crowds) to the pragmatic (Japanese homes tend to be so much smaller than those overseas that foreign guests would be uncomfortable in them, or Japanese hosts fear they would be). I stumbled upon a three-step solution to this problem:

> Step one: Be a single mother, so no husband (with corresponding presumptions of business matters) must be accounted for in hospitality.

Step two: Take your young child to a playground.

Step three: Wait an hour or so.

Inevitably, kids would gravitate toward my daughter and include her in their digging in the sand or tossing a ball. The kids, like Kendra, would touch base with their mothers regularly, as if hearing invisible alarms go off every five or ten minutes. Sooner or later, one of the mothers, the boldest or the one with the best recall of some English words, would approach me. A conversation of mixed vocabularies, body language, hand signs, and laughter would follow as we watched the children's antics. A child is bait, a playground a fishing hole. More days than not, in more cities than not, I ended up drinking coffee in one of the local mothers' homes while the kids looked at picture books, watched cartoons, or ate sweet snacks. Some of these bold and warm-hearted women made my life in Japan possible and fruitful; some became life-long friends even as all our kids turned amazingly into grownups. I have met their husbands, stayed in their homes, and hosted them on visits to America. But the crucial catalyst for the connection was our children. I cannot fail to acknowledge my debt to these women and their families who did so much to make Japan my family's second home.

Michiko-san agreed to help me try to find a place to stay but it was indeed challenging. Rooms were measured by the number of *tatami* mats (about three feet by six feet) that would fit in them (whether or not they were in fact covered by *tatami*). Four and one-half to six tatami spaces were considered good-sized rooms. One such room with a kitchenette and toilet/bath (likely shared) would be the most I could possibly afford. I had no income and was trying to get by on the proceeds of my father's small life insurance policy and the rental of my house in Washington, D.C. Furthermore, I would have to buy a refrigerator, gas ring for cooking, and a hot water heater as those appliances were usually not included. Rental agents required a two-year lease, with as much as six months' rent in advance, plus such items as "key money" and "gift money," not to mention deposits. And a foreigner needed a Japanese sponsor to ensure against any untoward alien behavior. To acquire a telephone required payment of a "bond" in the equivalent of hundreds of dollars. To try to avoid some of these upfront costs, Tashiro-san helped me search among the advertisements of departing Westerners and foreign students seeking to pass on their existing rental arrangements.

One day, though, as she was waiting for the bus to meet me, Tashiro-san ran into a neighbor of hers, Yoshiko Imaeda, and told her about my situation. Our time in Japan was filled with this sort of serendipity to which Quakers refer as "way opening."

Imaeda-sensei was the answer to my prayers. She lived in a suburban home near Tashiro-san, but still owned an apartment in an older Hiroshima neighborhood called Funairi-cho. She used the apartment for an after-school study/tutoring program that she ran, a *juku* (cram school) for kids in the neighborhood where she used to live. The apartment was large even by American standards. Two big rooms that served as classrooms, a dining room area, a fully furnished kitchen, a small den, a toilet, and a full Japanese bathroom. Imaeda-sensei invited us to stay at the apartment as long as we liked, simply putting away our futons and vacating the premises during the hours when she held school there.

She and my daughter fell instantly in love. She was, from then on, Kendra's "Japanese mommy." In short order, we stopped going out during the *juku*. Instead, I began teaching English, and Kendra began joining in the activities for the youngest students.

CHAPTER TWENTY-SEVEN:

If not for the pikadon

HIROSHIMA, JAPAN (1987) — IMAEDA-SAN'S GENEROSITY, and her kind support for my attempts to make a record of the experiences of my father and the *hibakusha* whom he filmed, were deeply personal. When she was ten months old, her mother was exposed to the bomb and died. During the time we lived at her apartment, Imaeda-san wrote a lightly fictionalized account of what had happened to her mother which she used as the basis for an illustrated children's book. She gave me this English translation:

If not for Pikadon

Chizuko was born at Hiroshima Red Cross Hospital. Soon after she was born, her whole family decided to evacuate to the country where her grandparents lived. Many people were fleeing to relatives in the countryside in search of greater safety. At that time, the war was intensifying.

Her father was a policeman; her mother a teacher in a girls' upper school. They both commuted by train to Hiroshima. Her father had a moustache that came to sharp points, giving him a severe appearance, but nevertheless he had a great sense of humor. Her mother was gentle, with a beautiful fair complexion. She also had an elder brother and an elder sister. The family lived happily all together. Their house was surrounded by a white fence with a big gate.

In the morning, after letting Chizuko have her fill of milk, her mother left for the school and her father left for the police station. They rode on the same train.

"Grandma, Grandpa, please take care of Chi-chan," mother said as she left. As the train passed the back gate of Chizuko's house, it tooted its whistle, as if to wave goodbye. Every day, the train carried so many people to Hiroshima and then brought them back again in the evening. In that quiet mountain town, Chizuko's family found a sort of happiness, but it was not to last.

On the morning of August 6, 1945, the air raid alarm had been lifted in Hiroshima. The rivers of Hiroshima sparkled in reflecting the rays of the morning sun. Suddenly, a bright flash appeared in the sky over Hiroshima: "*Pika!*" And then, "*Don!*" a sound as loud as if the whole world exploded. All the buildings exploded instantly. Everywhere fires broke out, and the town was consumed by flames.

What took the lives of immeasurable numbers of people and caused the devastation of the city of Hiroshima was an atomic bomb used then for the first time in the world. People called the atomic bomb which exploded then, lighting up the skies over Hiroshima, *pikadon*.

From Chizuko's village, twenty kilometers from Hiroshima, the large ominous mushroom cloud could be seen looming behind the mountains over Hiroshima, billowing out gradually. At that time, Chizuko's mother was working with girl students on the demolition of buildings. She was near Tsurumibashi, and Chizuko's father was at Ujina, when they met the *pikadon*.

It was a long, long summer day. The sad and frightening tidings found the village in the mountain already filled with anxiety. The train, which finally began to move around dusk, arrived loaded with badly burnt and wounded people. Among them was Chizuko's mother.

On hearing this news, her grandfather hurried to the station, pulling a hand-cart. "Oh, my God. How horrible!" Chizuko's grandfather cried out, mad with shock and grief, as he embraced her mother, who seemed completely changed. It took the help of several people to place Chizuko's mother on the cart, since she was burned over her entire body. When her shoulder bag was removed from her shoulder, only the mark of its strap remained white. Her skin peeled away. Her blood oozed out. Chizuko's mother hovered near death. At last, a few faint words came with difficulty from her open lips. "I . . . have to . . . nurse . . . So . . . I . . . came back . . . Chizuko . . ."

Fortunately, Chizuko's father soon returned home safely, not seriously burned. "I must . . . nurse . . . the baby . . .." So, said Chizuko's mother, but Chizuko was never again to taste her mother's milk. Her mother became resigned to death at any moment. Grandfather and grandmother cared for Chizuko's mother, wiping away the blood and pus, and crying out, "So cruel! So cruel! If only it could have been me instead!"

Chizuko grew thinner day by day, as her mother's milk had dried up. The happy house with the white fence grew grim, as it sheltered within two lives fading away. In time, the sad lament was heard: "Which will be the first to die?" so they sighed. On October 25 of that year, Chizuko's mother spoke her last words, "Children, love each other . . .," and with that, gave up the ghost.

Chizuko alone, among the wailing and grieving family, understood nothing. She sat sucking her little fingers. She sucked her pale fingers, innocently, as she listened to the violent anger and the agonized sorrow: "If only *pikadon* had never happened. . ..

If not for the *pikadon*!"

I include this story by permission of Imaeda-san. Its final cry continues to echo. The question of what might have been if not for the *pikadon* is an agonizing one for all *hibakusha*.

One of the ways that I began to realize that Numata-sensei was right when she told me that my father was *hibakusha* and that I was "second-generation *hibakusha*" was that I started to wonder who my father might have been, if not for the *pikadon*.

CHAPTER TWENTY-EIGHT:

Refrigerators and chewing gum

BEPPU, JAPAN (1946) — HERB FELL INTO A DEEP DEPRESsion as the train pulled out of Nagasaki. He gazed out of the window, hoping to see green again after the grey and broken landscape of the destroyed city. He scanned the scenery for some distraction from his thoughts as they rolled through small towns. Then he saw in the harbor of one hamlet – of all things – a refrigerator coming off a vessel.

The town was serving as the headquarters for the British Commonwealth Occupation Forces (BCOF). Troops jammed the streets from all corners of the British Empire – Sikhs, Gurkhas, Scots Highlanders, Aussies.

The ice car that held the film, as well as perishables, was hard to maintain and not all that effective. A refrigerator was just what they needed, and Herb decided they had to have it. He stopped the train, jumped off, and headed for the dock determined to get possession somehow. He was told that that the refrigerator was intended for the commanding general of BCOF. He describes the ensuing encounter:

> Well, I must explain that the British are very, very serious about the military. Americans get very informal at times. So, I reported to the commanding general of the British and explained our mission. I flashed our orders and said, "We require your refrigerator for our film." "You what?!" he spluttered. I saw the shock on the face of the Scots aide who stood at this side wearing a marvelous

tartan kilt as I demanded this precious refrigerator. It had been shipped half-way around the world for the general's express use. But I calmly repeated, "We require a refrigerator to keep our film cold. Our orders supersede everything and everyone, so we are requisitioning this one." He was on the phone to MacArthur's headquarters in Tokyo at once, asking over and over, "What can I do about these guys?" But he kept getting the same answer. So, we loaded the refrigerator on our train and were on the way.

They stopped next at a resort area called Beppu on the eastern coast. Hot sulfur water flowed down from mountain hot springs, making it a famous health spa. Visitors could cover themselves with the sulfur sands on the beach or soak in the hot springs bath. The town had colorful stores and lots of geisha houses. To Herb, Beppu was like Coney Island and 42nd Street put together. The clean rubble-free streets and neat intact houses were a wonderful relief after Nagasaki. The restored sense of order soothed him.

Not long before, Beppu itself had been crowded with refugees from Nagasaki. Many survivors fled there for help, believing in its healthful reputation. There was nothing in Beppu, or anywhere else, however, effective to cure the strange Nagasaki poisoning.

Herb strolled along a street and passed a house with a hand-printed sign in English that read: "G.I.'s! Bring us your used chewing gum!" Who could pass such a sign without finding out what it meant? Not Herb, who knocked on the screen door and was admitted by a Japanese man and his wife who spoke some English.

They were very appreciative of my coming in and nodded when I said, "I don't understand something.

You have a sign out that says something about used chewing gum?"

The man said, "Oh, yes, yes." "Well, what is it all about?" I asked. "After the bomb," he explained, "many people from Nagasaki came here because everything was destroyed for them. They walked across the island. We tried to help them in every way that we could. But there was nothing we could do. Many, many of them died. Then, shortly after, the Americans came. I have been looking out of the window here and watching all these American troops walk by. They all look very healthy. They all look very robust."

He went on in a confidential tone, "And, most of them are chewing their chewing gum. My opinion is that their good health and energy goes into that gum, which they just throw away."

"So," he concluded triumphantly, "I am collecting all of it that I can and I'm going to use it to help the atomic bomb victims."

How could one respond to that? Herb said, "I wish you well," and bade him goodbye. His heart was heavy once again as he hurried back to the train.

CHAPTER TWENTY-NINE:

Resilience

HIROSHIMA, JAPAN (1946) — IN MARCH, THE CREW'S train chugged into Hiroshima on the main island of Honshu. Hiroshima's terrain was flat, as opposed to the bowls of hills surrounding Nagasaki. Hiroshima was a larger city, sprawling out across its rivers and inlets. As a result, the circle of destruction was much wider and rounder since nothing blocked the blast. What immediately hit Herb was that here he could see in one glimpse the entire potential of an atomic bomb.

Figure 34: Hiroshima in 1946 from "Japan in Defeat." (Photo credit to U.S. Army)

Figure 35: Hiroshima in 1946 from "Japan in Defeat." (Photo credit to U.S. Army)

Figure 36: Hiroshima in 1946 from "Japan in Defeat." (Photo credit to U.S. Army)

Figure 37: Hiroshima in 1946 from "Japan in Defeat." (Photo credit to U.S. Army)

Figure 38: Hiroshima in 1946 from "Japan in Defeat." (Photo credit to U.S. Army)

Again, one of Herb's first encounters was with the station-master. A good-looking, middle-aged man, each morning he would line up the staff on the platform for inspection. As in Nagasaki, they always stood in descending order of importance: the first assistant followed by the second assistant, the trainmen, the porters, down to the toilet cleaners. Herb admired the organization and the respect for authority.

[When I first read my father's notes and noticed how much he was drawn to this sense of order and hierarchy, I thought it showed how different we were. I would find such discipline and ranking belittling to everybody – I would have to break ranks and show my individuality. In the years since he died, I have reflected instead about how profoundly upsetting the chaos that went on in our family must have been to him. My father's once thriving career in television collapsed by the late 1960's; my mother struggled with heavy drinking and bouts of depression; my teenaged brother constantly rebelled and repeatedly ran away; and, of course, I rejected his life and values in my teens, always making stubborn pronouncements about capitalism and pacifism, and then left home for good at sixteen. It was a time of social upheaval and generation gaps. I saw longstanding wrongs addressed and rigid systems challenged, but it was a bad time for Confucian respect for authority and for comforting structure. How painful he must have found it all! I imagine he envisioned himself as the benevolent leader of the family, providing guidance and meeting needs while receiving appropriate respect and appreciation. Both of his kids saw him as more of a clownish oppressor. He failed us; we failed him. It never occurred to me to consider his disappointments instead of my own disappointment in him until I found myself hearing these stories from the vantage of my own adulthood – of course, by then, he was gone.]

Herb quickly became very friendly with the stationmaster. He learned that the man had a special assistant, a young woman, with whom he had an unusual relationship. On the day of the bombing, she had been at the station waiting to take a train out to the countryside where she lived. At the moment of the flash, the stationmaster had fallen over her, knocking her to the floor and under a desk. She felt that this had protected her and saved her life.

As a result, she had decided to dedicate the rest of her life to serving this man as her savior. Odd as this attitude may seem today, Herb accepted it as simply another aspect of the Japanese culture. Among the services she provided for the stationmaster was a ritual Japanese bath. He invited Herb to join him in using the bathhouse. The bathhouse was just a rickety shack; but though not elaborate, or even attractive, it was quite functional. It contained a large wooden tub and facilities for heating the water to the boiling point. There, Herb first enjoyed this ancient custom of Japan late one night in ruined Hiroshima.

The Hiroshima stationmaster had an advantage over the one in Nagasaki. He still had a station. Indeed, despite its immense devastation, Hiroshima already felt to Herb more like a city, a functioning entity. By the time they arrived, clean-up was well under way. Hiroshima had started to reawaken and showed him the great energy that the Japanese had for rebuilding rather than concentrating on what was lost. He admired the diligence and focus he saw in everything in Japan.

Herb looked across from the train station one day and saw a line of people waiting patiently outside a recently constructed wooden shack, bigger than most. He crossed over to see what was being dispensed that had drawn so much interest. A movie theater had been set up. People were queued up to see the show. And the offering was an American western! Herb was astonished. How could such recent victims of an American bomb enjoy such entertainment? He wrote that he "always felt that if such a thing had happened in America, the hatred and anger against whoever had dropped such a bomb would continue for decades." He could not believe that, so soon after following their Emperor into surrender, these people could embrace such a quintessential bit of American culture.

[I suspect that the choice of films was controlled by the occupiers rather than by the people seeking whatever escape into entertainment was offered. What astonishes me, however, about survivors queuing up for movie night is how powerfully people need distraction even amid disaster. It explains why an army at war still needed the sort of shows that my father set up from Manila to Iwo Jima. What may seem frivolous in good times feeds the spirit in bad times as surely as rations feed the body. I take the ramshackle theater in hell as a sign of healing, resilience, and humanity.]

Something else was different about Hiroshima for Herb. Something subtle, but profound, that bound Herb to Hiroshima with feelings he had not experienced for Nagasaki, for all its horror. Something in Hiroshima spoke to him of home. Being a larger city, it had boasted more commercial buildings, more concrete structures, many larger than Nagasaki's small houses built in the traditional manner of wood, screens, and clay-tile roofs. Walking through the streets of Hiroshima, he saw burnt-out, blasted shells of seven- and eight-story buildings. They reminded him uncannily of Manhattan. Perhaps it was also the sense of being in a city surrounded by water. Even the climate was more like home, a chilly winter warming as March turned to April.

As he explored the ruins of the city, the thought kept going through his head: "This could be New York." When he saw the burnt-in shadow of a little man on the steps of a bank building in Hiroshima, he imagined men resting on the stoops of New York, burned forever into the concrete of their steps.

CHAPTER THIRTY:

Apologies

HIROSHIMA, JAPAN (1946) — HERB AND HARRY MIMURA set up cameras on the roof of the Communications Hospital to take advantage of the light. One victim after another was brought up to be recorded. The parade tended to merge into an agonizing "nightmare of scars, wounds, burns, missing limbs." Herb struggled to focus on the individuals here. He tried to talk with them. He tried to imagine their lives before and now. He had little success, but it matters that he tried.

One sunny spring morning, the nurses helped a tiny young woman hobble across the roof on crutches. She was pretty and unharmed on top. When she sat along the ledge, her kimono parted. She was missing a leg. The nurses drew back the bandages to reveal the raw stump, like a hideously swollen sausage. The contrast to her delicate face was so painful to Herb that he began to stammer apologies. This was Suzuko Numata-sensei. Neither of them ever forgot that day or each other.

Figure 39: Numata-sensei in 1946 from SBS footage (Photo credit to U.S. Army).

[Numata-sensei was, as I said, the first person whose *kataribe* I heard. It was she who helped my grandmother comprehend what my father had experienced in filming the aftermath of the atomic bombing. She opened her heart to me and to my daughter. Across four generations and so many decades, the bond born in pain and compassion on that rooftop continued to tie us together.]

*   *   *

HERB TRIED TO CAPTURE IN HIROSHIMA WHAT HE called "the beginning of democracy in Japan."

> We covered the changes in newspapers that had previously been controlled by the Japanese military authorities. A whole new wave of books coming into stores and newspapers being distributed to people that were no longer under the control of the Japanese government.

> One newspaper in Hiroshima had an editor who spoke English. I became well-acquainted with him. He had not been permitted to work during the war at all. He brought me very startling photographs that had been taken by the photographer from the newspaper. He had been in the mountains beyond the range of the bomb when it went off.

> He took those impressive photographs that most of the world has seen by now of what Hiroshima looked like one half hour after the bombing. The photographer had been outside the city, but he had a bicycle and, as soon as the bomb went off, he got on his bicycle and rode as far as he could go into the bombed area. I was told that most of the people in

these photographs, had taken some type of oil and were putting it on their bodies, but died afterward as a result of what had happened to them.

[My father did not know at the time, but this flowering of free speech was to be short-lived. The occupation authorities imposed their own strict press code which, among other restrictions, prohibited all published mention of the atom bombs in Japan from the fall of 1945 until the occupation ended in 1952. Even poetry about the atomic bombing was caught up in this effort to eliminate the entire topic.

The U.S. Government confiscated and suppressed black-and-white film footage taken by Japanese photographers closer in time to the bombing than the film shot by the SBS crew. The seized Japanese film was overseen by McGovern for years along with the secret color SBS footage.

Words and images alike apparently carried too strong a message to be tolerated.]

CHAPTER THIRTY-ONE:

War is waste

HIROSHIMA, JAPAN (1946) — A CONVERSATION WITH the same editor led Herb to one of the most moving visuals in the Hiroshima footage besides the records of individual survivors. He recounted that, in the weeks after the blast, Hiroshima's city government had scrupulously tried to account for all the victims. Teams worked through the scorched and blasted ruins searching for signs of the dead. Any remains they could find were placed in little wooden boxes and carefully identified with notations of where exactly each had been found. Solemn ceremonies were held to commemorate the return of these remains to the families that could be found.

> Near the hypocenter, the victims had been mostly vaporized, so I could not even fathom how they could find remains, but, apparently, they felt that they had. Then they attempted to locate and notify survivors. The families came in at some point to pick up these remains. They would have Buddhist funeral services before they left.

> We were permitted to record a reenactment of this beautiful ceremony. Again, the Japanese attitude was so astonishing to me. These families had all simply been called to bring these boxes back to City Hall and they did it without any pressure, without anybody, so far as I know, forcing them to

do it. Harry Mimura and I filmed the candles, the incense, the chanting.

I could never forget those boxes. That these little boxes – each no more than five or six square inches – contained all that was left of a human being! That was all that was left even of so many people who had been in bomb shelters. I thought it was very import-ant to film that because it would give somebody a sense of the people who had been destroyed, which there was no other way to obtain on film.

The impact of the scene, like the Mass in the Nagasaki cathe-dral, does not seem diminished by the fact that the scene was restaged. In Hiroshima, even more than in Nagasaki, Herb struggled to enter into the individual, human impact of the massive destruc-tion. And, even more than in Nagasaki, he found himself identifying with what such destruction could mean if it came to America.

*   *   *

WHILE STILL IN HIROSHIMA, HERB WAS CALLED BY DAN McGovern to get transport and come back up to Tokyo to meet someone from the States. At the Correspondents' Club in Tokyo, McGovern introduced him to "a writer from New York who wants to do something on Hiroshima." Over lunch, Herb told John Hersey about some of his experiences and gave him the names of people to contact in Hiroshima. [My father recognized many of the people who were ultimately included in Hersey's famous book, *Hiroshima*.]

*   *   *

ONE NIGHT IN HIROSHIMA, HERB, RESTLESS, COULD NOT sleep and went outside to smoke a pipe. He found Ando-san beside a large hole he had dug, just about to throw in a package of steaks from a big pile of food on the ground. For the first time, Herb realized what was being done with the excess food from the train. He was horrified.

> We had ten or twelve men on the train at different times, but American food could only be drawn from America depots in a very specialized, orderly way. One of the things I specifically remember is that they had prime steak, and you could only draw it in frozen 87-pound packages. Chickens you could only get in a package of fifty or seventy-five chickens. You couldn't draw any less. We did not have enough refrigeration to keep any supplies like that very long. If we might use ten or twelve pounds of steak one night for dinner, more than seventy pounds would be left over. Ando-san was going out at midnight and burying it all.

> I grabbed his arm and insisted the food should be given away. The people were living on practically nothing — in most cases, rice and little else, if they could get the rice. It was heartbreaking, absolutely heartbreaking, to see how difficult the situation was for people throughout Japan, and especially in the cities we were in. And then to have this man burying the food.

But he shook his head and explained. Despite all we had, we simply did not have enough to begin to take care of the thousands and thousands of hungry people in the city. If word got out that we had extra food, we could never handle the terrible food riots that would result. It was far wiser that the food simply be buried.

And he was right.

Herb nevertheless found it painful to see the desperation of the people and to know that the over-abundance of his own food was going to waste.

[My father could never stand waste, whether lights left on in empty rooms or food left on the plate. As he learned, war was at its core waste. Waste on a massive scale. Waste of planes, and trucks, and fuel. Waste of food. Waste of lives. I think this was at the root of his reaction to the atomic bombs. To throw entire cities over the cliff in a single instant, squander all their resources and peoples, and leave poison behind was more waste than he could bear to imagine happening again. It is more than I can bear, too.]

CHAPTER THIRTY-TWO:

Scattering his story

HIROSHIMA, JAPAN (1987) — IT WAS SUNNY AGAIN IN Hiroshima on September 2, 1987, the second anniversary of my father's death. His ashes were not in Hiroshima, despite what my brother had shared about his last wish. Nevertheless, a small group gathered in his name in front of the mound holding the unidentified remains of atomic bomb victims near Ground Zero. This gentle grassy hillock with a railing in front to hold flowers and candles was the resting place of the unidentified remains of bomb victims. Even though I could not, under Japanese law, bring his ashes to scatter, I needed to find some way to honor his last wish. My new friends in Hiroshima, including the World Friendship Center directors, Michiko and her daughter Mirei, and Yoshiko Imaeda, joined us to observe the anniversary by a memorial service.

Figure 40: In front of the Atomic Bomb Memorial Mound, created in 1955 to mourn the ashes of the unidentified dead from the bombing, (from left to right) Michiko Kitayama, Kendra Parham, Bill and Jeanne Chappell (then WFC hosts), Leslie Sussan and Yoshiko Imaeda. (Photo from author's collection)

I told my friends about my father's last wish. I believed he had wanted to try, in one last way, to come to terms with his experiences by symbolically becoming one with the city and those who come to it in a search for peace. I shared my new understanding of how to carry out his desire. Instead of scattering his ashes to the winds here, I decided that I had come to Hiroshima to spread his story. I thought that story might bring meaning and completion to his life and his death and make up somehow for the suppression of his films.

I read aloud a few excerpts of my father's typewritten notes which later became part of the raw material for this book. We sang a song I had loved since I went to Ethical Culture summer camp as a child. Called "Last night I had the strangest dream," the song imagines a world where all the people dance in the streets as all the guns and drums and uniforms lie abandoned on the ground.

I read a poem by Tamiki Hara, himself a *hibakusha* who committed suicide after hearing public discussion about the possibility of the United States dropping an atom bomb during the Korean War:

Engraved in stone long ago,

Lost in the shifting sand,

In the midst of a crumbling world,

The vision of one flower.

Just so the memory of the atom-bombed cities was engraved in my father's heart long ago. And the vision of the old man carefully watering his garden in hell gave birth to his own vision of revealing the truth to the world so no one would ever again think of wreaking such destruction. A vision trampled by the arms race and hidden away by the government, and so lost in the sands of time. He still thought until the end, despite everything, he would be able to produce a documentary from the footage that would convince mankind to change its suicidal course. I tried to imagine how the persistent seeds of the vision might still bloom, still bear some fruit.

Kendra, then four years old, recited her own poem:

Balloons are like people.

Can't you tell why?

Balloons pop and people die.

Kendra had been hearing for weeks about her grandfather, about the story of the making and the hiding of Pempah's films, about atom bombs and *pikadon*, and about people burning and dying. What seeds had I planted and watered now?

I closed by dedicating a small stone I had picked up near Peace Park and painted white. I had written on it my father's name and dates of birth and death, and decorated it with a drawing of a little flower in bloom, a small seashell collected from the riverside in Hiroshima, and, perched on the shell, a tiny origami peace crane. We ended in the Quaker manner with a moment of silence.

And then, for me, the work began.

Figure 41: Kendra's kindergarten story illustrating her understanding of why we were in Japan. Text reads: "My grandfather went to Japan to film what had happened when the bombing had hit. And the radiation were still around. And a couple of years went by and my grandfather got sick and died." (Photo by author)

CHAPTER THIRTY-THREE:

Finding the hibakusha

HIROSHIMA, JAPAN (1987) — ACROSS FROM ME SAT A middle-aged man in a suit, dignified and serious but with a current of energy palpable from across the room. His face was round with soft eyes and a half smile. The place to begin gathering the stories I want to preserve, everyone has agreed, is in this small office in the Hiroshima YMCA building. I could see why. Dr. Nagai of its International Institute for Peace clearly cared deeply about his special responsibility of serving in Hiroshima.

I never thought about how difficult it would be to identify specific individuals from the painful images in the old footage until Dr. Nagai told me about the many months he had dedicated to locating *hibakusha* whose faces are visible in the hospital scenes. Dr. Nagai obtained some of the names from the thirty or so caption cards from Hiroshima, but these names were written phonetically in English. The sounds, even if the American ears caught them correctly, might be represented by several different Chinese characters. Each of those *kanji* variations represented entirely different surnames. Then, too, many of the names were common ones. Frequently, even when someone of that name was found, he turned out not to be the "right" Mori or Tsukamoto. And, after all, just because someone was exposed to the bomb in Hiroshima, that person was not obliged to still be there decades later.

Then there was the problem of the women. Only men were likely to be found by poring over phone books in Japan, Dr. Nagai said with a sigh. Those women who had married would have changed their names.

Dr. Nagai spent every spare moment and used all his weekends going out hunting for hibakusha in Hiroshima, while Mr. Iwakura conducted a similar hunt in Nagasaki.

One couple that was immediately recognizable in the footage was the Kikkawas. Mr. Kikkawa had become famous in the months after the bombing as "#1 Atom Bomb Victim," not always spoken with affection. He opened a tourist stand not long after the war near the structure now known as the Atom Bomb Dome, originally a commercial exhibition hall for the prefecture. He sold fragments of houses and other debris left from the atom bomb, along with other souvenirs. Some viewed this business as exploiting disaster, but the Kikkawas needed a way to support themselves and pay for medical treatment. They lived in a shack in the shadow of the Atom Bomb Dome for years.

Mr. Kikkawa had died by the time I came to Hiroshima, but I met Mrs. Ikumi Kikkawa, who was still able to get around at the time of my first visit. On later trips, I visited her after she was confined to the special nursing home maintained for the hibakusha in Hiroshima. She had clear memories of the black rain falling around them. She also remembered the cameramen filming her. Her memory of my father was that he was good-looking with pale white skin. He did not frighten her, she said. She told me that being filmed was a "not-good feeling" at the time but "now precious." Perhaps, she hoped, the films will help toward peace and, had the footage not been shot, no meaningful record might remain as the hibakusha themselves grow old and die.

Mrs. Kikkawa said that Dr. Fumio Shigeto at the Hiroshima Red Cross Hospital persuaded the patients to allow the filming. At first, Mr. Kikkawa said: "Why should I show my back to those whose country did this to me? I have suffered enough." In the end, he felt the pictures of the keloids on his back might serve to alarm others enough to realize what really happened and could happen again. He was ill when my father visited in 1983, and Mrs. Kikkawa told me that her husband regretted missing the chance to talk to my father. They might have argued, she said, or they might have talked about peace.

She and her husband showed their injuries publicly when no other *hibakusha* would, and some accused them of "selling their wounds and selling their country." She insisted to me that they were misunderstood and were always trying to make a statement for peace. Her husband used to say that *hibakusha* came in two types, those who speak out and those who shut their mouths like clams. They only met a year before the bombing, but she loved him for his "broad heart" and his love of books. She was a "country girl," she said, but he taught her to be able to talk to anybody. Near the end, he told her she must keep reading after he died.

The Kikkawas had each other and did not worry about discrimination against them as *hibakusha*, so they persevered in their approach. She saw them as trying to create a pinpoint of light in the darkness. In later years, attitudes became more open and other *hibakusha* began talking about their experiences leading eventually to the *kataribes* I observed.

Kikkawa-san presented me with a roof tile she saved from the bombing which she autographed on the back in black ink calligraphy. Japanese roof tiles are about a foot long. They are heavy, made of clay and curved. The hard, ceramic surface, where this tile had not been overlapped by the next, had bubbled from the incredible heat near the hypocenter. Something about the concreteness of this memento in my hands made the reality of the *pikadon* come home to me in a new way.

Figure 42: Roof tile with surface bubbled from the flash heat of the atomic explosion, requiring more than 3000°F. (Photo by J.C. Penney Portrait Studio, March 2020)

Figure 43: Reverse of exposed roof tile inscribed by Kikkawa-san to the author.
(Photo by J.C. Penney Portrait Studio, March 2020)

In his search, Dr. Nagai also contacted the widow of Dr. Michihiko Hachiya, who had worked at the Communications Bureau Hospital (the hospital where Numata-sensei was treated) during the war and who had struggled to do something to help the victims. Japanese law required retention of hospital records only for five years. Nevertheless, Dr. Nagai and Mrs. Hachiya were able to unearth some fragmentary records of the hospital staff from post-war days. Mrs. Hachiya located a few former hospital staff members who searched their memories for names and clues. This strategy successfully identified three or four more patients from the films.

In addition, Dr. Nagai studied the black-and-white footage of the Japanese film crew. This footage was also seized by the United States military during the occupation and suppressed for decades, but it had been released earlier than the color Strategic Bombing Survey footage; some stills from it had appeared in the Japanese press as early as 1970. He compared the faces of victims in the Japanese film to the people in the U.S. color footage. Where a person appeared in both, Dr. Nagai was able to find the correct name from the Japanese film records.

Next, Dr. Nagai turned to the press. He publicized his efforts through the newspapers and television. He soon learned, however, that the sensitivity of the subject meant that he had to go alone first to any *hibakusha* who came forward as they would not speak to journalists. The shame of being publicly viewed as damaged and the fear of discrimination or rejection remained daunting. Like many Holocaust survivors, some *hibakusha* simply could not bear to speak about the unspeakable events of their past.

In May 1981, a public announcement was made for people to gather at the Memorial Hall of the Hiroshima Peace Museum, where the original footage of medical scenes was to be shown for the first time. About sixty doctors and nurses attended along with many survivors. In July 1981, another showing was held at Hiroshima Red Cross Hospital for elderly doctors and nurses and more *hibakusha* and their relatives.

Despite all these efforts, Dr. Nagai said, of all those they looked for, only twenty were found. Of those found, more than half refused to have their pictures used in the films produced by the Hiroshima-Nagasaki Publishing Committee using footage obtained through their Ten-Feet Campaign. Two documentaries resulted, called *The Lost Generation* (completed in January 1982) and *Prophecy* (completed in May of the same year). The committee felt strongly about respecting human rights and privacy, so they were careful about obtaining consent from those whose pictures would be used. (Respecting this concern, I have included only accounts from those *hibakusha* who chose to speak with me in awareness that I was compiling stories to be shared and used only pictures with faces of those who chose to be public.)

In *The Lost Generation* and *Prophecy,* bits of the original footage were interspersed with narration and interviews with those few *hibakusha* willing to speak about their memories and about the impact of seeing the films of themselves as terribly injured young people. The Ten-Feet Campaign and the showings of these documentaries in Japan brought the voices and faces of the *hibakusha* out of silence and darkness, according to Dr. Nagai.

Dr. Nagai told me that the lives of all *hibakusha* were split into two stages by the bomb, a before and an after. Ever after the day of the *pikadon*, they were changed. They all carried scars not only on their bodies but also in their minds. One woman's son approved use of her footage after her death, but told Dr. Nagai that while she lived she had refused to speak even to him about her experience, saying it would be like "prying open an eye" that had been burned painfully shut.

But a very few, perhaps 0.1%, have reached a third stage in life, as Dr. Nagai sees it. They have found the courage to tell their true stories, speaking to the young and traveling into the world. He believed that these *hibakusha* found spiritual healing for themselves through this truth-telling and witnessing, doing *kataribe*. Numata-sensei was a leading member of this brave, activist minority among the survivors.

Dr. Nagai told me that, around 1956, *hibakusha* first began to organize into groups, partly to seek desperately needed care for themselves but also to call for an end to nuclear weapons. Dr. Nagai volunteered in 1969 to help form the Institute of Hiroshima Peace Education, which invited schools from other prefectures throughout Japan to bring students to Hiroshima for "peace trips." Busloads of schoolchildren have been arriving ever since, swarming through Peace Park twittering even more than the clustered pigeons. They often visit more than once, in sixth grade, in junior high school and in high school. Dr. Nagai also worked on several programs over the years that enabled *hibakusha* who felt called to speak out to carry their message to the United Nations, to the United States, and to other countries that have deployed or are developing nuclear arms.

When he told me that only a miniscule percentage of living *hibakusha* speak publicly about their experiences, I was deeply struck by the frustration Dr. Nagai seemed to feel about that fact. He said that if "even 1%" of *hibakusha* spoke out about the meaning of their experiences, it could change the political situation in Japan and perhaps the world.

I wondered why most *hibakusha* would not be shouting about the things that had happened to them. Then I wondered what would happen in the world if one percent of the rest of us screamed, and pleaded, and prayed, and worked for peace, and why don't we? After all, we have the health, the youth, and the energy that are in such short supply for the survivors.

Perhaps one reason I went to Hiroshima was to find my voice.

CHAPTER THIRTY-FOUR:

Hibakusha toxic humor?

HIROSHIMA, JAPAN (1987) — DR. NAGAI ARRANGED A dinner for me with a group of the *hibakusha* who appeared in my father's footage. We had a private room at a traditional-style restaurant with low tables and a tatami floor with thin cushions to sit on. The other guests, although all older than 60, folded smoothly into their places. I was too fat and too stiff. I managed to fit myself on to a corner cushion with my legs crossed clumsily. I knew it was rude to stick your legs out straight, so I tried to unobtrusively undo and re-cross them when they went numb.

Listening to the flow of talk, I was surprised at the laughter mixed in the telling of sad stories. These survivors seemed to have become good friends despite sharing nothing but the experience of having been filmed by enemy soldiers at the worst moments of their lives.

The food arrived in waves of small plates. Soup, sushi and sashimi, fried plates, grilled fish. All tasty seafood dishes. I explained what I was doing in Hiroshima, about my father's wish, about my wish to understand and spread the story of the films. They all knew this already.

They knew because it was on television. When I returned to Hiroshima, I encountered the same media interest that my father had. We were met by television cameras and reporters with microphones. Nothing had prepared me for the idea that I would encounter my Andy Warhol fifteen minutes of fame in Hiroshima. I had not reckoned with how well-known the Ten-Feet Campaign had made my father's story in the city. An NHK (Japanese television) reporter and her photographer were with me in Peace Park when I first heard Numata-sensei's *kataribe*. I walked forward while the photographer skittered backwards to film me and my daughter entering the park. Being filmed while simply walking is strange. I felt as if I ought to dance a jig or make a speech or do something interesting to justify to onlookers why a camera was pointing at me.

I did not know until weeks later what I ate at that dinner with the *hibakusha*. As it turned out, the restaurant specialized in a single kind of fish. Every dish was made from *fugu* (blowfish). *Fugu* is a Japanese delicacy that has the distinction of bearing a tasteless toxin in its internal organs. You would never know if a trace remained in the flesh when served, at least until it was too late. Chefs require special training and a license to serve it because the poison is deadly if the fish is not properly prepared.

I wondered if survival made *hibakusha* fearless about such things or if the choice of venue was a private joke. The food was excellent.

CHAPTER THIRTY-FIVE:

Motherhood in Hiroshima

HIROSHIMA, JAPAN (1987) — FALL ARRIVED, STARTLING me. I forgot that Hiroshima had seasons other than summer and that not every day dawned sunny. Living in Hiroshima was a peculiar balance between the ordinary and the sacred. I learned to shop for groceries daily, the Japanese way. I learned to ride the streetcars and to find the things needed for daily life.

Yet every day, as I came to a bridge or stood by a building, I would come across a wall-mounted bronzed picture showing the same view as it had looked after the bombing. I would stroll beside the river and stumble on yet another monument or shrine tucked between bushes and draped with chains of paper cranes. Hiroshima is full of life, stores, restaurants, work, laughter, but burned on to it is a shadow city still frozen at the moment of the *pikadon*. At times, the bomb seems utterly past, but it is never forgotten.

Kendra attended a *yochien* (kindergarten) called Mikune-en, run by a Japanese Christian Church in our neighborhood. The principal, Reverend Shozo Muneto, was dubious at first, having never accepted a foreign student before. The main problem for him was not the child but the mother. Mothers have many responsibilities to the school, and a foreign lady was unlikely to understand, much less fulfill, them. Hiroshima had an international school but the tuition was quite high, at least for someone like me with no regular income. Besides, I did not like the idea of living in Japan but enclosing Kendra in an English-speaking bubble.

A cousin of Imaeda-san, Emiko Morikawa, lived near the school and became a close friend to me. She had three children, an older boy, Hidehiko, and two girls, Fumie and Aya. Aya-chan was near Kendra's age, and they became regular playmates. I discussed with Imaeda-san and Morikawa-san the problem of kindergarten – and of me. Morikawa-san promised the principal that she would see to it that I did things correctly.

The first step involved preparing Kendra for school. She needed two uniforms with light blue blouses and dark blue skirts and two hats, straw for warm weather and felt for cold. With her name embroidered on each. Her name spelled out phonetically in katakana characters – ke - en - do – ra. She had to have special rubber soled canvas shoes to play in, with her name embroidered on them. She needed four different sizes of bags — for her large drawing pad, her shoes, her school papers and books, and her lunch. They all needed her name embroidered on them too, and two of them had to be made from scratch to specifications. All this Morikawa-san arranged.

Figure 44: Kendra (on right) and classmate in kindergarten school uniform.
(Photo by author)

And then Kendra must have a plastic lunch set with compartments for rice balls and for little matching chopsticks. At first, I tucked sandwiches cut in little triangles into the compartments. Soon, though, Kendra wanted "normal" lunches like the other girls. I had to buy *o-nigiri* (seaweed-wrapped rice balls) at the corner store since I was too incompetent to make even the simplest correct food.

These elaborate preparations were only the beginning. Mothers were expected to play an active role in the operation of the school. Once a week, we were to come in and assist the children in cleaning the schoolrooms. The children cleaned up every day, but the heavier work was left to the mothers. I bumbled through this job, not sure what to do, but got the hang of it watching the other mothers at work.

The children's cleaning duties gave me a clue about how differently Kendra approached learning Japanese at four than I did at thirty-four. One day, I was picking up our things at the apartment before the time for Imaeda-san's *juku* to begin. Kendra watched me and sang out "*O-katazuke-o shimashoo!*" Stumped, I asked her what *o-katazuke* meant. I knew *shimashoo* meant "let's do," but let's do what? She looked at me puzzled and explained that it *didn't* mean in English. The next time, I got the question right: "Well, who says it and what do they say it for?" Relieved at being asked a coherent question, she informed me that the teacher says it when it is clean-up time. Clearly, she was not composing lists of matched vocabulary words in her head as I was, trying to learn how to say English ideas with Japanese words. She paid attention to the sounds that got results and repeated them until she could get results too.

Each day, I waited at the heavy sliding iron gate outside the schoolyard, along with the other mothers, many with younger children in strollers. I knew I did not hold up my end of all the school mother duties, even with Morikawa-san busily filling in gaps.

Nevertheless, the other mothers were fascinated by such alien creatures as my daughter and me and never seemed to resent any extra load they may have carried on my behalf.

Expectations of foreign efforts to speak Japanese, much less become literate in the language, were low. Anyone exceeding those minimal expectations hovered between the statuses of freak and genius. Meanwhile, Japanese efforts to speak English were marked by a mix of painful shyness and shock at discovering that the language they had studied for so many years at school and in which they had achieved flawless grammar bore no resemblance at all to the language Americans actually speak. The resulting communication was often difficult on both sides but also frequently hilarious.

English was all around on signs, t-shirts, and advertisements but much of it was what I called "Janglish." Janglish looked like English and almost meant something in English, but not quite. The false appearance of meaning was nerve-wracking because an English-speaker could not help investing some mental effort into trying to understand it. For example, a department store section for "ladies characters" turned out to sell designer fashions. A sweatshirt may proudly assert "Good feeling thought" or "For beautiful my pace." Then there are the startling drink names like Calpis (pronounced cow-piss) and Pocari Sweat. I was brought up short by this phenomenon so many times that I began to wonder if clothing in the U.S. decorated with random Chinese characters was just as aggravating to those who understood the *kanji* and found them nonsensical.

In the mornings, the mothers did not meet at the gate. Kendra instead joined her classmates in the play yard across from our apartment building. They walked together unsupervised, holding hands, about five blocks to school. The side streets had little traffic, but they also lacked real sidewalks. I was terrified at first by the practice of letting four- and five-year-old's make their own way, but Kendra was adamant that mommies did *not* walk their children to school. I stalked the little parade of serious-faced children for several days, spying on them from around the corners of buildings. Oddly, the group of children seemed collectively more mature and responsible than any one of them appeared alone. Eventually, I relaxed and allowed Kendra the same freedom as her friends. After all, I had been able to cross streets, run to the playground, and buy candy or pickles at the newsstand in New York City before I was in grade school.

CHAPTER THIRTY-SIX:

The angry jizo

HIROSHIMA, JAPAN (1987) — ONE DAY I TOOK KENDRA to the Hiroshima Children's Library and Museum. We had just come out after an enjoyable visit into dazzling summer sunshine when I heard a deep voice intoning loudly to my left. Puzzled, I turned to see a group of children circled around a thin man beside a bicycle to which was strapped a large cabinet. The somewhat ragged, bearded man looked like a medieval magician. Opening his cabinet, he pulled out little toys for the children and made them sweets shaped like bunnies with cookie ears and chocolate syrup faces.

He was an itinerant storyteller, illustrating his tales with dramatic gestures and colorful picture cards, a rare phenomenon in modern Japan. Of course, we hurried over to join the waiting children and see what would happen. I expected a chance to sample traditional fairy tales.

Instead, his tale was of the atom bombing of Hiroshima, "*Okori-Jizo*," the Angry Jizo. We had seen *jizo*, the little rotund statuettes, often about a foot tall, near shrines or beside roads. Sometimes they had red kerchiefs tied around their necks; sometimes offerings of rice or children's toys were placed at their bases. They looked cute and cheerful, but I was told they were set up in memory of lost or aborted children. Despite our limited Japanese, the storyteller's expressiveness and the striking pictures made the meaning clear:

The Angry Jizo

A sweet little girl loved a small stone statute with a red kerchief under his chin. He seemed to her to always be smiling gently at her. She would smile back at him.

But then, the bomb knocked the *Jizo* to the ground. All around him he heard the cries of a dying city.

At his feet, he saw his little friend. She was badly burned and begged for water. "*Mizu, mizu!*" She cried. The *Jizo's* stone heart broke with anger and sorrow. Tears rolled from his eyes to the child's lips.

She drank the water eagerly . . . and died.

Living in Hiroshima means that you can never tell when you will be reminded that it is Hiroshima in which you live.

CHAPTER THIRTY-SEVEN:

Community and belonging in Hiroshima

HIROSHIMA, JAPAN (1987) — I JOINED THE FUNAIRI-CHO neighborhood association as its first foreign member, to make an effort to be fully part of daily life there. I could tell from posters when a meeting was planned, even though I never could read the topic. One of my neighbors, however, would be sure to turn up before the meeting and accompany me to it and give a running explanation of what was decided in some mix of stiff English and baby Japanese tailored for me. The main activities of this association, or at least those that I was able to comprehend, surrounded planning traditional seasonal and cultural events, keeping the neighborhood clean, and organizing rituals such as a Shinto blessing when ground was broken for a new building. It was also clear to me that the biggest pastime was that staple of neighborhood associations everywhere, gossip. I am sure I was a capital topic for gossip with all my comical or inexplicable behaviors. All the festivals gave me the idea of sharing an American holiday.

Halloween is not celebrated in Japan although a few commercial echoes of it had just begun to show up in department store decorations when we lived there. As October 31st approached, we had been telling *juku* students about what Halloween was like in America. I explained about trick-or-treating door to door in the neighborhood, about costumes ranging from scary to silly, and about bobbing for apples at parties. We decided to invite the whole neighborhood to a Halloween party as a small way to express gratitude for our welcome.

With Imaeda-san and Morikawa-san and other neighborhood friends, I set about planning a Halloween party. I bought paper lunch bags, construction paper, and glue, and began making masks of lions, cats, dogs, pandas, and other animals as well as devils and angels and other fanciful designs. In one store I managed to find a blue wig and clown nose for me to wear. We set up in the park, and Imaeda-san helped organize the kids into different games, like relay races. We had apple bobbing from a big plastic tub. I bought lots of candy which we gave out as prizes. All around me I heard squeals and shrill giggles. I am not sure how much the excitement added to any real understanding of America culture, but I am certain that at least one neighborhood's worth of now-grown Japanese kids knows that "Ha-ro-e-en" involves lots of sweets and laughter.

Later in the winter, several friends began telling me eagerly about an upcoming festival called the "Pay-Ah-Say-Low-Vay." Every time I asked what that meant I was met by a puzzled stare and the answer that "But it is English!" I could not figure it out until I arrived and saw the large banner over the entrance gate reading "Peace-love Festival." The syllabic rendering in Japanese never had connected in my mind with the words "peace" and "love."

The celebration, unique to Hiroshima, featured live music. Many of the bands regularly played at Clementine's, an entirely incongruous country-western bar with faux Texas food and décor that might resemble Tex-Mex ambiance if you squinted. The tunes they offered at the festival had nothing to do with peacemaking, but the general spirit seemed to be an imaginary American hippie summer-of-love be-in. Booths around the field offered easily carried food such as broiled baby octopus or teriyaki chicken strips on bamboo skewers. Since eating while walking around is frowned on in Japan, most people would squat nearby to consume the treats.

In one corner, Kendra discovered a young woman giving lessons in tea ceremony. The instructor of the little outdoor class patiently included my eager four-year-old. Kendra copied each step with careful concentration, folding the napkin just so, placing the little pile of powdered green *macha* tea in the bowl without spilling a fleck from the tiny bamboo spoon, ladling a cup of hot water with slow graceful movements, and then whisking it cheerfully in the bowl. She turned her bowl three short turns before taking a cautious sip and wiping the edge with her little fingers before passing the bowl to the teacher. By the time she finished, she had drawn quite a crowd to gawk at the improbable sight of a biracial American kindergartener so studiously mimicking the tea ceremony ritual.

We stumbled one time on a frenzied street parade. We had seen the elaborate portable shrines called *mikoshi*, like soaring airboats with colorful faces and carvings in a cultural museum in Nagasaki. Viewing them reposing on stands did not get across their real purpose. The gods within rode out on special days carried by a dozen sweating men in loincloths through a crowd to driving drumbeats. As the crowd's excitement rose, the bearers did spins and dips, and threw the heavy boats into the air. Primal energy surged through the onlookers, vibrating between joyous and terrifying. I wondered about how such raw displays coexisted with, or perhaps made possible, the careful politeness of everyday life in Japan.

Living in the community, instead of within one of the enclaves of foreigners, brought a deeper understanding of the ways that humanity connects even when culture divides.

As always, though, community life in Hiroshima included regular reminders that our home was indeed Hiroshima. Peace activism is woven deeply throughout the web of connections. Before and after exist side by side. Happy parties alternate with somber protests.

CHAPTER THIRTY-EIGHT:

Looking sideways

HIROSHIMA, JAPAN (1987) — IN THE MIDDLE OF MODERN Hiroshima, I came upon a timeless enclave called Shukkei-en. The garden with its central pond and winding path, detouring to hidden tea houses, was first laid out in the 1600s near Hiroshima castle. The bomb dried the fishpond, seared every plant, and cut down the trees in the garden. Its bones remained, though, and life regrew around them.

The trick of its design is that, when viewed from the proper angles, miniature scenes appear. Tiny mounds artfully suggest mountains; trickling rivulets mimic wild streams. A pebbled curve captures an ocean beach. It is essential that you not raise your eyes to see beyond the frame of the illusion, however, or it vanishes. Its beauty is that fragile.

* * *

HOW DO YOU SPEAK THE UNSPEAKABLE OR PICTURE THE invisible?

I saw pictures that did exactly that once. The images were more like negatives than photographs, but they were not blank. They had form, texture, and presence. There was something there to see but you could not see what it was. Alice Miceli, the artist who made them, explained that these exposures were taken in the contaminated area around Chernobyl, in an attempt to make visible the unseen radiation that fills the space without inhabiting it. (Projecto

Chernobyl can be viewed in part online at https://www.as-coa.org/alice-miceli-projeto-chernobyl.)

Could a picture like that of my father have made visible what from Hiroshima permeated his life? Was it the radiation that poisoned him, or was it the memory of his proximity to suffering? Or maybe the real poison was his own enforced silence, separated from his footage for a lifetime, stifling his vision of speaking through film?

What if I could have seen a picture exposing the invisible pull that Hiroshima would have on me? Would I have avoided it, or would I have gone sooner? We were both filled by Hiroshima. We were both changed by it. But I still cannot say what it is.

*   *   *

I USED TO GO HIKING WITH A FRIEND WHO WAS AN Army captain. He taught me how to walk in the dark without a flashlight. The secret is to get the most from moonlight by not looking straight ahead at the path. Peripheral vision is more effective in low light. You have to look sideways to see clearly.

I wish I could see, or show, or speak the thing that seeps from Hiroshima into the heart, but I can only see it by looking sideways.

CHAPTER THIRTY-NINE:

Kataribe

HIROSHIMA, JAPAN (1987) — I HAVE TRIED TO UNDER-
stand the power this city had over my father's life and over my imagination. I talked to Numata-sensei about this mysterious bond. She
introduced me to a man who had helped create the *kataribe* program, Tamotsu Eguchi.

He was a short man, with a round bald pate, bright eyes, and
an infectious smile. I never saw him anything but cheerful. It was
easy to see that he loved children from the natural way they crowded
around him and listened to his tales. His storytelling was so gentle
that one could almost forget how sad the stories were. His favorite
spot was next to one of the riverbanks, so the water could be heard
gurgling in the background while he told his story. The water comforted him.

In late July and early August 1945, he said, everyone knew that
the Americans were in Okinawa and expected them to land next
in Kyushu. A life-size wooden model of a tank was made so that
the people could train in how to destroy the treads with explosives.
One day, a bomb was dropped on the fake tank. People guessed that
perhaps the Americans thought it was real. Students trained with
wooden rifles and bayonets. Eguchi-sensei said that as a student,
he was an "enthusiastic believer" in what the authorities taught and
"had no reason to suspect no one was telling the truth."

Eguchi-sensei was exposed in the courtyard of Keiko Middle
School in Nagasaki, a wooden building 800 meters from the

hypocenter. He found himself under debris, having lost consciousness. No one helped him so he must have crawled out himself, but he had no memory of having done so. Amazingly, he did not die in the flames that were flaring all around. Nevertheless, he was burned on his upper arm and suffered other injuries from the debris falling on him.

About eighty or ninety percent of the people at the school died, he told me. Two of his friends were in the yard too, along with seven or eight other people. One, Shoichiru Okada, was not hurt at all. Kazuki Yamamoto was also in the yard with him, trapped between rafters and crying for help; Okada-san was able to move the heavy wood off him.

Yamamoto-san remembered how he and Eguchi-sensei climbed, slipping and scrambling, over ruins of houses near the gate of the school. They reached a well and drank a little water. They saw many people passing by dazed and bleeding. Eguchi-sensei was covered with cuts on his face and body. A glass fragment pierced his left eye. He lost all his hair. He had a huge hole where his nose had been (and the bridge of his nose later had to be reconstructed with bone from his hip). Children cried that he was a ghost.

His home and family were located three kilometers away. Happily, they were all well. Three days after he reached them, the whole family went to relatives in Saga Prefecture, where he recuperated. He became a teacher and, in 1951, was married in Tokyo.

Six months later, when his own injuries had healed, Eguchi-sensei went back to Nagasaki and tried to find Okada-san. He learned that even though Okada-san had made it through that awful day unscathed, he died on September 2, 1945. Okada-san's mother said that, before he died, Okada-san was anxious about Eguchi-sensei because he thought that Eguchi-sensei's injuries were so serious that he must not have survived.

Eguchi-sensei pondered his experiences for a long time. Especially he wondered, since it was possible to train warriors, could pacifists be trained? He concluded that the essential thing was to teach children to feel others' pain and consider others' feelings. To that end, he believed that when schoolchildren come to Hiroshima and hear *hibakusha* talking to them, the children will feel the pain that others have suffered.

Eguchi-sensei came to this sense of a duty to share his pain only slowly and over many years. In his case, it was the receipt in 1960 of an official certificate of his status as a survivor that first caused him to feel an identity as a *hibakusha*. After that, at the start of each new school term, he introduced himself to the students and told newcomers about Nagasaki. On special days, instead of math, he would discuss the war in his classes.

In 1976, he began to arrange school trips to Hiroshima and Nagasaki, working with Dr. Nagai. At first, he planned to have the students listen to mothers who had lost their children in the bombing, but it was difficult then to find *hibakusha* who would talk to the children for fear that other people would disapprove. Also, over the years many of the first generation *hibakusha* had died or became bedridden. Eguchi-sensei continued to visit them, in their beds or their tombs, but they could not speak to children.

He retired from teaching a few years later. One day, around 1982, he was in Peace Park when he came across a high school group from Miyaga (a city that he knew had a nuclear plant). The students were looking for roof tiles by the river. Eguchi-sensei spoke to their teacher and learned that they had had no opportunity to hear testimony. He arranged for them to listen to Numata-sensei give *kataribe*.

After that, he realized that, since not enough *hibakusha* were available to speak to students, he must do so himself. Even as an old man, every year he left his wife, children, and grandchildren in Tokyo and joined a survivor group in Hiroshima to speak to students during the times when the most students visit.

Figure 45: Eguchi-sensei in reflective moment in 1987. (Photo by author)

Eguchi-sensei invited us to visit him in Tokyo when he went home at the end of the school visit season. His family hosted us for lunch at his apartment. Eguchi-sensei's face was deeply expressive. He could fall into a distant sorrow, but when a child sought his attention, whether his granddaughter or my daughter, he would suddenly glow with kindness.

While we were in Tokyo, Eguchi-sensei took me to see the museum housing the fishing boat called *Daigo Fukuryū Maru*, or "Lucky Dragon No. 5." The museum in Tokyo is built around the boat itself and has a dramatic sloping form echoing a graceful sail. (The unique museum and the ship inside can be seen at the museum's website at http://d5f.org/en/. There is even a memorial set up to the radioactive tuna that had to be destroyed.) The tuna fishing boat was an early casualty of the race to escalate the power of nuclear weapons in the 1950s as part of the unfolding Cold War with the Soviet Union. Once America knew that Stalin had tested an atomic bomb, the U.S. government poured resources into a secret program to develop an even stronger, even "better" weapon. "Mike," the first successful hydrogen bomb tested, carried a force of ten megatons, which was more than eight hundred times the power of the Hiroshima explosion, according to the primary sources cited in NPR's "The Race for the Superbomb." A program of testing in the Pacific ensued, starting with the "Bravo" test on the Bikini Islands on March 1, 1954.

The twenty-three-man crew of the Lucky Dragon was unluckily close enough to see the flash and the cloud that followed the explosion. CNN interviewed one of the survivors, Yoshio Misaki, and his description of what he saw has been widely quoted: "The sky in the west suddenly lit up and the sea became brighter than day. We watched the dazzling light, which felt heavy. Seven or eight minutes later there was a terrific sound — like an avalanche. Then a visible multi-colored ball of fire appeared on the horizon."

Radioactive ash fell on the ship eighty miles east of Bravo. All the crew members sickened from acute radiation poisoning, and one man, Aikichi Kuboyama, died seven months later from symptoms of radiation poisoning. Many other crew members reportedly died young though the etiology was harder to prove by then. Misaki-san himself died in 2016 at the age of 90.

Despite initial denials, the United States ended up paying two million dollars in compensation for the damage done to the Lucky Dragon and its crew. This was accepted as part of the price of staying ahead of the Soviets. Yet only a year and half after Bravo, the Soviet

Union also had a hydrogen bomb. The endless cycle of arms race and escalation and proliferation continued.

I could not help but wonder at the irony of a Japanese fishing crew being the victims of another American nuclear bomb. Many historians suggest that the atomic bombs used in Hiroshima and Nagasaki are better understood as the opening salvos in the Cold War than as the final attacks to end World War II. But the last shot in every war is the first shot in the next, it seems.

The Lucky Dragon brought home to many *hibakusha,* as well as to other people in Japan, the message that the continued development of nuclear weapons was a threat not just to the superpowers but to Japan and to the whole world. The testing and potential use of these weapons could sicken and kill noncombatants far from any war zone. The incident provided part of the impetus that led to the first World Conference Against A- and H- Bombs held in Hiroshima the next year.

I am not a scholar of World War II. I am often confronted with arguments about "what about Pearl Harbor," and "how many more people, especially Americans, would have died in an invasion," and whether "Japan would have surrendered anyway." Anyone can read the same books as I have about these debates, and nobody can change what happened.

Every one of the stories I have included here is part of what happened. That is all I can say. Each person must decide what message to draw from those stories. Compassionate listening can open the heart to lessons for now, even if it cannot rewrite errors from the past.

CHAPTER FORTY:

A single memorial

HIROSHIMA, JAPAN (1987) — THE WOOD FLOOR OF THE classroom bounced and the tables and chairs vibrated as a group of teens, plus my energetic four-year old, enthusiastically put their left feet in, put their left feet out, and jumped around as they turned it all about. By the time the song finished, kids were draped over the wooden chairs gasping for air, trying to recover more from the hilarity than the exertion. The English lesson was clearly over for that day.

I started to gather the picture books and notes I used to give volunteer lessons at the Hiroshima Christian Social Services Center. I was pulling on Kendra's coat to get ready for the twenty-minute walk across the river back to our apartment, when a heavy-set young woman approached. She had a broad face, flattened features, and her black hair did not hang straight down like that of most Japanese people.

"Excuse me, please. I want to ask. How is it in America? For African peoples?"

I looked down at my daughter. "Life is better for most African American people now than when I was a girl, but many things are still not fair."

"I want to go to America. I want to know African peoples."

"You do? What makes you want to do that?"

Many Japanese people peeked at my daughter's tight braids and glanced back and forth between us, obviously puzzled by the contrast with my long reddish blond hair. No one had previously broached the subject of race out loud.

"Korean peoples in Japan same like African peoples in America, I think this."

The same, yes, and, of course, quite different. And impossible to explain either in my limited Japanese or her limited English. I smiled at her. "Please come visit us in America and see for yourself someday." She grinned.

Instead of heading straight home as I had planned, I walked toward Peace Park. The walk was longer this way, and I did not enter Peace Park. I stopped on the other side of the river, where a single memorial stands as if banished from the rest just over the bridge.

More than ten percent of the people who died in the atomic bombing in Hiroshima are thought to have been Korean, many of whom had been brought there forcibly during Japan's colonial control of Korea. This memorial, a stone obelisk engraved with many symbols mounted on a stone turtle, is a cenotaph for the Korean victims. An inscription on it translates as: "Souls of the dead ride to heaven on the backs of turtles."

Eguchi-sensei had brought me here and explained that the construction in Peace Park of any remembrance of Korean victims of the bomb had been hotly opposed. The location was a compromise. I had been shocked at the time to find that racism infected even this.

By this time, I knew a little more about the history of internal Japanese discrimination. Korean and other Asian people living in Japan, sometimes for generations, were not assimilated and were long considered inferior. People looked down as well on the Ainu, the indigenous residents of northern Japan, and on *burakumin* people, an historically outcast group. I had learned much of this from Reverend Mutoi Munakata, who ran the Hiroshima Christian Social

Services Center, which served many Korean and burakumin residents, and who recruited me as a volunteer. One day he finally told me his own memories of discrimination against Christians during the war.

Munakata-sensei was born in 1924 to Japanese parents in Taiwan. The family returned to Japan in the 1930s. His parents were Christian, and he used to attend church in Taipei. In the run-up to the war between the United States and Japan, however, Christians in Japan came under government surveillance, and incurred hostility from the general population, because they were associated with a Western religion. To deflect suspicion, he was sent instead to the Shinto shrine and made to participate in military training from middle school on.

Children were taught that they must work hard for the Emperor and that any actions were justified if undertaken for the Emperor. Killing other people, including other Asian people, was not wrong if it served the Emperor. Christians were required to answer the question of which was greater: Jesus Christ or the Emperor. If they said Christ was greater, they would be punished. But if they said the Emperor was greater, they were required to explain why they followed Christ when he was dead and was not a great man. The only viable answer was that it was impossible to compare the two. Had any Christian of the time criticized the Emperor, the punishment would have been severe. Almost all Christians therefore obeyed the Imperial system at that time, and those who did not were segregated from society.

The Japanese forces occupying Korea began to build Shinto shrines in Korea. The Japanese government sent leaders of the Christian communities to Korea. Their mission, according to Munakata-sensei, was to tell the Korean people that the shrines were not "religious" buildings and that they must all attend the shrine, regardless of their religion.

After graduating from middle school, Munakata-sensei entered the naval military academy close to Hiroshima. After completing the naval program, he served as chief of a small submarine until the war ended. He worked hard for the imperial system, following the oft-repeated instructions to ignore one's own needs and serve the needs of the country. On August 6, 1945, he was working at about 120 miles away from Hiroshima. He was startled by a flash, and then he saw the mushroom cloud growing over Hiroshima.

About a year after the war ended, he entered the theological seminary in Tokyo and became a pastor. He found compassion for those who had discriminated against the Christians, but he came to despise the imperialistic oppression of the war years. After graduation, he returned as a missionary to Hiroshima serving Ushita Church. He was gripped by the idea of peace-making, and the conviction that war should never return to Japan.

Before the war, children were taught to look down on *burakumin* people, a group at the bottom of the imperial caste system. Although ethnically Japanese, they inherited a status similar to the Dalit people in India, whom Gandhi championed and who similarly were restricted to "unclean" tasks such as handling waste and leatherworking. Children were also taught contempt for the "little brother" Koreans and Chinese. Disparaging attitudes toward other Asian peoples had emerged in the post-Meiji era in Japan (after 1912). In fact, many key cultural components in Japan were imports from China and Korea, including the kanji writing system and the Buddhist religion. Munakata-sensei believed Japan felt insecure, with a landmass too small for its large population and therefore a need to obtain control of more land. Patronizing ideas about these

neighboring people justified actions which treated them as less entitled to autonomy. In this, he concluded, Japan followed the same
approach as the European colonizing powers. Japanese were taught
to see themselves as the top of civilization, with Europeans relatively
high (a nod to their displays of military strength), and other Asian
people at the bottom. Japanese pre-war society, he told me, simply
"floated in an ambiance of cultural discrimination."

He opposed the return of the imperial system after the war for
two reasons: (1) because war should never again be forced on the
people and (2) because Japan should never return to the prior social
and cultural discrimination against Asian and *burakumin* people.
Of course, during the war, Japanese children were also taught that
Americans were like animals and did evil things. This message was a
new and temporary one, though, Munakata-sensei felt, without the
long history behind it of negative attitudes against Asian and *burakumin* people. Before the war buildup, people thought that European
countries and America had highly developed cultures. The Japanese
government had to work hard to reverse people's impressions. He
believed that explained why Japanese attitudes toward Americans
reverted to mostly positive almost immediately after the war. The
contemptuous attitudes toward *burakumin* people and other Asians
were deep-rooted, however, and did not change as quickly after
the war.

The two westernmost rivers in Hiroshima historically marked
the boundaries of the *burakumin* area. These sections were the most
vulnerable to flooding. This arrangement was viewed as a flood pro-
tection measure. In case of flooding, the water would merely wash
out the *burakumin* and not threaten the city. The dampness caused
many illnesses among the residents. (After the war, in the early 1950s,
a project was undertaken to redirect the rivers and create landfill.

In the course of that work, the original residents were scattered.)
Immediately after the bomb exploded, disaster and panic created
a sort of a temporary equality as desperate people fled toward the
burakumin areas. The Army Marine Transport company was then
stationed at Ujina Port, which played an important role as a military
launching point during the war. They dispatched a unit called the
"Akatsuki Corps" to the *burakumin* area after the bomb. Opinions
among the *burakumin* differed about this deployment, with some
believing the Corps came to help the people and others convinced
that the Corps came to impose security control on the *burakumin*.
When it came to medical treatment for survivors, *burakumin* and
Korean people clearly came last.

In 1957, Munakata-sensei went to Brazil as a missionary. While
he was away, anti-discrimination measures began to be adopted by
the national government beginning in 1963. When he returned, he
found the atmosphere improved but equality still elusive, and so
he worked on creating a center to support those suffering from the
persistent negative attitudes. The children who came to Hiroshima
Christian Social Center include *burakumin* and North and South
Koreans, as well as handicapped children, joining in activities with
ordinary Japanese children. Munakata-sensei taught them all about
how Japan was before the war. He encouraged Korean children to
use their real names, their Korean names, rather than the Japanese
names they usually are known by in Japan. Korean people were
forced to change their names during the Japanese occupation, and
many parents continued to fear allowing their children to use their
Korean names openly in school.

After the war, according to Munakata-sensei, *hibakusha* too
faced discrimination. Radiation sickness was not well understood so
people worried it might be contagious or spread by physical contact.

Some thought that anyone exposed would be unable to bear children or would only conceive stillborn or deformed babies. No one knew what the impact would be on life expectancy. In Japan, prospective employers and marriage brokers commonly investigated the backgrounds of those being considered and ruled out those with foreign or *burakumin* ancestry. After the war, being *hibakusha* could also be considered a taint in such screenings. After measures were passed to assist *hibakusha*, some people also resented the special benefits granted to *hibakusha*. To a large extent, the United States occupation policy, he believes, fed the discrimination by hiding scientific information about the actual range of effects of exposure to the bomb on human bodies. Fear fills a void.

Munakata-sensei was not always widely embraced, even by some in the peace movement in Hiroshima. For one thing, he was open about his desire to see an end to the imperial system after the death of Emperor Hirohito at a time when most people would refer to this subject only in whispers and by code names such as "Zero Day." He opposed right-wing campaigns to reinstate the wartime flag, the *Hinomaru*, and to make "Kimigayo," the song dedicated to the Emperor during the war, again the national anthem. He feared popular pressure for remilitarizing Japan and argued that the slogan "No more Hiroshimas" must have two meanings. "One is that we should never repeat the atomic bombing. But the other is that we should never repeat the aggression that led to the war."

For the same reason, he argued that Peace Park must include an exhibit on Japanese aggression. The Hiroshima Peace Museum, he complained, fails to present any of the history of why Hiroshima was bombed. Hiroshima had several military installations during the war, including a depot storing 120,000 tons of ammunition. His arguments about presenting this aspect of history elicit a lot of opposition from those who feel that only the suffering of the *hibaku-sha* should be shown there.

At heart, his message was a call to repentance by all sides. That message spoke deeply to me. I was not in search of victims and villains. I wanted to understand how we come to hurt each other so deeply and how the effects of racism, war, and violence can echo down so many generations only to breed more of the same.

CHAPTER FORTY-ONE:

On top of the world

NIKKO, JAPAN (1946) — HERB CLUTCHED THE DOOR OF
the military ambulance as it sped around yet another hairpin turn
on the narrow, rocky road up the mountain. Praying that a car did
not appear coming the other way, Herb wiped the mist from the window with an elbow. Outside was a desolate landscape of windblown
pines and rocky crags with steam rising from all the crevices. The
mountain itself was exhaling into the chilling atmosphere. He shiv-
ered despite the heater.

At lower levels, they had rushed past resort hotels which had
been taken over by the Occupation as rest stations for troops. For
some time now, though, he felt as if the unpaved road had left the
real world behind and carried them off into an unearthly realm. He
was not sure if they were still solid themselves.

A few weeks before, about six months after leaving Tokyo,
Herb's crew had returned their train to the rail yards at Yokohama.
By now the occupation had taken on a new formality. The train was
required to be turned over to the regular occupation authorities –
only no one could find any record of its having left Tokyo, or of its
very existence for that matter. No one, therefore, would take responsibility for officially accepting its return. Finally, the crew just left
the train that had been home for so long in the Yokohama yards and
walked away from it. The crew scattered, and Herb loaded 100-foot
rolls of sixteen-millimeter Kodachrome, in several large footlockers,
into their Jeep and drove it to their offices back in the Meiji Building.

Herb sat at his desk and looked at the mountains of paperwork to be completed. Day after day, he pulled out the log he had kept of their travels. He tried to fill in the gaps for the string of cities they inventoried on the return trip. In his mind, it was blurring already. More vistas of rubble, more burns and wounds, more broken buildings and grieving people, more signs of slow recoveries under way. He sat at the typewriter. He did not hit a key.

He tried to think of a few bright spots. They had managed to arrive just at the reopening of Kirin Breweries. He smiled at the memory of filling every receptacle they could find – jars, basins, pots, anything – with the delicious beer to take along for the rest of the trip.

There was Kokura, the city that missed being the target of the bomb thanks to a cloud bank. The Americans had pinpoint bombed the coke ovens at the heart of Kokura's steel mills two years before. Without the coke ovens, Japan could not run a steel industry, and it took years to bring them fully back online. At the time of Herb's visit, some furnaces were just beginning to operate again. Another brief smile, thinking of the metal from all the guns and armament of the Japanese military machine refashioned into . . . cooking woks.

Herb met the president of the steel company. Not the sort of person Herb would ever have been likely to meet back home. In normal times, he would have been the equivalent of an American multi-millionaire, Herb figured. Now the man could not stop thanking Herb for arranging to get him a case of condensed milk for his little granddaughter.

And Kyoto — the most beautiful of Japanese cities — was mercifully undamaged. If the bomb had hit Kyoto, many of the most treasured cultural artifacts of Japan would have been gone.

Herb chewed on an unlit cigar. He looked out the windows. Words would not come. While they had been on the move, he had been able to get his job done. Looking for things to record on film, meeting people, making plans. Now, when the work should be easy, it had suddenly become impossible.

He could not work; he could not sleep; even sitting still had become hard. And yet, he pulsed with the need to do something. These films had to be released, quickly. No one at home knew, even all these months later, how horrendous the effects of this weapon were on people or how it engendered an invisible, poisonous illness. To get the film they had shot ready for viewing was the most important thing in the world. But instead of rushing to do that, he felt paralyzed.

At last, he decided to visit a doctor.

I confided, "Doctor, I can't get the horrors of Nagasaki and Hiroshima out of my mind — one scene after another. Especially the faces of the survivors, melted into weird configurations — they haunt me. I can't sleep at night, because every time I close my eyes, I see their faces."

This was no way to talk to a military doctor, but luckily Dr. Bowman was unusually kind. He told me he had no medicine he could prescribe that could help me, but he invited me to join him the next week on a furlough to an isolated spot in the mountains which he described as "another world."

Since I had had more than enough of this world, I accepted gratefully.

He held on tightly as the doctor pulled the ambulance around the last hazardous curve, and then caught his breath as they stopped at last in a clearing. He unfolded himself from the car and looked around — a grassy plain, towering ice-capped peaks, a forest of pines, a tiny lake. Reflected in the motionless mirror of the lake was a picturesque little inn that looked as if it had been on that spot for more than a hundred years, and it had.

He was on top of the world and beyond its reach. The silence and the peace washed over him. He could stay in this spot forever. Surely the natural beauty and sulfur baths would bring back the buoyant, confident young man who had departed from Tokyo half a year before. The innkeeper and his daughter prepared a dinner with the food that the guests had brought with them: American beef for sukiyaki, fresh vegetables, and American coffee.

Afterwards, Herb strolled outside and breathed deeply. Warmed within by sake wine, he wandered along a solitary lane through a virginal grove of miniature maple and pine trees. He was glad that no other guests were at the inn. This spot was his secret cure. He was free of war at last. He told himself to stop feeling guilty for those holocausts below; the atom bombs were not his doing. He was convinced that he just needed time alone, here close to heaven, to get his balance back.

CHAPTER FORTY-TWO:

Orders from Washington

NIKKO, JAPAN (1946) — THE SUN SHONE THROUGH THE branches the next morning. The air was thin and crisp, scented by pine needles and sulphur from the hot springs. Around noon, he heard an engine laboring up the unpaved road. Abruptly, its horn blared out. He came out to see what the noise was about. A military police sergeant stepped down from the Jeep, walked straight up to Herb, and held out papers.

They were orders to return to Washington immediately, by the fastest possible transport. Herb knew what that meant: uncomfortable bucket seats on an air transport plane for an interminable flight. What could all this rush be about? The war had been over for months; the film was all safely in the footlockers in Tokyo. He figured it was another case of the Army adage: "Hurry up and wait."

When he hesitated, the sergeant said, "Look, lieutenant, I don't want to do this. But if you don't come with me immediately, I have orders to place you under arrest and bring you down." As he bounced back down the mountain and sped the seventy-five miles south to Tokyo, Herb tried to imagine what was going on. The sergeant had nothing to offer. Herb rushed into the Meiji Building to find Daniel McGovern and ask for an explanation. But when he knocked on the office door, he got no reply. Inside he found the two rooms completely empty, except for two of the footlockers left in the middle of the room.

One of them was stuck with a note from McGovern saying simply that he had been ordered back to Washington and that Herb should report to General Anderson with the remaining film. He checked the footlockers and found that those with the thousands of feet of color film he and Mimura had shot seemed intact. The lockers with Dan Dyer's footage were missing. Also missing was Herb's log. The disappearance of the log sickened him.

> I searched and could not find it. In it I had expressed my inner reactions to the places we had visited and the sights we had seen, and those certainly did not accord with the prevailing military view. If it were read by the military, neither it nor I would be very popular.

He collected the footlockers and headed home on a beat-up DC-3. For 60 hours, he crammed his big frame into a bucket seat against the wall and stared down at the flat open space in the middle of the plane. The only stops were for refueling: Guam, Johnson Island, and Hickam Field in Hawaii. At Hickam Field, he asked to get out and have a milkshake – the taste of America. He was not permitted to leave the plane. When they arrived at San Francisco, California, he was transferred with the footlockers to another airplane. They stopped at Wichita to refuel and finally arrived on a Saturday at the relatively new National Airport at Gravelly Point outside Washington.

He unloaded his footlockers and his gear and looked up. He was alone on the empty apron of a field in the military zone. Finally, a Jeep drove up with two military police. He was suddenly self-conscious in his crumpled uniform that was now too tight to button, with his overfull duffel bag, carrying two Japanese swords he had acquired as souvenirs.

The MPs asked where he was going. He answered, "I don't know. I'm supposed to report to the Pentagon." They took him to a phone booth to call in. He called General Anderson's office at the Pentagon. The operator said nobody was in. The war was over in the United States too, and they did not work on Saturdays anymore.

He explained to these new MPs about the footlockers with this film. They knew nothing about it. He asked if he could lock the footlockers up somewhere so he could go up to New York for the weekend and see his mother. The MPs took him to a mostly empty building in Gravelly Point near the airport that had served as a temporary Army Air Corps headquarters. They found a custodian mopping the wide hall.

Herb asked the custodian, "Is there some place I can put this away?"

"I only have the key to the broom closet."

So, he got the key to the broom closet and put the footlockers in there. He found it ridiculous that he could not stop for so much as a milkshake but now the rush seemed to be over along with the war.

The MPs took him back to the airport to catch a military flight to New York City. He had not seen his mother for three years. The first she knew of his return was a call from the airport. By the time Herb arrived at her door in Manhattan, the family had gathered. He was so exhausted he hardly spoke to them and slept most of the time until Monday.

Then he returned to Washington, DC, to report to the Pentagon as ordered.

CHAPTER FORTY-THREE:

Classified

WASHINGTON, D.C. (1946) — GENERAL ORVIL ANDERSON had been the military commander of the Strategic Bombing Survey, but its reports had been made and the survey was breaking up. Herb called him from Gravelly Point and reported that he had arrived. The only answer was this demand: "Where's the footage?"

"Well, to tell the truth, it's locked up in a broom closet here at Gravelly Point."

"Don't leave there!" the general shouted. "Don't leave!"

Herb waited. Less than thirty minutes later, two Jeeps and a small truck screeched to a stop in front of him, sirens blaring. An MP captain jumped out, followed by three sergeants, and demanded the film. Herb stared at them, puzzled by all the ruckus.

"What is all this excitement about?"

"This film has been classified 'Top Secret,'" the captain snapped, "and no one — no one — is to view it without the express permission of General Anderson. We're to take it to the Pentagon, and we've got to be sure that it gets there all right."

Herb said, "Well, there it is." And they took it.

> So, the film which I thought would change the attitudes of the people and the governments of the world about nuclear weapons went from a broom closet at Gravelly Point directly to Top Secret vaults in the Pentagon. I began to suspect from this hasty official classification of film which hadn't even been

developed yet, and from the mysterious disappearance of my log, that some powerful forces intended
to keep the true effects of the atom bomb out of the
public view. And that was the first step in what I
believe is the cover-up of this material that went on
for 30 years.

Some people argue about this, but it was not shown
to the American people at that time. And that is the
time that I felt it should be shown to the American
people, and the world. They should have been made
aware of what they were dealing with.

I can't tell you the exact moment in time that I realized that the things I hoped to do with this film
were totally against what the military wanted to do
with the film. The impression was that the military
thought the best thing that could be done would
be to make more bombs as quickly as possible and
drop them on the Soviet Union and have that out of
the way.

There was also a notion that what occurred was so
horrible that nobody should see it. Well, if nobody
saw it, the only image anybody in the world had of
an atomic bomb was a large mushroom cloud. That's
all that was released; that's all that anybody saw.

It is impossible to feel or understand or calculate or
have any idea from a big cloud or even from degrees
of heat or other numbers what the bomb meant. You

have to do this in human terms for human beings to understand. Not a foot of the film of human beings was released. After the classified training films were made, the footage remained classified as top secret.

Herb rode along with the film to the Pentagon. He was handed a small building map with which to find General Anderson's office where he was greeted by a WAC Major whom he described as "the most beautiful woman he had seen in three years." (It turned out she had been an editor at *Vogue* Magazine before entering the service.) She was to be Herb's secretary while he was working at the Pentagon.

The general rushed out around his desk to shake Herb's hand. Herb was dazzled by his decorations. The right side of the general's uniform was adorned with about every possible ribbon that an officer of his rank with twenty-five years of service could attain, topped with his pilot wings. On the left was the presidential citation ribbon with five stars. He told Herb that the color film would have to be sent to Kodak Laboratories in California for processing, which would take "some weeks, especially now that it was classified." Thousands of black and white photographs had already been printed up in the Pentagon's own labs, however.

The general asked him to sign a piece of paper stating that he would stay in the service as long as needed. Herb was to write a complete report "to the President with special emphasis on Hiroshima and Nagasaki." When Herb held back, the general promised that, any time Herb wanted out, he would arrange it. It was hard for a young lieutenant to argue with a general, especially one with this long pedigree and impressive awards.

Herb debated with himself. On the one hand, he had been in the service for more than five years. On the other hand, he was convinced that the films were crucial. He looked at the man across from him. And he understood that their motives could in no way be the same.

After the general hurried out, Herb asked Major Mitchell, "Is that true? He'll let me out any time I want?" She said, "Don't believe it." He never signed the paper.

But lieutenants take orders, and Herb set to writing his report. He was assigned a space in the second sub-basement of the Pentagon. For eight weeks, he did not see sunlight — coming in early and leaving late. Words did not seem to work, so finally he made a three-volume photographic book, using the black and white images that had been printed from the footage or from still photographs taken at the same times, and adding textual notes. The report was entitled "Japan in Defeat." Herb was given to understand that it was to go only to General Anderson, to the head of the Air Force, and to President Truman. ["Japan in Defeat" consists of three bound volumes, nine by 12 inches, with three themes: Strategic Air Attack; The Atomic Bomb; and The People. He retained his own copy, which remains in the author's possession.]

He was asked to help make training films using the footage. He declined. Four films were eventually made, also all classified, on subjects such as the military use of the bomb and its medical effects. If the footage was too graphic for the public to see (as he was told), then all the public would have to imagine an atomic bombing was that image of a big mushroom-shaped cloud. The human message he wanted to communicate was stifled. He decided to leave the service.

As an American, Herb felt America could make anything bigger and better. He knew what he had seen was "only a little example of how the tiniest of these things that they had concocted would act." He pushed to get out real images of what a bigger and better bomb would mean to human life. But the answer was no, and stayed no.

He was not allowed to even see any of the developed film. It was classified, and would stay classified, and he did not think he could do much about that.

And with that, he returned to New York City and civilian life.

CHAPTER FORTY-FOUR:

Daruma

HIROSHIMA, JAPAN (1987) — ON A SPECIAL SHELF IN A bookcase in my dining room sits a big round red ceramic doll. His two round eyes, black pupils in white circles, stare impassively back at all comers. He does not rest, or grow impatient, or give away any of his secrets.

The one area of Hiroshima that was not smashed or burned to the ground by the bomb lay in a sliver hidden behind Hijiyama Hill. Roofs were blown off, and the houses tended to lean to the east, but many structures remained useable. When I was first in Hiroshima, that area alone preserved how the city was before the bomb leveled it and people rebuilt it into its modern incarnation. Wooden houses huddled along narrow, illogical streets. Small shops, identified by colorful door curtains called *noren,* squeezed randomly in among the old residences.

The air was brisk when Kendra and I came one day with an interpreter. In one hand, I clutched a long page of notes explaining how to find the house we are seeking; with the other hand, I held on to my daughter. Suddenly, Kendra yanked me to a halt with an excited cry. Through the doorway of one tiny store, she had spotted dolls. Sets of *hina ningyo* dolls, the women in tiny silk robes and the men wearing high black headgear. She dragged me inside the airless space filled with odd objects from that netherland between leftover junk and treasured antiques — woven straw sandals, bamboo implements for tea ceremony, and innumerable ceramic sake cups.

I had been surprised before that Japanese culture, which seems so devoted to tradition, nevertheless put little value on mere age of objects. At a flea market, for example, I bought exquisite old wedding kimonos for less than $50. Friends explained that such items were of little use since no one would want the bad luck of wearing a used wedding kimono. Apparently, similar thinking applied to *hina ningyo* dolls that had, for some sad reason, wandered off from their ancestral families. The shopkeeper carefully wrapped the dolls and accessories of the set my daughter had spied in the glass cabinet at her eye level. She carried the bag proudly as we followed the shopkeeper's advice to arrive at last at Kenjiro Nishikubo's house.

Figure 46: Hina ningyo doll set. (Photo by Gorosan/shutterstock.com)

A hunched and wrinkled man with alert eyes, Nishikubo-san welcomed us. His daughter (fairly elderly herself) brought us tea and then hovered protectively over him. They shared with us their remarkable story, which might have been titled "the oldest living *hibakusha* tells all."

Figure 47: Nishikubo-san and daughter, 1987. (Photo by author)

He was born in 1884 and spent twenty years in Los Angeles (from 1902 to 1922) working as a farm manager. In 1912, he returned to Hiroshima to marry and then took his wife back to America. His four brothers and one sister remained in Hiroshima. He had seven children, but the three eldest died before our visit. In addition to the daughter caring for him, he had a son also living in Hiroshima and another in Nagoya, while his oldest son still lived in Los Angeles.

By 1945, then 62, he had retired and was back to Hiroshima, living close to his present house. (He pointed out to us the lot where a store now sold electric appliances.) The house he lived in now already belonged to his family during the war but was rented out. One of his sons was in an internment camp in America and another was serving as an Allied soldier. During the war, he warned that Japan was wrong to fight against America, where, he knew from his years living there, "everything was bigger." He always felt Japan would lose and told his family so. He never made any comment in public, though, fearing the power of the military police.

On August 6th, he was at the Hijiyama-mae trolley stop on the "wrong" side of the Hill, about 1.5 kilometers from the hypocenter. He saw a blinding explosion and, after a few seconds, heard the thunderous *don*. His right ear went deaf. Everything was dark. He was feeling for his air raid hood as things began falling all around him. His left hand was cut, and three fingers became useless; his right elbow and wrist were injured. All his clothes were torn off except his trousers. Fragments of glass became embedded in his chest. He was severely burned, his face was swollen, and the skin had peeled off his arms and was hanging down in shreds. Many of those exposed at Hijiyama-mae died immediately, but those who were alive crossed together over to the sheltered side of the hill.

His daughter, Tomie Okuda, nineteen years old at the time, was home with her mother. Her body was lifted into the air by the shock wave and then thrown down. The earth moved as if in an earthquake. Though her eyes were open, she saw nothing but darkness. Her mother was standing in the corridor and hid from the blast. She was not hurt and did not get any of the symptoms about which they were later warned in booklets distributed after the bomb. Okuda-san had lost a lot of blood, though, and needed bandages and disinfectant. They had no medicines, and all nearby hospitals had been destroyed.

Her youngest brother, seventeen years old, had been mobilized as a student worker tearing down buildings. (Many students in the late stages of the war were made to work in demolition to create firebreaks to contain possible fire-bombings. Old men and women were also often ordered to help.) He came home with his face badly burned accompanied by a friend whose head had been torn open.

Okuda-san and her brother fled with their father to the rural town of Fuchu where their paternal grandparents lived. Their mother stayed at home. So many people were coming along the road, bare-foot and without clothes, injured and burned. All of them were begging for water, water. Her mother gave them shoes and water until it grew dark, and then she too fled to Fuchu. She later told Okuda-san that she regretted what she had done because she heard that those who drank water died.

For months after the bomb, the whole family felt weak, lost their hair, and suffered from diarrhea and loss of appetite, even his wife who had been uninjured. Nishikubo-san's burns healed, but Okuda-san's wounds remained raw and pus seeped out of them off and on for a year. While recuperating, the family stayed in the rural area, but the men came into town from time to time to repair the house. They finally returned to it after about three months. They drank an infusion of Chinese medicinal herbs instead of tea to combat germs and infection. They still drink it every day. They used grated cucumber on their skin injuries having no oil or ointment.

Nishikubo-san adopted his own regimens to which collectively he credits his amazingly long life. For example, he took no tobacco or sake, and only indulged in *mikan* oranges and plum wine. He ate lots of vegetables and miso with ginger and garlic. As a result of this diet, according to him, he was spared sickness, though he admitted he did have high blood pressure.

The family read articles saying that not even grass would grow in Hiroshima for seventy years, which caused them great fear. It was thought that everyone would die. The rumors and uncertainty about the likely fate of those who lived in Hiroshima after the war and of their future children haunted all the *hibakusha*. Many people, Okuda-san reported, feared that not only *hibakusha* but their children and even grandchildren might yet suffer. The taint was thought to pass down in the blood. When Okuda-san's daughter wanted to marry a man from another prefect, the man's parents refused to attend the *o-miae* (a formal meeting between families to consider and sanction a relationship between two young people). She eventually married a man from Hiroshima who was not put off by such prejudice.

Nishikubo-san announced that he never thought America was "bad," but he did feel that the atom bomb was awful and powerful. He asked himself why it is that *hibakusha* can forgive when so many Americans are still bitter about Pearl Harbor. He believed that Japanese people forgive more easily because they do not keep hatred in their hearts.

He offered this plea for me to take to the wider world:

> Nuclear war would destroy the earth and eliminate the human race. There must be no more nuclear war, and we must never make such bombs to kill people again. Hiroshima's bomb was very small, yet so many died in an instant from its terrible power.

> So please never let people forget Hiroshima and Nagasaki. If people forget the fearfulness of the deaths, the souls of *hibakusha* cannot reach heaven but will wander forever in hell. I will pray no other people will ever suffer nuclear war.

As we finished listening to the story, Nishikubo-san signaled his daughter to get something. She brought out a ceramic doll about two feet high and round except for a flat base. She explained to us the myth of Daruma (the Japanese name for the Indian saint Dharma).

It is said that Daruma struggled for years to reach enlightenment. He finally sat down to meditate and vowed that he would not get up again until he had achieved enlightenment. He sat still so long that his arms and legs fell off, but eventually his determination was rewarded. That is why Daruma dolls are always round with no arms and legs. Thanks to the weighted bases, when you push them over, they right themselves. The Japanese say that Daruma is seven times falling down, but eight times getting up. He is a symbol of persistence and patience. Daruma dolls are always red with big empty white eyes. By custom, the black center is painted into one eye while making a wish or a vow. When the goal is fulfilled, the other eye is also painted in.

Usually the dolls are then burnt. In November, we had attended an *aki-matsuri*, a fall festival in the neighborhood park. Wood had been stacked into a huge pile that was lit at dark into a bonfire. Neighbors fed the fire with Darumas that had fulfilled their purposes. When the fire died into smoldering coals, sweet yams wrapped in foil were buried to bake. Sweet yams were a big favorite here. Kendra's teacher took her class on a field trip to a farm to dig them. In one corner of the park, the white altar of a corner shrine had been decorated with attractive displays of unblemished vegetables, perfectly shaped *mochi* (pounded rice balls), and small bright oranges. Late in the evening, a priest arrived in white Shinto robes and a black lacquered peaked hat. People gathered round him, and young children were pushed to the center of the circle in front of him. He waved a branch over them, apparently in blessing. Daruma was an integral part of the celebration of harvest and plenty.

This doll had both eyes painted in but had not been burned. Nishikubo-san explained that he had wished on this Daruma that he might live to be 100 years old. He painted in the second eye when he achieved that milestone. He was 104 years old when we met. He gave his Daruma doll to my daughter to bring back to America. He hoped that the Daruma would make us patient and persistent in working for remembrance of the *hibakusha* and for the end of nuclear weapons.

Figure 48: The Daruma presented to Kendra by Nishikubo-san. (Photo by J.C. Penney Portrait Studio, March 2020)

The shelf on which the doll now sits is a sort of shrine for me. Daruma has waited there for many years now, along with the stone from my dad's memorial service, the bubbled roof tile which Kikkawa-san gave me, and a picture of Numata-sensei. Daruma speaks of the courage and resilience of survivors and the duty their sufferings press on us to prevent another nuclear war. Together they remind me of my duty to be a faithful messenger.

I would not have believed then that I would wrestle for so many years to learn how to tell this story. I hope Daruma forgives my slowness and approves of my persistence.

CHAPTER FORTY-FIVE:

Never again

HIROSHIMA, JAPAN (1987) — ONE OF THE MEMORABLE activists I met in Hiroshima was a woman in her twenties, Yoko Kitaura. From her home base in Osaka, she organized volunteer groups that traveled to the United States offering peace messages from *hibakusha,* leavened with various bits of Japanese culture meant to build human bonds to the American public. The name of her organization, the Never-Again Campaign, chilled me, with its echoes of the vows of Jewish Holocaust survivors.

* * *

WHEN I WAS A GIRL, NANNY TOLD ME THE STORY OF A young couple in London, relatives of her husband, to whom she sent socks during the hard days after the war. The socks could be sold to buy eggs for their baby son. The couple had been in love and planned to leave Poland, but before they could find a way out, the young woman was seized with her family and taken to a concentration camp. The young man joined the resistance and at last helped her escape, although her mother and sister were murdered before they could be rescued. The couple managed to flee to England. Their son was my prom date in 1969.

I was shocked to learn at age twelve that I was not Jewish like Nanny and my father, having absorbed so many Yiddish expressions and heard so many family stories of the Holocaust. At the time, we lived in Los Angeles, in one of the few high-rise buildings then on Wilshire Boulevard. Across the street was Sinai Temple.

My father had recently lost his position as a television producer at Screen Gems, and things were tense at home. Bitter quarrels raged half-heard behind closed doors; tears erupted in the middle of the day; doors were slammed; fingers were pointed. My mother hated California; my father blamed her for not playing role of a Hollywood wife. My mother drank too much; my father stayed out longer and longer. I found a refuge after school at the temple where I hid and began reading the Pentateuch I found in the pew racks. The custodian got to know me after a while and would let me stay until he finally locked up the building. Then I had to go home.

What I read comforted me and gave me this talisman for my life:

See, I have set before thee this day life and good, and death and evil; in that I command thee this day to love the Lord thy God, to walk in His ways, and to keep His commandments and His statutes and His ordinances; then thou shalt live and multiply . . . . I call heaven and earth to record this day against you that I have set before thee life and death, the blessing and the curse; *therefore choose life,* that thou mayest live, thou and thy seed; to love the Lord thy God, to hearken to His voice, and to cleave unto Him; for that is thy life and the length of thy days . . . .

Deut. 30: 15-20.

This edition of the Pentateuch included commentary on the verses delving into deeper meanings of each word. The commentary on this verse quoted Maimonides: "Free will is granted to every man. If he desires to incline towards the good way, and be righteous, he has the power to do so." I took this to mean that I could see what a mess my parents were making of life and still be free to do something good with my life. What that might be, I had no clue. The guideline I embraced was: In everything, "choose life."

I wanted to become bat mitzvah at this synagogue, but the rabbi broke the news to me that I was not Jewish. Even though my grandparents had fled Russia in the face of Jewish conscription and oppression by the Czar. Even though relatives died in both Stalin's and Hitler's camps. Even though the one time I remembered my father striking me as a girl was when I said "*Oy gevalt*," and he told me it made me sound like "dirty ignorant Jew." Even though virtually all the relatives I knew of were Jewish. Under Jewish law, only a child born of a Jewish mother is born Jewish. My mother was not Jewish. Neither of my parents considered the costly process of conversion an option for me. My father mocked the very idea of spending money on such "absurd superstitions." Did I really believe that God had hopped down to a mountain and given Moses the rules on a rock?

I had no idea what I believed about God and mountains. But I knew Hitler would not have cared which parent was Jewish – I would have died as a Jew like all the others. I could not understand how I could be Jewish enough for Hitler and not Jewish enough for the rabbi. I did not know then that my father's bar mitzvah was so closely followed by his father's death. It did not occur to me to wonder in those days what lessons my father might have drawn from the Holocaust as a son of Jewish immigrants to America. His own notes used the word Holocaust several times to describe what he found in Hiroshima and Nagasaki. I knew the words "Never Again" meant something resonant and important to him, but I never asked him what.

*   *   *

BUDDHIST MONKS BEAT PRAYER DRUMS BY THE Cenotaph at Peace Park. The beat feels too slow to me. I sit cross-legged on the ground in my gray wool coat pulled tight around me against the chilly breeze. I close my eyes and try to slow my heart and breathing down. Threads of incense sweeten the air. Whenever a nuclear test took place anywhere in the world, a small group of Buddhist monks convened here for meditation. As soon as I learned of one of these vigils, I joined them. I am not good at meditation, or patience, and I hoped they would pull me along. We all sit still and send up our hopes for peace.

Figure 44: Author (second from left) participating in a protest against atomic-bomb tests in 1988. Dozens of tests were conducted that year alone by the United States and the Soviet Union. (Photo provided by The Chugoku Shimbum and used by permission)

"Never again" never seems to prevail, despite all our prayers, and the same mistakes are made over and over.

CHAPTER FORTY-SIX:

Choose peace

HIROSHIMA, JAPAN (1987) — WHEN THE STUDENT IS ready, the teacher appears, they say. Teachers appeared to me on every hand in Hiroshima. I started the journey to Japan thinking, perhaps somewhat resentfully, of what I owed my father, of filial obligations. I slowly moved to thinking of what I might owe my daughter, of parental obligations, of the duty to preserve and pass on the lessons of this history to another generation. Munakata-sensei convinced me that a new kind of education is crucial. Peace may take root only when children are taught the costs of war and the values of peace with the same kind of organized focus that children were taught to believe in the honor of war and the values of power.

To understand the importance of this kind of education, I went to visit a school that had tried to resist militarism during the war. From outside metal gates, I looked in at a concrete building under the direct sun of an early afternoon. Beside the entrance is mounted the bronzed photograph of this spot in the bomb's aftermath, another of the shadowy mirrors that reflect the past at passersby.

Jogaku-in was a Christian mission school that had experimented with putting peace in the curriculum even at the height of imperialist power. As a result, the school became the target of growing suspicion as the military gained increased power from 1937 through the end of the war. Jogaku-in's foreign teachers were regularly followed by military police. School administrators were called in repeatedly by the military authorities to answer charges as seemingly minor as the insufficiently prominent placement of the Emperor's portrait and as serious as being a school for spies. The use of Christian hymns and prayers was declared unpatriotic. By 1939, the remaining young missionary teachers were repatriated back to America, some of them quite unwillingly. The students were mobilized for war work in munitions factories and demolition.

Twelve of the teachers and 320 students died when Enola Gay dropped its payload over Hiroshima. My father filmed the ruins of the school. By that time, clusters of survivors, some of them orphaned by the bomb, had crept back to their school. Classes were held in the shell of the building on days when rain was not pouring through the broken walls and windows. Students scavenged and fought wild dogs for food.

A memorial to the dead was erected in the yard of the rebuilt school. A visit to the school made clear that, even more than forty years after the bomb, the dead were still very much in the hearts and minds of the present faculty and administration. And the survivors continued to suffer.

I was invited to speak with one of the much-loved teachers from the war days, Tasu Shibama-sensei. She told me that, on the morning of the bombing, she was eating her usual breakfast alone in her kitchen. She was supposed to leave shortly for the school. The day was terribly hot, so her clothes lay ready nearby, but she ate barefoot, wearing only her underwear.

That year there had been no summer vacation. About half of the 700 high school girls were sent to Kaitai-chi, where cars are now manufactured but where bullets were then made. The girls were to pack the ammunition as part of their contribution to the war effort. Even younger students of twelve or thirteen were sent to work in the center of town, where Peace Park now stands. Their job was to demolish tightly packed houses to prevent the spread of fire.

Some girls, however, were physically weak or ill and could not do the assigned jobs. They were required to get a doctor's excuse and to spend a half day at the school in order to be counted as excused absences. About one hundred girls came to the school each day. Shibama-sensei's job was to watch over these girls.

The school was more than just a job to her, however. When she was sixteen, her mother had died. Miss Rachel Gates, then a missionary teacher at Jogaku-in, comforted her, saying "I will try to be your American mother." Shibama-sensei became a Christian at age seventeen. But in April 1939, Miss Gates was forced to leave on the last repatriation boat. Later, Shibama-sensei learned that Miss Gates died in California only a month after the United States declared war on Japan.

Shibama-sensei's home was less than two miles from the school, near the Hiroshima train station. She was alone because her sister had taken their elderly father to Gion. He was past eighty, and they agreed it was better for old people to be in the quiet countryside during the dangers of wartime. She would have liked to go with them, but the neighbors complained that, if she went, the house would be empty. Her neighbors scolded her. "If a bomb falls at night on your house, you should be here to put the fire out with buckets and water. If you wait even five minutes, your house will burn up. And if your house burns, ours will too. So, you may work during the day, but at night, when the danger of bombing is greatest, you stay right here!" So, she did. And so, there she was on the morning of August 6th.

Suddenly, the house collapsed. At the same instant, she saw a bright flash. Strangely, she did not hear a sound. Some survivors who experienced this silence concluded the sound was too big for human ears to hold. She was in complete darkness. She found she could not move to get out of the house under which she was now buried. Then, she felt someone begin to move close by. How peculiar, she thought, when no one else was in the house! It turned out that her neighbor, Miyahara-san, had been blown from his garden into her ruined house. Miyahara-san was strong and determined. He dug them both out from under the debris. When he rushed to his house, he found his wife and two daughters buried beneath it. When the flames rushed over the area, his house caught fire. He could not save them. All three burned to death.

Shibama-sensei was shocked when she looked around to discover that nothing remained of the city around her. Even two- and three-story buildings were smashed. She learned later that many girls at the school were crushed under the school building. They had nobody like Miyahara-san to help them, and they were only young girls. So, they had to die. Her only explanation for her own survival is: "I was just a very lucky, lucky one that I can escape."

Barefoot and half naked as she was, she began to walk like a mechanical doll. She felt nothing. The glass from her kitchen window had pierced her right side, but she was not aware of any pain. She walked to the train station where she found many people gathered. The shock was so great that nobody spoke. Like ghosts, they had all lost their words. She thought she would take the train to her family in Gion, but of course, despite the hundreds of people crowded around, no trains were running.

She did not know what to do. Finally, she started walking again, heading to the countryside on foot. She saw hundreds and hundreds of people lying dead on both sides of the road. But still she did not feel afraid, only numb. After an hour, she became terribly hot and thirsty. Outside the city, she found some farmhouses still standing. She joined others in looking for the wells behind the houses. Four or five times on the way, she says, she stopped at such farmhouses to drink, and wash, and refresh herself. At about 5 p.m., she finally arrived in Gion.

She rested in Gion for two weeks. A doctor told her that it helped to wash out the "bad thing" that she had been breathing. She drank and washed her mouth over and over. She was easily exhausted. Out in the country, though, she was able to get fruits and vegetables and eggs to eat. She believes that this regime saved her from radiation effects and prevented leukemia.

After two weeks, she went back to her house. She learned that only six of the thirty-six members of her neighborhood ration group (*tonari-gumi*) survived. After the repressive treatment the school had received from the Japanese military powers, she was surprised to find that the occupation forces were friendly and kind. Japanese officials and soldiers had been strict and severe, but she found the American soldiers generous. They gave her more food than the Japanese government had. Ordinary Japanese people had gone hungry throughout the war. She could speak a little English and had some understanding of American manners from spending time around American missionary teachers. The soldiers appreciated this.

For fifteen years after the war, Shibama-sensei found herself picking glass out of her skin. While washing her face, she would feel something hard in an earlobe or cheek and out would erupt a needle-like sliver of glass. In the 1960s, Shibama-sensei traveled for seventy-five days with Barbara Reynolds, the founder of the World Friendship Center in Hiroshima. She visited eleven different countries, including the United States, Canada, England, and other European nations. This is the message she carried then and that she still wants to send to the world:

I could escape from a primitive atomic bomb. New-type nuclear weapons, I am sure I could not survive. No one could survive. It was terrible for us. It was terrible enough. But with the present developments of the hydrogen bomb, it is getting worse and worse.

These weapons will not bring peace. They will destroy everything.

We must build friendships and loving hearts. We must build peace instead of bombs.

As I left the school, the sunlight slanted, and shadows stretched toward me. The school had become again a place for children to learn and build loving hearts.

CHAPTER FORTY-SEVEN:

Lessons to take home

HIROSHIMA, JAPAN (1987) — I RODE A TROLLEY THAT rattled to our area, Funairi-cho, and climbed down in time to pick up Kendra from her school. We stopped for our favorite dinner, *okanomiyaki*, called Japanese pizza. To me, the dish more resembles a hearty variant of crepes. Cabbage and veggies are cooked on a grill in front of you (eggs and bacon too, for non-vegetarians), batter is poured over it all, the whole is flipped, and then served with a special sauce squirted from a plastic bottle. Every city has its own style, but I am sure Hiroshima's is the best.

Spring had come. Cherry blossom season. Haiku about the evanescence of the pink snow and the brevity and preciousness of life in the moment came to mind. I looked forward to peacefully viewing cherry blossoms while sipping traditional sake and contemplating philosophy. Blossom-viewing parties turned out instead to involve dozens of families picnicking on cheap plastic tarps under a few trees in a small park as radios played. I missed the lush pink and white clouds of blossoms surrounding the Tidal Basin back home in Washington.

One warm evening, Kendra sat on my lap, taking advantage of the longer daylight, and asking for just *one* more story before bed. I picked up one of the children's books from home and began to read to her again. Suddenly, she gasped and pointed at one of the pictures in the book. "Mommy! Those children are wearing shoes! In the house!"

"You don't remember wearing shoes in the house?" But she insisted, "I would never wear shoes in the house!"

Too far east too long, I thought, remembering the title of one of the funnier books I read about adjusting to life as a foreigner in Japan. After the incident with the picture book, though, I started to wonder how funny it was. By this time, Kendra could chatter away in Japanese. It turned heads. I was told she spoke with a Hiroshima *ben*, apparently an accent as distinctive to Japanese listeners as a Texas twang or Southern drawl is to Americans, though I could not hear the difference.

Gradually, I realized that she considered herself Japanese. She thought that she was just like her friends at kindergarten or would be if I would just send proper homemade *o-nigiri* for lunch. She had little memory of America. Japan is not a country that embraces diversity, however, and no one else would mistake her for Japanese. Time to go home, I decided.

Kendra did not want to leave Japan. In Hiroshima, everybody knew her, and everybody liked her. She could tell because everywhere she went grown-ups would pat her, talk to her, and give her candy or pretty little handkerchiefs. I realized I had to teach her all over again not to talk to or accept gifts from strangers and not to go off with anyone she did not know. But everyone in America had become a stranger to her by then.

She asked me, "Mommy, is everybody in America bad?"

The answer is a resounding no. But it was not an easy thing to explain to a little girl in tears.

* * *

TOWARD THE END OF OUR TIME IN HIROSHIMA, WE MET a couple from Europe on a four-month tour of Japan with a multi-media exhibition entitled "Shadows from Hiroshima." A thirty-year old Swiss journalist, Gauthier W. Loffler, was accompanied by Ilka Dohrn, a younger West German artist. Their project began in 1983 when Gauthier came to Hiroshima as a freelancer and began asking *hibakusha*, "What did you do with your atomic bomb experience?" Ilka captured their answers in eighteen oil and charcoal pictures. The couple focused on the feelings of shame and inferiority that many *hibakusha* expressed and the discrimination they encountered.

The graphic images meant to capture these themes, which included slides and drawings of deformed children and damaged parents, one-eyed babies, and dreadful injuries, were controversial in Hiroshima. Some scientific researchers, such as Dr. Naomasa Okamoto, formerly of the Hiroshima University Institute for Nuclear Medicine and Biology, denied that any genetic effects had been identified in the children or grandchildren of *hibakusha*. The artist may have aimed only to show graphically what mental images were used against *hibakusha*. Some *hibakusha* protested, however, that public displays of such images only add to the discrimination from which their children still suffer, and indeed some felt that even scientific research into medical aftereffects caused more harm than good to those most affected. Gauthier and Ilka were stunned since such issues had never arisen in their prior presentations of the exhibition in fifty other cities, including Paris, Leningrad, Warsaw, and elsewhere through Japan. But then no place else is Hiroshima.

Ilka and Gauthier took an interest in the story of my father's films, and the U.S. government's long suppression of the disturbing images in them. Ilka created a charcoal sketch of my father's face. She worked from a picture I had of him when his cancer was fairly advanced. The drawing captured the hollowness and tensely stretched skin that I have learned to associate with cancer. Somehow, the drawing, unlike the source photograph, managed to depict the haunted look that was often in his eyes. I saw his soul in those eyes.

* * *

SHORTLY BEFORE WE LEFT JAPAN, WE MADE A PILGRIM-age to a gallery about twenty-five miles from Tokyo in Saitama Prefecture. I had seen an exhibition in Hiroshima that made me beg for an appointment to visit the artists and see more of their work. I was stunned by the wall-size paintings (1.8 by 7.2 meters), at once stylized and brutal. When I first came upon them, they seemed powerful abstract images of red and black filled with dark masses and burning intensity. Then, body parts and faces began to swim forward. Within the red, blood trickled and flames roared. Tiny squiggles turned into perfectly detailed line-drawings of dead babies. From the unformed darkness peered completely formed faces of individuals in scenes of agony. The pain is matched by the compelling beauty. One critic, John W. Dower, has described the Marukis' panels as "hell scenes" reminiscent of "medieval Buddhist scroll paints of damnation, where the torments of hell are as gruesomely varied as Dante or Bosch ever imagined them to be." Mingled in the nightmare are bursts of humanity and hope, rescuers with stretchers, embraces, even a rainbow. The panels were born from the lifetime collaboration of this husband and wife who have used their artistic ability over more than three decades to release the visions burned into them in Hiroshima.

Iri Maruki was eighty-seven when I visited. He was born in 1901 outside Hiroshima. He was a Tolstoy-esque figure, swathed in layers of sweaters over what looked like long woolen underwear and a cotton robe. He exuded quiet concentration, moving slowly and deliberately over the stone paths of his country retreat. Toshi Maruki was younger, more energetic, and more rooted in this world. She was born in 1912 in chilly Hokkaido, the child of a Buddhist priest. They were not living in Hiroshima when the bomb exploded, but already working as artists in Tokyo. Nevertheless, as soon as they learned of the disaster, they rushed back to find Mr. Maruki's parents and other relatives who remained near the city. Most were dead or dying. His mother survived, but his father died slowly over six months. Mr. Dower reported what the Marukis told him they did in Hiroshima: "We carried the injured, cremated the dead, searched for food, made roofs of scorched tin sheets, wandered about just like those who had experienced the bomb, in the midst of flies and maggots, and the stench of death." The paintings embody that visceral intense experience. When the Marukis began painting and displaying them, the Occupation press code was still in effect and the titles were changed several times, partly to avoid scrutiny.

Mrs. Maruki pulled Kendra to her and guided her hands to roll brown rice into *nori* wrappers to make *o-nigiri* for us to share. She served us a tea which tasted slightly of barley and grasses. She explained that she picked and dried wild herbs herself to make it. She believed that these natural plants were efficacious in protecting her and her husband for so many years from the long-term effects of their exposure to radiation. With a bit of cloth and a wide ribbon, Ms. Maruki improvised a kimono for Kendra's Cabbage Patch doll and played with her while I was looking through the gallery.

Their gallery was filled with the huge panels full of black lines and red and gray washes, capturing vividly scenes of devastation. They included panels representing the Korean victims. In addition to the Hiroshima Panels, they painted panels on the rape of Nanking and on Auschwitz. They believed it was important to express the universality of suffering that war brings and to avoid any implication that the Japanese were blameless victims. Instead, they focused on the hope that such destruction should not befall people anywhere in the future.

They allowed me to visit their workshop and watch their technique in action. An enormous white sheet of paper lay on the floor in a room that seemed ageless and rustic, filled with smells of oil paints and ink and cluttered with brushes and piles of paper. Before my eyes, Mr. Maruki's body language changed from slow deliberation to barely controlled energy. Mr. Maruki used large brushes with traditional black *suiboku* inks and fluidly danced over the paper, leaving confident lines that came to life before me. His whole body moved in rhythms that somehow flowed into not only the black lines but into the white spaces. The still forms on paper seemed to contain within them movement and life. Later, Mrs. Maruki would go over the same area with colors using quite different styles. Each painting by the two artists grew organically as a merged whole. Layer after painful layer peeled back to find truth; then layer after layer laid down to bring that truth to visual life. (You can visit their gallery virtually and see many of the panels at http://www.aya.or.jp/~marukimsn/english/indexE.htm.)

The *pikadon*, the cries of sufferers, and the screams of the dying seemed to surround them on every side every day. These two were among the most gentle, earthy, and humane people I have ever met. Yet, in their work, anger fights with deep compassion — the human is monstrous but fragile; the horrific has beauty as well as the reverse. They made me think of *bodhisattvas*, enlightened souls who need not have remained in a world of suffering but who chose compassion for other beings over personal nirvana. I took their lessons home with me.

CHAPTER FORTY-EIGHT:

Coming home

NEW YORK CITY (1947) — HERB IS BACK HOME IN THE city he has known all his life. Something has gone wrong with his city, however.

Manhattan is a mix of low brownstones and distinctive high-rises. New glass office buildings have popped up next to old brick apartments. The streets are full of cars and taxis, speeding and honking. The sidewalks and crosswalks are crowded with rushing people. Kids are playing; men are lounging; music comes from the bars.

Everything seems normal as Herb walks down the streets of his hometown. Suddenly, buildings explode. Men evaporate. Shadows remain.

He sees each type of structure destroyed in a specific way. Town houses on the east side of New York look like a four-story house he saw in Hiroshima. All that had been left of it was a wrenched metal frame, as if God has just taken the house and twisted it. That is what the red brick town houses turn into now.

The glass buildings shatter into thousands of pieces of flying glass hitting people's bodies at tremendous pressure and speed. In Hiroshima and Nagasaki, people went through dozens of operations trying to get glass pieces out of their flesh. These crowds are sliced to bits; the survivors covered with shards.

The faces of the passersby are weird rubber masks. Herb sees on them the enormous keloid formations that had distorted the faces of people he photographed in Japan. Their skin melts and freezes permanently into hideous contortions.

He is terrified. He cannot get out of his mind the fear that the same thing could happen here. He cannot stop seeing it happening here.

A year passes before the visions fade.

CHAPTER FORTY-NINE:

Pioneering a place in early television

NEW YORK CITY (1947-1960) — AS HE BEGAN TO ADJUST
to civilian life, Herb went looking for a job. He found it at Grand
Central Station, his original point of departure from New York, but
in 1947, housing production studios for what would become the
CBS television network. He got hired based on his experiences in
occupied Japan to make documentaries, but television was new then
and lines of responsibility were not yet clearly drawn.

His first production was called "Television Today." The film
was made to explain to sponsors what television was, since no one
had quite figured out yet what to do with it. He cast himself in the
role of the television director, appearing in a real control room —
one that did not have live equipment yet.

> I was not a director; I played the part of a director.
> I went into television taking the lowest level job I
> could get — purposely, because I wanted to learn
> about it.

> But this film started to be shown, and everybody
> wanted that director. So, one day, CBS called me and
> said, "You're a director now." That's how I became
> a director.

> They put me on a musical show as the first show I
> directed, called "The 54th Street Revue." [Among the

stars was dancer Bob Fosse.] I told them, "I can't dance. I don't know how to do this."

They said, "Well, if you can't do this, you can't be a director."

So, I just learned how to do things.

He worked with the pioneers of early television, was one of the first members of the Directors Guild, and found it all exciting. One of his programs, "The Ken Murray Show," opened up Saturday night for television. Eighty-five episodes aired from 1950 to 1953. Before that, there was no television programming on the weekend. Murray, who had been a popular vaudeville and radio entertainer, hosted the variety show bringing in lots of acts from Buster Keaton to Marilyn Monroe. Many Hollywood stars made television debuts doing ten- or twelve-minute dramatic skits on that show.

All shows were produced in New York then and sent out to other cities on kinescope, which meant poor-quality images. CBS only later became a true network with different cities connecting to a feed. Herb sat in a control room watching as Chicago, and later Washington, came online.

[Once when I was about twelve years old, I watched one of the surviving kinescopes at Ken Murray's house. In the program, Ken invited my father on screen and announced his marriage to my mother, who was a production assistant on the show. My father looked to me as if he had stepped out of the skin I knew and into a sort of costume. He was recognizably himself, but some other self — standing straighter, looking smoother and surer and beaming with the expression of a well-fed cat who has caught a catnip toy. My mother looked wide-eyed, like a pin-up girl surprised by the camera in mid-step, her beauty not surprising since she had previously been a model. How peculiar to see these people who resembled but were not, at least not yet, my parents, flickering before me in black and white.]

By 1954, Herb was married with two children. He had moved to NBC, where he produced "Wide Wide World," with Dave Garroway as host. It was the first show to take viewers live on location all around the country. The concept came from my father, who always loved the idea of live shots. He never got over the amazing thrill of: "This is happening somewhere else in the world, but now YOU are there!" As senior producer of the show, he gave Americans an entirely new and concrete sense of the breadth and diversity of their country. Each show had segments from multiple spots. A presentation of the famous underwater dancers of Weeki Wachee Springs in west Florida might be followed by the sight of hundreds of thousands of mallard ducks startled into flight above Claypool Reservoir in northeast Arkansas. You might be looking down from the top spire of the Golden Gate Bridge or floating along looking up at the Grand Canyon, or suddenly watching molten steel poured in Cleveland or a performance of a Broadway show in your own living room. Gene Kelly made his television debut on the show. Tennessee Williams came on to talk about his plays. Viewers got to visit Mickey Mantle at his training camp. Justice William O. Douglas escorted viewers on the first televised tour of the Supreme Court chambers and courtroom. Unprecedented access was granted to film a missile launch at the White Sands Proving Grounds narrated by Dr. Werner von Braun.

[When much network television has become the same situation comedy or police procedural repeated under different names, cable television offers endless channels to watch infomercials and unreality shows, and the Internet makes the whole world accessible if not understandable, it is hard to imagine how novel people once found it simply to discover places and meet people they would never otherwise have seen. Wide Wide World, which won multiple awards and Emmy nominations, was the show of which my father was proudest. The only thing he did not love about it, as far as I know, is the nickname he was saddled with as a result, given his life-long struggle with his weight, the "Wide Wide Producer."]

On March 4, 1956, Herb received a Freedom Foundation Gold Medal "for outstanding achievement in bringing about a better understanding of the American way of life" in honor of his production of the "Birth of an American," which showed an actual birth on television for the first time. Altogether, his shows received six Emmy nominations, two Edison Foundation awards, a Peabody citation and the Sylvania Award. By the fall of 1958, Herb had been promoted to executive producer and the head of specials at NBC. Professionally, this period was the pinnacle of his life. The war was long over; the money was more than he dreamed of; everything was just as it should be in this best of all possible worlds.

CHAPTER FIFTY:

Making a list to survive the bomb

NEW YORK CITY (1952-1973) — WHEN I WAS A LITTLE girl, my father went to work every day in a big office with huge glass windows at Rockefeller Center. He wore a suit and a white shirt and a tie and polished shoes and carried a briefcase. The briefcase was never to be touched; an aura of adult importance surrounded it.

My father let me visit him at work a few times. Once when I was quite young, I visited him at a studio set. My father was producing "The Eddie Fisher Show" then. Mr. Fisher was kind and patient, sat me on his lap, fed me a cup of soup, and sang to me. Later, my father arranged for me to join the "Peanut Gallery" of forty kids on one episode of "The Howdy Doody Show." I found these experiences obscurely disappointing, though, as if the magic leaked out of TV-land once I saw behind the curtain.

I grew up in the acknowledged capital of the world, at least as New Yorkers all modestly viewed it. The United Nations finished building its home in lower Manhattan the year I was born. Our family lived in an apartment complex called Sutton Terrace on the East Side in Manhattan. A uniformed doorman called me Rusty (after my reddish hair). Three tall apartment buildings surrounded a courtyard, which we called "The Garden," with a wall closing off the fourth side.

Near that wall was a covered area and pool with a small fountain. In the summer, I played handball against the wall and listened to the fountain splash. Girls would jump rope, play clapping games, or chalk hopscotch boards on the cement. We had lots of chants about Miss Mary Mack, Mack, Mack; and, A - my name is Alice and my husband's name is Alan; and Miss Lucy had a baby. I remember: "Dodgers, Dodgers, boo boo boo! Kick 'em in the trash can, two by two!" and "Whistle while you work. Hitler was a jerk. Mussolini bit his penie, then it wouldn't work!" None of us had any clue what Dodgers were, who Hitler or Mussolini might be, or what a "penie" was or how it worked. Somehow, the street culture passed down among kids preserved resentment against a disloyal team and contempt for former enemies, independent of any understanding of the adult context.

I rode my tricycle, and later roller-skated, around the paths between the grassy areas. We kids were supposed to stay on the paths, but in the corners and under the bushes were secret hiding places that only the kids knew about. Inside them, I could listen to a transistor radio or read a book by myself. Our apartment was on the seventh floor. From its tiny balcony, you could look down and see the garden and its paths, but not the hidden places.

When it snowed, the garden paths were lined with snow cliffs that towered over our heads. We dug tunnels into them and built igloos. Early on snowy mornings, my brother and I would hurry down to the garden with a big kitchen bowl and a serving spoon. We would scrape off the top layer of snow, already speckled with Manhattan soot. Then we would shovel in the clean middle snow, being careful not to dig down as far as the dirt. Our mother would add a couple of spoonfuls of sugar, a dab of vanilla extract, and some milk. We would stir it all quickly and eat "snow ice cream."

My father was mostly absent from my world. He was at work. He was traveling. In the 1950s, fathers were expected to be away in the world while mothers were to keep the home. Sometimes, he was home, but we were not to bother him. He sat in a bathrobe and watched TV. Sometimes more than one TV at a time. You have to watch the competition, he said.

In my elementary school years, everybody knew New York City was a target. We were the biggest city in the world, the richest city in the world, and the most famous city in the world, so of course the Russians wanted to blow us up. The Communists hated us, and they had the bomb. We graduated from Duck, Duck, Goose, to Duck and Cover. Our classrooms all had signs posted about nuclear war – the kind that explained with pictures the drill for nuclear war, as if it were another sort of fire drill. Children were to scramble under their desks and curl up with their heads tucked in. We practiced this. A parody sign circulated later that made more sense to me, advising, in the event of nuclear war, to get under your desk, curl up in a ball, and "kiss your ass goodbye." Those years were full of inexplicable activities orchestrated by adults with straight faces.

I loved to read. My parents constantly complained that I read so intently that I paid no attention to things around me. I favored books with feisty, self-sufficient girl heroines, like Nancy Drew, or Francie in *A Tree Grows in Brooklyn*, or Margaret in *A Wrinkle in Time*. Jo was my favorite sister in *Little Women*, even though I cried every time I read the chapter where gentle Beth dies. I sat at the white vanity table in my bedroom with its curved bench and spread out booklets about surviving nuclear war. I made a list of the places near our building where I had seen the distinctive yellow and black signs that meant fallout shelter. I never went inside to see where in the buildings the actual shelters were, but I imagined they must be in the basements with the laundry rooms and storage spaces. Would they have enough food for us? And water? What about toilets and what about blankets and medicine? I read the brochures carefully and compiled lists of what would be needed. I tried to calculate how much of each item we might need for four people to last at least two weeks. Somehow, I had the idea that two weeks was the critical amount of time we would need to hide to survive the worst of the deadly radiation.

Finally, I took my lists to my father and asked him to buy the things on them to be ready, just in case. "Are you out of your mind?" he responded. "If the Russians bomb us, shelters aren't going to save you! It's ridiculous!"

"But we should do what we can. What's wrong with trying to prepare the best we can?"

"Prepare?! You don't know what you're talking about!" And he threw down my lists and left the room. He did not tell me the things I did not know about nuclear weapons, and he did not tell me how he knew them.

But he had not forgotten Hiroshima and Nagasaki and the films. In the notes he left behind after his death, I found this account of some of his efforts to get access to make the film that would convince America to reject nuclear weapons. It begins in the late 1940s and carries into the 1970s:

> The best-known newsperson then was Edward R. Murrow. Since I had joined CBS, I arranged to get a meeting with him. I wanted to try and get his great weight, his great ability, and his great influence to get the films released. But he was no help to me at all. I learned years later that David Lilienthal, who was head of the Atomic Energy Commission at that time, was a close friend of his. I also found out that Edward R. Murrow had narrated one of the military training films, called "Strategic Attack," which was

in complete opposition to what I would have liked to do with the films.

In about 1950, I wrote a letter to President Truman, asking him to authorize release of the footage for use in a full-length motion picture to show what had happened in Japan. I felt, as I said then, that the times screamed for the people of the world to see what nuclear war really was. I thought that the hatred against the United States abroad for having used the atom bombs had waned a bit and that it was imperative that the American people understand what they were dealing with. In October of 1950, I received a reply from Dallas Halverstadt, a Presidential assistant, which again denied that the public would or should have any interest in seeing this film.

In 1955, I left CBS and went to NBC to produce "Wide, Wide World." While I was there, I approached Chet Huntley of the NBC news team who had wide contacts in Washington. I was told that NBC news did not want to get into this subject. By now I was not surprised. I was no longer quite so naïve. The American government was still being criticized worldwide for having dropped the bomb and was sensitive on the subject. Furthermore, we had a growing stake in the development of new atomic weapons and in the new atomic industry. In those days, no network would seriously challenge the establishment when it claimed that the material was classified information and would not interest people even if it were not.

In 1956, I produced "Force for Survival," which saluted the armed forces. I met the Joint Chiefs of Staff and asked again about the films. Secretary of Defense Neil McElroy informed me that the footage was still classified and could not be released.

In 1962, while developing a TV series called "The Law Enforcers," I met with then-Attorney General Robert F. Kennedy and asked him about the films. Again, I was told that the material was classified, and his office could not, or would not, get it declassified.

In 1963, while making "The Decisions of Harry Truman," I asked the former President about the films in person. Truman told me he would "check on it," but later also said that it was still classified and would not be declassified.

In 1964, a Pentagon-connected friend finally arranged for me to view one of the training films made by Warner Brothers in 1948 that used some of our footage. Their message was that nuclear war could be survived. I could not sit through it because it made me literally physically ill.

The following documents (many obtained by Greg Mitchell in his investigations) demonstrate what Herb confronted:

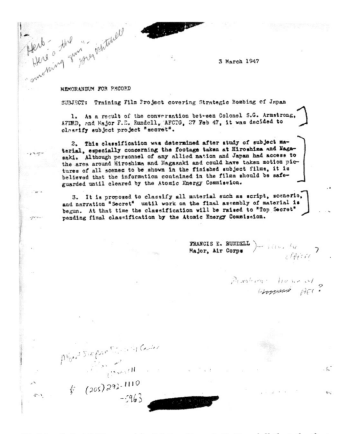

Figure 49: March 3, 1947 record by Major Francis E. Rundell that the footage was indeed classified as top secret.

CBS TELEVISION NETWORK
A Division of the
COLUMBIA BROADCASTING SYSTEM, INC.
485 MADISON AVENUE, NEW YORK 22, N.Y.
PLAZA 5-2000

September 25, 1950

The President
The White House
Washington, D.C.

Sir:

The recent release of the government's book
for civilians in reference to the possible effects
and preparations for atomic bombings has justifiably
received the publicity it deserves. I respectfully
suggest that now is the time for release of an even
more vivid and directly informative report to the
American people on this momentous subject.

As Production Manager for the United States
Strategic Bombing Survey in 1945-46, I had the unique
opportunity to direct thousands of feet of color
motion picture footage on the medical, morale, and
physical damage effects of the atomic bombs in Nagasaki
and Hiroshima. Although our mission was specifically
outlined in a letter from the Office of the President,
during production we were ever mindful of eventual
public release of these films by the government. The
War Department, however, placed a blanket "Top Secret"
classification on the entire footage, regardless of
the fact that fully sixty-five percent of it comprises
human interest and general coverage parallel to still
pictures released earlier. Major General Orville
Anderson, recent Commandant of the War College at the
Air University, was the officer-in-charge of our project
at that time.

I respectfully submit that this is the time for
release of a full-length motion picture in color, which
can effectively be produced from the aforementioned
motion picture material now in government hands.

CBS TELEVISION NETWORK
A Division of the
COLUMBIA BROADCASTING SYSTEM, INC.
485 MADISON AVENUE, NEW YORK 22, N.Y.
PLAZA 5-2000

—2—

Such a film would vividly and clearly reveal the implications and effects of the weapons that confront us at this serious moment in our history, and would be a unique visual document many times more powerful than the recent book release for informing and preparing American cities and the American people for the ever-present possibility of atomic attack.

I would be honored to assist in any way possible in production of such a valuable motion picture at this crucial time. It is my feeling that the times fairly scream out for release of this motion picture material. If there is any way that I can be of service in expediting this mission, I am available at your call.

I have the honor to remain,

Most respectfully yours,

Herbert Sussan

HS/js

Figure 50: Two-page letter from Herbert Sussan to Harry S. Truman dated September 25, 1950, from the official Harry S Truman Library.

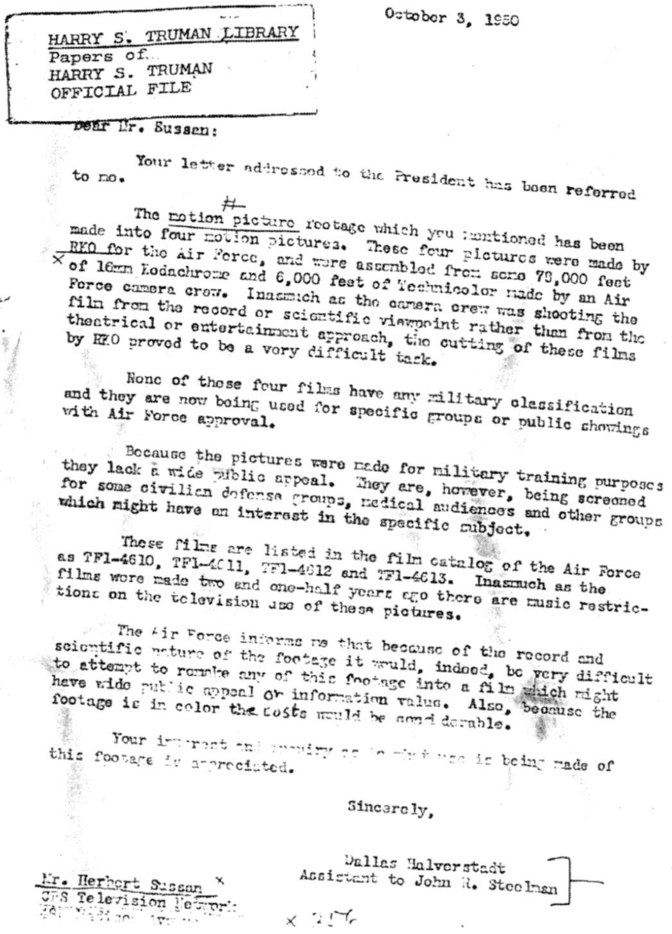

October 3, 1950

HARRY S. TRUMAN LIBRARY
Papers of
HARRY S. TRUMAN
OFFICIAL FILE

Dear Mr. Sussan:

Your letter addressed to the President has been referred to me.

The motion picture footage which you mentioned has been made into four motion pictures. These four pictures were made by RKO for the Air Force, and were assembled from some 79,000 feet of 16mm Kodachrome and 6,000 feet of Technicolor made by an Air Force camera crew. Inasmuch as the camera crew was shooting the film from the record or scientific viewpoint rather than from the theatrical or entertainment approach, the cutting of these films by RKO proved to be a very difficult task.

None of these four films have any military classification and they are now being used for specific groups or public showings with Air Force approval.

Because the pictures were made for military training purposes they lack a wide public appeal. They are, however, being screened for some civilian defense groups, medical audiences and other groups which might have an interest in the specific subject.

These films are listed in the film catalog of the Air Force as TF1-4610, TF1-4611, TF1-4612 and TF1-4613. Inasmuch as the films were made two and one-half years ago there are music restrictions on the television use of these pictures.

The Air Force informs me that because of the record and scientific nature of the footage it would, indeed, be very difficult to attempt to remake any of this footage into a film which might have wide public appeal or information value. Also, because the footage is in color the costs would be considerable.

Your interest and inquiry as to what use is being made of this footage is appreciated.

Sincerely,

Dallas Halverstadt
Assistant to John R. Steelman

Mr. Herbert Sussan
CBS Television Network

Figure 51: Halverstadt letter of October 3, 1950 replying to Herbert Sussan letter to President Truman.

* * *

NO WONDER MY FATHER BECAME FURIOUS AT MY FALL-
out shelter lists. It would have been in about 1965 that I proposed
planning for us to survive nuclear war with enough juice and toilet
paper. As I went through high school, through assassinations, riots,

and Vietnam, my father was still trying to find the footage and make the film that would awaken the world.

> In 1973, I discovered for the first time that the film was stored at the Defense Department's film depository at Norton Air Force Base in California. I went to the base and found that my old superior officer, Dan McGovern, now a retired colonel, was there as a film producer. He admitted to me that he had "guarded" the film for the Air Force all these years. He directed me to the files where records on all army films were kept. I found the card on my film, and it was indeed marked "Top Secret." No change in classification. I still couldn't see it. I couldn't touch it. Period. Once again, I had to walk away frustrated and baffled from the one project I really wanted to do.

In 1973, I graduated from college. I had protested for civil rights, organized against ageism and sexism, and marched against the Vietnam war. I was frustrated and baffled by my father's opposition to my activism. I resented him; he worried about me. We did not understand each other. At least, not yet.

CHAPTER FIFTY-ONE:

Ground Zero again

NEW YORK CITY (2001) — SEPTEMBER 11, 2001, WAS ONE of my lucky days. A Tuesday so I could skip the commute and work from home. I was at the computer in my home office, and the radio was playing in the background. A strange note in the announcer's tone made me stop and pay attention.

A plane had flown into one of the World Trade Center towers. I visualized a small plane, a private pilot. Had he lost his bearings? Had a heart attack? Then, another plane. How could two planes get so lost? Not small craft but commercial airliners! Then the entire WTC crumbling, one tower after the other! Oddly, unlike most people, I did not think to turn on television, so I did not immediately see the images. Even though I saw them later, I still hear rather than see the shocking news in my mind.

And then I froze. Was my brother at work yet? Almost 9 AM. I knew his subway stop was under the WTC. He worked as a computer developer on Wall Street. I called his cell phone and his home number; sent emails, tried to reach his wife and children. Where *was* my brother?

In the afternoon, at last, he walked in the door as I was instant messaging with one of his sons. He had walked up the length of Manhattan island from Wall Street to my grandmother's old cooperative apartment on the Upper West Side where he now lived with his wife and two boys. He came on the computer:

blinkstare2001 (3:29:09 PM): Hi sis . . .

> Goldylox41: oh god I was so scared for you. I have hit redial for hours.

> blinkstare2001: I was two blocks from the trade center, at 75 wall when the center came down. I was in the last subway train that made it into the wall st station before they stopped service.

> Goldylox41: thank god . . .
> blinkstare2001: All of downtown ny is covered with dust and millions of pieces of paper. Survivors were taking refuge with us, covered with inches of white dust.

> The most scary thing I have ever seen. We did not know if we were next as JP Morgan is just as big a symbol as the WTC. I am probably in shock somewhat.

> As I walked uptown, behind us was the huge black cloud where the center used to be. It felt like walking away from Hiroshima . . .

Paul was unhurt. At least that day, although he had respiratory problems afterward. His boys spent a long day wondering if they still had a dad. No one can know how long the ripples will spread from that one explosion as they have from that earlier Ground Zero.

Even that first day, both of us realized that our father's worst nightmare — those images that had ambushed him in the streets of New York City — had materialized before his son's eyes. Manhattan was the new Ground Zero. My father's war had followed him home after all.

As perhaps all wars do in the end, as long we continue to fight them.

CHAPTER FIFTY-TWO:

Seeds for peace

HIROSHIMA, JAPAN (VARIOUS DATES) — I MET NUMATA-sensei often in Peace Park during our return visits to Hiroshima over the years. We usually met by the parasol tree. The parasol tree is another part of her *kataribe* story.

During the long months she spent in the Hiroshima Communications Bureau Hospital, she could see the burned trunks of the trees from her window. She felt as hopeless and burned out as the trees for a long time.

Figure 52: Parasol trees in Hiroshima Peace Park. (Photo by author, 1987)

When doctors arrived at last from other prefectures and set up a temporary relief station in the burned-out hospital, Numata-sensei was carried into one of the filthy rooms. By then, gangrene had turned her leg black to the knee. The only way to save her was to amputate above the knee, and to do it without anesthesia or antibiotics. She fainted during the surgery and awoke to unbearable pain. After the operation, her wound would not heal. Maggots grew in her leg and pus seeped out through the bandages, turning them a putrid green. She lost her hair, ran high fevers, and suffered from diarrhea and bleeding gums. She ate food from buckets so covered in flies that the contents looked like solid moving black masses. Around her, the living and dead existed side by side. She tells of days "punctuated only by the anguished screams of the conscious, the raving of the delirious, and the cries of those in the throes of death," and nights breathing "the stench of blood, pus, and the burning of corpses which continued day and night on the burned-out desert which was once Hiroshima."

Then one day, her mother pointed out to her that a few green leaves were unrolling from the branches of the parasol trees outside the window. She had thought the trees were dead. She felt life begin to stir in her too. Her life energy, which shines so indomitably in her when she does *kataribe*, revived.

When she was a teacher, her students could tell that she walked strangely, but they never knew the reason. Wearing a false leg and a long kimono, she hid her injury and kept silent for decades about the bomb. People did not suspect that she was *hibakusha* because she had no burns. Once, she fell in love and had hopes again of marrying. One day, however, her lover told her that his mother opposed the match. The prospective mother-in-law advised her son that plenty of other, able-bodied girls were out there to marry. After that, she decided never to marry and to keep her silence. She could not bear to speak out when she thought of the dead who could not be happy with the living. She told me many emotions filled her heart over the years of silence, but she could not express them through her lips. Besides, she thought, so many people were working for peace. Surely, she need not be outspoken.

Although she went on with her life, the health effects of her exposure to the bomb were not so easily left in the past. Over the years, Numata-sensei lost her womb and ovaries to cancer and developed a degenerative disease affecting her back, knee, and hands. She could no longer use a false leg because the stump would not tolerate it. For thirty-eight years, her leg ached, and she took medication to control the pain. In 1983, she had to undergo another amputation of a section of the injured leg. Numata-sensei seemed to move around quickly and easily on her crutches, but her sister told me that every day Numata-sensei came home with her underarms badly swollen from the pressure of the crutches.

Numata-sensei remained close to her sister whose health also continued to be affected. Pieces of glass worked their way out of her body. A spot on her skin would get red and tough from time to time, and then yet another fragment would have to be removed. She also had to have both breasts removed because of cancer. Numata-sensei's sister shared her reluctance to speak out publicly, saying: "Our suffering will be enough." She carried no grudge, however, against any country, and sincerely wished for world peace. It is impossible, she would say, to retrieve a healthy body, but nevertheless one must try to be independent and positive. She wrote haiku to console herself and Numata-sensei. They both adored cats and loved to play with kittens, finding comfort in such small pleasures.

After the release of the Ten-Feet Campaign film changed her mind about telling her story, Numata-sensei said, she began talking constantly to anyone who would listen. She described her new self as "a talking doll, with my mouth opening and closing like a goldfish," spilling out her message, even to foreigners who may not understand a word of her Japanese but may absorb some of her urgency for peace. She believed that peace is something that must be taken in on a daily basis, like vitamins, to train us in a healthy love of life. She said she would always regret that the adults in the time before the war did not have the right understanding of how to bring about peace so that they might have stopped the war from happening.

So, she gathered every day with schoolchildren and tourists spread around her in the shadow of the parasol trees. The trees continue living. Their trunks have begun to curve around the deep hollows where they were burned, as if cradling their painful scars. She would tell her story and show her pictures one by one. The photo of her in the lovely wedding kimono. A picture of the building where she once worked and where she met the bomb. Snapshots of her family members. The trees in their original location. The one of my father's face and a new picture of their reunion in New York in 1982.

She always told her listeners that every day she talks to the parasol trees, to let them know they are not forgotten. The trees cannot speak of the agony which they felt and saw. The multitude of the dead likewise cannot speak. She was preserved alive. She decided she was not meant to live for herself alone, but for all those who died. She urges every audience to carry the story and tell it to someone else, as she is doing now.

"What I have told you," she explains, "is a seed, a seed for you to grow. Grow it into an invisible tree of peace. You too can sow seeds for peace wherever you go."

Figure 53: Numata-sensei next to Kendra in the Hiroshima Hibakushas' office.
(Photo by author)

The parasol trees are not in a prominent place in Peace Park and are likely overlooked by most visitors, despite the small explanatory sign in front of them. The students who hear Numata-sensei's story drape long chains of folded paper cranes over their branches and pray before them. Anyone who has heard her talk cannot help but regard the trees in a new light, as almost human personalities. They seem, like her, to have dedicated their remaining lives to spreading the hope for peace. To some of those touched by her message, Numata-sensei has also given seedpods from the parasol trees. She hopes that offspring of the trees that gave her hope are now growing in many places around the globe.

The last time I saw Numata-sensei at Peace Park, she gave me a copy of her autobiography. She asked why I had not yet finished my book. I was ashamed. I composed these haiku in honor of Numata-sensei's *kataribe*:

> Three parasol trees,
>
> Leafing, mute, from keloid trunks,
>
> Strain to hear your voice.
>
> These trees remember,

Too, but cannot speak of it.

Summer sun – too hot!

My quarrel with my father, at bottom, was the same as Numata-sensei's students quarrel with her. He did not tell me the things that mattered the most. My father's quarrel with me, at bottom, was that of all the *hibakusha*. I did not pay attention to the things his experiences could have taught me. We were both right.

We must meet our history at a human level across generations. We can ask parents and grandparents and elders what they were like, what their lives were like, what they learned, what they did, what they saw, before their memories are lost and their era is pressed between the pages of textbooks. I believe that, when we come to feel the human continuity of lived history, we will also understand that neither the causes of wars nor their costs and effects can be comprehended in snapshot form. Understanding requires the full movie to show the long, linked chain of actions and consequences. One action, one bomb, can send ripples for decades, across continents and generations.

Lived history teaches us lessons. If we do not learn from them, our children may have to learn them anew living through the repetition of history. The lessons of our parents are the legacy of our children. My daughter's is a nuclear legacy, and I owe it to her to preserve and pass on its lessons. The reason *hibakusha* speak is to pass hard-won understanding on to the next generation.

The mourner's *kaddish* is traditionally said the year after a death and on the anniversary of the death. Part of the *kaddish* translates as: "May there be abundant peace from heaven, and life, for us and for all Israel; and say, Amen." (This translation is excerpted from https://www.myjewishlearning.com/article/

text-of-the-mourners-kaddish/; some other versions add a plea for peace for all who dwell on earth.) As a non-Jew, I have not been able to pray the *kaddish* for my father, and given his avoidance of religion generally, he probably would not mind the omission. Still, I feel that this book is in part a fulfillment of a duty as a daughter to try to make of his death a blessing and a message for peace for us all.

This is my *kataribe*. This is my *kaddish* for my father. *Therefore, choose life . . ..*

AFTERWORD

I HAVE DEPENDED FOR MUCH OF THE STORY ON EYEWIT-
ness accounts from my father and from the *hibakusha*, and, of course,
my own. As a judge, I know well that eyewitnesses are not always
reliable and memory is not always perfect. I have verified what I
could but cannot eliminate all subjectivity. Recent neuroscience has
shed light, or cast doubt depending how you look at it, on the trust-
worthiness of all eyewitness accounts. Of course, we always knew
eyewitnesses may lie and that one's point of view (literally, as in how
far away one is standing and whether the line of sight is obstructed,
as well how attentive or emotionally involved one is) affects what
one can actually see and hence report. What has now become clear,
though, is that we do not record our experiences as if by a mental
video camera (however imperfect) or play them back like rerunning
a film (however deteriorated). Instead, we construct perception and
reconstruct recollection. In other words, our eyes do not merely take
in what is in front of them. Rather, our brains select the input that
matters to us for attention and structures it into patterns that give
it meaning to us. Once we do make a memory of something, we do
not simply retrieve and then reshelve the stored impressions. Every
time we pull together a recreation of earlier impressions, we alter
those impressions themselves at a neurological level. In short, we
truly cannot swim in the same memory twice.

If the point of revisiting memories is to achieve precision, as
it is in court, then these characteristics are defects, sometimes fatal.
But if the point is to try to enter into someone else's experience, then
the fact that their impressions and recollection are shaped by their
point of view (in all senses) is actually a benefit. We find each other's
stories more absorbing than mere recordings of events; hearing an

account of a traveler's journey is much richer than looking at a perfect postcard of a famous location. I hope the accounts here bring that kind of meaning to the reader. If, in the process, any errors have occurred, I take responsibility for them.

One area of dispute of which I am aware relates to Daniel McGovern, the man who selected my father for the mission. He stayed in the military when my father quit. He passed away without my having ever met him, but I know he and my father did not see eye to eye about the footage. My father used to mutter about McGovern "sitting" on the films and blamed McGovern for blocking every effort he made to make them public. My father's plan, as he repeated over and over, was to make a movie "from the American point of view," that would be designed to help Americans understand what was wrong with these weapons. When my father told the story of the film crew, he portrayed McGovern mostly as the boss sitting in Tokyo. I understood that McGovern felt my father was more of a bit player in the crew (a writer and poker player, I have heard McGovern described him). McGovern thought my father claimed too much credit for himself for a project McGovern conceived and led. I knew, though, that they did communicate over the years. Among my father's stacks and files, I found some correspondence with McGovern in which he sent my father photocopies of some of the scene descriptions from the footage. I also found many still photographs. They included many aging prints of Hiroshima and Nagasaki scenes from 1946, some stamped on the back: "Credit to Daniel McGovern" and some annotated with helpful information about persons, time, and place.

Greg Mitchell was the first journalist to interview my father and wrote about him in magazine articles and book chapters. Greg was also involved with the making of "Original Child Bomb," a movie which included some of the footage. We had been in touch occasionally over the years, and I knew that Greg continued to be outraged by the government's suppression of the atomic footage. In 2011, Greg published a book himself, entitled *Atomic Cover-up: Two U.S. Soldiers, Hiroshima & Nagasaki, and the Greatest Movie Never Made*, exploring the history of the films. He had watched all the footage, communicated with McGovern and his son, as well as my father, and visited Hiroshima and Nagasaki himself. Greg, unlike me, is an investigative reporter, good at asking questions and ferreting out information and unthreatened by sorting out competing versions of truth. Greg wrote that McGovern indeed stayed with the footage, but also that he saw himself as preserving it:

> "I always had the sense," McGovern told me, "that people in the Atomic Energy Commission were sorry we had dropped the bomb. The Air Force — it was also sorry. I was told by people in the Pentagon that they didn't want those [film] images out because they showed effects on man, woman and child. . .. They didn't want the general public to know what their weapons had done — at a time they were planning on more bomb tests. We didn't want the material out because . . . we were sorry for our sins."

This quotation confirmed for me the core of what my father saw in the suppression of the footage. When I read Greg's accounts of the differences in the way McGovern and my father recall the making and hiding of the atomic footage from Japan, what seems clear to me is that they both told the truth about what they perceived initially, as best they can remember it, from where they stood and that their memories of each other were affected by their emotional stances.

McGovern's account is of the central role he played in organizing the expedition and directing the filming, but he says he traveled back and forth to Tokyo and delegated a lot. My father did not mention McGovern being on the train or directing filming on the scene. But neither does he ever deny that McGovern organized the whole venture and controlled the orders or that McGovern was present in Nagasaki or Hiroshima or on the train. McGovern reportedly described my father as relatively unimportant, not the "producer," just a "writer." Of course, the great bulk of the film was taken of physical effects of strategic bombing, and my father never claimed to play a role there. What he did assert was that he worked with Harry Mimura on the human effects footage and that he took the initiative on that. I find it understandable that McGovern would have an overview of the whole enterprise whereas my father would attend only to the parts in which he was most involved. (When I learned that McGovern viewed him as the group's writer, though, it makes me think of the painstaking log that my father kept which vanished when the film was taken to Washington. My father suspected McGovern of having taken the log, or at least knowing what happened to it. It is not an unreasonable suspicion since McGovern was in charge of the office where the footage and materials from the trip remained while my father left for his brief rest break in Nikko, but I am aware of no evidence to support it. So far as I know, no information about the fate of the log has ever surfaced, which means that the only documentation of exactly what role my father played in the actual shooting cannot be verified.)

McGovern also told Greg that my father was wrong about bringing the film back to Washington because he himself brought the film to the Pentagon. But what my father actually said is that McGovern left behind just the footlocker with the footage shot by Harry Mimura, so again the versions can be reconciled. McGovern saw himself as rescuing and preserving the footage while my father saw him as helping to withhold it from the public. McGovern saw my father's efforts to get at the film as motivated by self-promotion; my father saw his drive as born in some mix of patriotism, truth-telling, and art. I doubt anybody's motives are unmixed, and I do not know how to dissect them with both men dead. I do not think it matters very much in the end. No matter who played what role with what motive, the footage contains the most compelling record of what nuclear war really means for human life.

Greg checked out what could be found objectively about these questions and published the results. I recommend his book to those who are interested in the details. I felt freed by it to tell what I heard from my father, and from the *hibakusha*, and saw for myself with all the limitations inherent in accounts by honest eyewitnesses.

This story has been 75 years in the making, starting with the terrible instants of *pikadon*, followed by my father's experiences filming in Japan in 1946, his efforts over the years to get access to the footage, his final illness when he opened up about his memories and revisited Japan, and his last wish to have his ashes scattered in Hiroshima. My part in it began with trying to carry out his wishes and finding instead a calling to complete his mission to communicate the significance of what happened in Hiroshima.

* * *

AS I PREPARE THIS MANUSCRIPT FOR THE PUBLISHERS, I am making plans for another visit to Hiroshima. Kendra and I will be at the 75th memorial ceremonies. I will bring copies of this book to the Hiroshima Peace Museum and to those who helped bring it to fruition. I will have kept at last promises made there to myself, to my family and to the *hibakusha*. But the call to work and pray for peace and freedom from the threat of *pikadon* will not end.

NOTES ON SOURCES AND MATERIALS

Footage — The raw footage shot by the Strategic Bombing Survey crew, consisting of about 90,000 feet of color film, is now accessible in its entirety to the public at the National Archives. It is identified as item #342 USAF and viewing requires prior arrangement. Among the films that have used images from the footage (mostly fairly small excerpts) are the following: *Lost Generation* and *Prophecy* created by the Ten-Feet Campaign, as described above; *Original Child Bomb* by Carey Schonegevel (McKenzie); *Dark Circle* by Chris Beaver; and *Pictures from a Hiroshima Schoolyard by* Brian Reichhardt. I would be glad to learn of others of which I am not aware.

Photographs — The photographs of Nagasaki and Hiroshima were taken by members of the Strategic Bombing Survey film crew. According to the introduction to "Japan in Defeat," in addition to over 90,000 feet of color film, the crew compiled about 2,000 still photographs. It is impossible now to know who shot each photograph. Some of the still prints were sent to my father by McGovern and, as mentioned, some of those have on the back a stamped request that they be credited to him. Since McGovern appears in some of the stamped photographs, it is clear the stamp was not necessarily intended to show which ones he personally shot. (On some, McGovern included identifying notations which I have referenced in captions with gratitude.) Some were simply in my father's possession when he died, and a few of those had notations in his handwriting. Other photographs I have scanned directly from the "Japan in Defeat" report that my father compiled before leaving the Army of which I have an original set of the three volumes. All of these are United States Government works, having been created while on an official mission, but I am grateful for their existence and pres-ervation. During one of my trips to Hiroshima, I provided all the photographs I could locate to the Hiroshima Peace Museum at their request for copying and study.

I have also included a few of the photographs in my father's collection that date from his 1983 return visit to Japan sponsored by the Ten-Feet Campaign. I have tried to contact the sponsoring group (Hiroshima-Nagasaki Publishing Committee/Japan Peace Museum) without success so far. I have not been able to determine who shot the photographs or sent them to my father at the time or to obtain specific permission from the photographer or those who appear with my father (most of whom I believe are deceased). I will make corrections or updates in future editions or on the website if I can obtain more information about any of the photographs or if I am notified that the use of any of them for this educational project is objectionable.

My father's voice — The chapters told from my father's view-point refer to him as "Herb." They rely on his notes and oral history, and, in a few cases, stories he told me. The indented portions use his own words from those sources to allow his voice to be heard more directly. The words in those portions are all his, but the quotations are not verbatim in that I condensed for space and flow and merged multiple accounts he gave. I have bracketed my own reflections or comments in those chapters in order to clearly distinguish them from his own story. The chapters told from my own viewpoint refer to him as "my father." I realized as I worked on the book that I never called him either Herb or father when he was alive, but only "Daddy." The childish name perhaps reflects the reality that comes through in this book that we never fully found an adult-to-adult relationship. In my heart now, Daddy has grown into my father, of whom I am proud.

Disclaimer — The information and opinions in this book come from the author personally and do not reflect any official positions of the United States government.

Website — I hope readers who want to know more about the events discussed in this book and to reflect more on challenges for the future implicit in the destruction of Hiroshima and Nagasaki will visit my website at https://wordpress.com/post/lesliesussan.wordpress.com/4. The website and blog will house more images, links, and background information than could be included in the space of this book (and will also note any corrections of which I become aware). I also hope that readers will contribute to expanding and enriching the dialogue about our shared future through that website.

I focused in this book on the reverberating impact of one instant in one war on a personal scale. So much writing about war in general, and nuclear war in particular, is abstract, focusing on strategy, justifications, and large-scale events. As an antidote, I have tried to avoid the aerial view and the intellectual perspective. In addition, I wanted to feel and share the human emotions involved rather than engage in a debate. Nevertheless, history matters, and moral issues deserve serious debate.

Rather than weigh down this book with footnotes and bibliographies, I have opted to put these resources on the website, where you can link to some of the primary sources and many in-depth materials now available online. I have and have used dozens of books about the use and effects of the atomic bombings, the Occupation, the cultural contexts in Japan and America, and the *hibakusha*. I plan to list and review many of these on the website. Among those, a few I particularly recommend (besides those cited in the text) that have informed or been quoted in my writing are: Dower, J.W., and Junkerman, J. (eds.). (1985). *The Hiroshima Murals: The art of Iri Maruki and Toshi Maruki.* Tokyo, Japan: Kodansha Int'l Ltd.; Dower, J.W. (1986). *War Without Mercy: Race & power in the Pacific war.* New York, New York: Pantheon Books; Ham, P. (2014). *Hiroshima Nagasaki: The real story of the atomic bombings and their aftermath.* New York, New York: St. Martins Press; Hiroshima-Nagasaki Publishing Committee. (1978). *Hiroshima-Nagasaki: A pictorial record of the atomic destruction.* Tokyo, Japan: Hiroshima-Nagasaki Publishing Committee; Lifton, R.J. (1964). *Death in Life: Survivors of Hiroshima.* New York, New York: Simon and Schuster; Lindee, M.S. (1994). *Suffering Made Real: American science and the survivors at Hiroshima.* Chicago, Illinois: The University of Chicago Press.

Glossary — A glossary of foreign words used in this book is included for the reader's convenience. The definitions in the glossary are my own simplified versions and should not be viewed as definitive. In compiling them, I have drawn on Sanseido's *Junior Crown Japanese-English Dictionary,* Webster's *New World Compact Japanese Dictionary,* the glossary in *Ultimate Japanese* by Hiroko Storm (Living Language, 1998) which I used in studying Japanese, and ever-available help of Google Translate.

ACKNOWLEDGEMENTS

IT IS IMPOSSIBLE TO THANK ALL THE PEOPLE WHO helped over the long years of gestation of this project, but equally impossible not to try to acknowledge their generosity and kindness. Books, like children, turn out to take a village. My first thanks must go to my father for blazing the path I followed and to my daughter who accompanied me on every step of it. I am grateful to my brother, Paul, for his help in finding and preserving our father's materials and encouraging me on the way.

Next, I owe a tremendous debt to every survivor whose sacred story was entrusted to me. I hope I have done them some justice and apologize for any mistakes or missteps which are my own. Among them are Suzuko Numata, Sumiteru Taniguchi, Fumiko Sora, Michiko Yamoaka, Chiyo Takeuchi, Ikumi Kikkawa, Tamotsu Eguchi, Yoshiko Imaeda, Rev. Mutoi Munakata, Kenjiro Nishikubo, Tomie Okuda, and the Marukis. Their courage and dedication to peace cannot help but be inspiring.

Innumerable people lifted me up in Japan to make it possible for us to live there without financial support, to learn about and come to love the culture, and to meet and communicate with the *hibakusha*. Among those who are personally dear to me are Masahiko Sumiya and his family, Yoshiko Imaeda, Emiko Morikawa, Michiko Kitayama, Mirei Tashiro, Shizuo Tachibana, among many others. Kendra and I cherish warm memories of our neighbors in Funairicho and the teachers and classmates at Mikune-en kindergarten.

The exposure of the footage to the public and the identification of the survivors who were filmed would not have occurred but for the tireless work of Mr. Iwakura, Dr. Nagai, and the Ten-Feet Campaign. I also received helpful information from Ronni

Alexander, who worked with the Ten-Feet Campaign and assisted my father during his return visit in 1983.

I appreciate the help and coverage of the media in Hiroshima, especially The Chugoku Shimbun (which published many articles on the Ten-Feet Campaign, the hibakusha in the footage, my father's visit, and my own visits to Hiroshima, with special thanks to Akira Tashiro) and NHK-Hiroshima.

I want to also thank the following groups in Hiroshima which helped me while I was there and which have long been among the beacons of the city's commitment to peace-making: Hiroshima Peace Museum, YMCA International Institute for Peace, World Friendship Center, and Hiroshima Interpreters for Peace.

I have not been able to locate the student, whose name was P.K. Smith, who recorded her interviews with my father. If she ever discovers this book, I would love to send her a hug. Without her project and its preservation by the Columbia Oral History Archives, there is so much I would never have known about my father.

I also owe a tremendous debt to Greg Mitchell, for bringing the story of the film crew and the suppressed footage to public awareness. He has stayed with the cause of making people understand the horror of nuclear weapons and exposing government efforts to cover up these images over decades. And I thank him for contributing the foreword to this book.

I am also grateful to the work of the D.C. Hiroshima-Nagasaki Peace Committee, founded by John Steinbach and his late wife Louise Franklin-Ramirez, and others, out of the D.C. chapter of the Gray Panthers. John has gently encouraged me to press forward on this project for many years and has been a diligent and faithful messenger for disarmament.

The two faith communities to which I have belonged both offered discernment and validation. My thanks to Arlington Presbyterian Church which commissioned my first journey and to Rev. Robert Harris who took pastoral care to the point of visiting us in Hiroshima. My gratitude also goes to my current spiritual home at Bethesda Friends Meeting and particularly to the members who served on a clearness committee for this book.

Much help in learning to write better and frame narrative, as well as time and space to practice those skills, came from residencies and retreats, though none of them are responsible for any failures in those regards that may be evident in the text. I thank the Atlantic Center for Arts in New Smyrna Beach, Florida (and the two master memoirists who selected me for and led my residencies there: Honor Moore and Nick Flynn, as well as the fellow residents); The Porches Writers Retreat in Norwood, Virginia, and Trudy Hale; and Shalom House Retreat Center and its staff in Montpelier, Virginia.

I am grateful to the many people and workshop groups that provided advice, offered cheerleading, and read and commented on drafts all along the slow passage to completion of this book. They include the inspiring women writers' Facebook network of groups (you know who you are); my friends and my understanding bosses at the Departmental Appeals Board; the Silver Spring Writers Group; the Washington Biography Group; Sandra Lambert; Leslie Taylor; Steven Malone; Neil Kaufman; Laura Macklin; and Samuel Pickands.

I received generous and helpful assistance from two editors: Pat McNees and Deanna Nikaido.

Carolyn Reines-Graubard did an amazing job proofreading the manuscript on a tight schedule.

GLOSSARY

Aki-matsuri – autumn festival

arigatoo – thank you

ben – accent (regional)

benjo – toilet, lavatory

bodhisattva – this term has many meanings in different strands of Buddhism and may encompass all who commit to seeking enlightenment, but one sense to which I refer is of a being who has attained enlightenment but delayed entering into nirvana out of compassion in order to serve other beings who have not yet become enlightened.

-chan – a diminutive ending for children's names

dai ichi – number one

daruma – Daruma was the Japanese name for Bodhidharma, a Buddhist monk in India. The legends about his diligent meditation led to the *daruma* dolls.

eki – station

ekiben – train station boxed meals

fugu – blowfish

Gambatte, kudasai! – Good luck! Really something more like "please be strong and do your best!"

Genbaku Otemi – Atomic bomb young women, known in English as Hiroshima Maidens

genkan – foyer, entryway

hab mein ebben tsuris – tsuris is Yiddish for trouble; as my father used the expression, it meant "I have troubles of my own"

haole – generally, a Hawaiian term for individuals who are not Native Hawaiian, although it has sometimes come to have negative connotations.

hibakusha – usually translated as atomic bomb-affected person or bomb survivor

hina ningyo – A set of dolls dressed in formal garb as the Emperor, Empress, and courtiers of the Heian period. Sets are passed down in families and are displayed in careful arrays for Doll Festival.

Hinamatsuri – Doll Festival, also known as Girls' Day

irashaimase – welcome

itai – hurt

jizo – Jizo is a much-loved *bodhisattva* who seeks to protect against evil and whose statues are believed to guard children in particular (both living and deceased children) *joozu* – skillful, good at something

juku – cram school

kaddish – Jewish prayer in memory of a deceased person

kamikaze – literal meaning is divine wind; the reference in World War II was to pilots who undertook suicide flights against enemy targets

kataribe – *kataribe* were storytellers in olden times in Japan but the term has come to refer to the stories of those *hibakusha* who pass on their experiences.

katazuke – tidying up

kawaii – cute

kouban – small neighborhood police buildings or boxes

matsuri – festival

mikan – Mandarin orange

mikoshi – portable shrine

mizu – water

mochi – soft pounded-rice cakes

nisei – refers to a child of Japanese immigrants who is born in the United States

nori – dried seaweed sheets, commonly used to wrap sushi and onigiri

noren – colorful fabric hanging often used in the entrance to businesses signaling they are open

obento – (or just *bento*) conveniently packaged box meal

O-Bon – Summer seasonal observation during which people often travel to ancestral homes and shrine and visit family, and during which the spirits of ancestors too are believed to return and visit. The community dancing regularly held during the days of *O-Bon* is called *Bon Odori*.

ofuro – bath, hot tub

okonomiyaki – Sometimes called Japanese pancakes, they are savory and prepared on a grill with cabbage, noodles, often pork and egg, and other options (the name means as-you-like-it grill). The best okonomiyaki is definitely Hiroshima-style, but don't say I told you.

onigiri – prepared rice balls, sometimes wrapped in seaweed and sometimes with pickled plums in the center

pikadon – coined in response to the atomic bomb explosions from the words for bright flash (*pika*) and thunderous boom (*don*)

salariman – generally, a white-collar corporate employee

-san – polite ending to a last name (equivalent of Mr., Mrs. or Ms. without implying gender)

sayoonara – goodbye

-sensei – teacher or master, used as an honorific ending to a last name

shimashoo – let's do [something]

Shinkansen – bullet train

suiboku – ink, in particular monochromatic black ink used in traditional style painting

sukiyaki – hot-pot beef dish

sumimasen – excuse me, forgive me

tatami – straw floor covering mat

Takushii-wa doko? – Taxi, where?

Tojo baka – statement that Hideki Tojo, Prime Minister of Japan during much of World War II, was crazy

tonari-gumi – neighborhood association (such associations existed before and after the war, as with the one I belonged to in Funairi-cho, but during the war they were mandatory and were responsible for assigning rations and policing conformity; see https://en.wikipedia.org/wiki/Tonarigumi)

wasurimono nain desho – "Do not forget any belongings"

yochien – kindergarten

yukata – lightweight, informal kimono for summer wea

INDEX